Third Edition

Keith Harding and Alastair Lane

INTERNATIONAL EXPRESS
INTERMEDIATE

Student's Book
with Pocket Book and DVD-ROM

OXFORD
UNIVERSITY PRESS

Great Clarendon Street, Oxford, OX2 6DP, United Kingdom

Oxford University Press is a department of the University of Oxford.
It furthers the University's objective of excellence in research, scholarship,
and education by publishing worldwide. Oxford is a registered trade
mark of Oxford University Press in the UK and in certain other countries

© Oxford University Press 2014

The moral rights of the author have been asserted

First published in 2014

2018 2017

10 9 8 7 6 5 4

No unauthorized photocopying

All rights reserved. No part of this publication may be reproduced, stored in a retrieval system, or transmitted, in any form or by any means, without the prior permission in writing of Oxford University Press, or as expressly permitted by law, by licence or under terms agreed with the appropriate reprographics rights organization. Enquiries concerning reproduction outside the scope of the above should be sent to the ELT Rights Department, Oxford University Press, at the address above

You must not circulate this work in any other form and you must impose this same condition on any acquirer

Links to third party websites are provided by Oxford in good faith and for information only. Oxford disclaims any responsibility for the materials contained in any third party website referenced in this work

ISBN: 978 0 19 459760 9

Printed in China

This book is printed on paper from certified and well-managed sources

ACKNOWLEDGEMENTS

The Publishers would like to thank the following for their kind permission to reproduce photographs and other copyright material: Alamy Images pp.6 (couple/Image Source), 11 (woman in office/OJO Images Ltd), 11 (man on laptop/OJO Images Ltd), 16 (man smiling/Blend Images), 21 (woman at counter/Mauricio Jordan), 22 (picture framer/Juice Images), 34 (Kindle/Krys Bailey), 36 (handshake/OJO Images Ltd), 42 (Louvre Museum/John Kellerman), 44 (Bhutan Taktsang Tigers Nest monastery/travelib prime), 45 (bamboo/Chad Ehlers), 48 (balloon safari/Steve Bloom Images), 54 (flight attendant/imagebroker), 54 (pit stop/Bill Cheyrou), 54 (businessman/OJO Images Ltd), 57 (St Patrick's Day Parade/Steve Vidler), 57 (Bastet figurine/Elena Kovaleva), 60 (Nan Lian Garden/Iain Masterton), 60 (market/Travel Division Images), 67 (women carrying water/Jake Lyell / Water Aid), 78 (man in office/OJO Images Ltd), 78 (woman in office/OJO Images Ltd), 79 (home office/Adrian Sherratt), 81 (banking website/Eric Carr), 81 (banking app/Ian Dagnall), 81 (mortgage application/Brian Jackson), 82 (man with laptop and bills/Image Source), 90 (cocoa picking/Peter Bowater), 90 (cocoa beans roasting/Bon Appetit), 104 (Pelé/Interfoto), 105 (web designer/Cultura Creative (RF)), 105 (checkout girl/BWAC Images), 106 (call handler/UK Stock Images Ltd), 107 (job interview), 114 (Neil Armstrong & Buzz Aldrin/NASA Photo), 114 (Sgt Peppers Lonely Hearts Club Band cover/Jeff Morgan 04), 114 (iPad/CJG-Technology), 114 (Chanel perfume/Bhandol), 119 (teleconference/Cultura Creative (RF)), 120 (colleagues/PhotoAlto), 120 (Mobile World Congress Barcelona 2013/rosmi duaso); Corbis pp.8 (sign/Radius), 12 (businesspeople/Hero Images), 20 (Jimmy Choo/Steffen Thalemann), 33 (Discovery launch/Mark M. Lawrence), 34 (couple/John Smith), 34 (senior couple/John Lund/Marc Romanelli/Blend Images), 42 (Trafalgar Square/SOPA), 44 (Kinkaku-ji (Temple of the Golden Pavilion), Kyoto, Japan/Ben Pipe/Robert Harding World Imagery), 54 (Josh Lewsey/Mario Pietrangeli/NewSport), 71 (presentation/Hero Images), 79 (meeting/Image Source), 79 (man with laptop/Marco Cristofori), 83 (woman at desk/Image Source), 84 (warehouse/Rick Gomez), 90 (cacao beans/Owen Franken), 102 (London 2012 Olympics/Christopher Morris), 102 (Olympic Stadium/Mark Chivers/Robert Harding World Imagery), 102 (Usain Bolt/Christopher Morris), 114 (Harley Davidson/Doug Meek), 116 (emergency landing/Brendan McDermid/Reuters), 117 (woman cooking/Marnie Burkhart), 117 (man with laptop/Wavebreak Media Ltd.), 117 (gardener/Tim McGuire); flpa p.54 (whale researcher/Flip Nicklin/Minden Pictures); Getty Images pp.11 (Asian businessman/Robert Daly/OJO Images), 18 (Zaha Hadid/John Stillwell-WPA Pool), 18 (London Olympic Aquatic Centre/View Pictures/UIG), 18 (Guangzhou Opera House/View Pictures/UIG), 18 (Galaxy Soho,Beijing/View Pictures/UIG), 19 (Nada Debs/Kaveh Kazemi), 20 (John Rocha/Ben Stansall/AFP), 21 (man in warehouse/ColorBlind Images), 23 (meeting/Jon Feingersh), 25 (interactive shopping window/Johannes Eisele/AFP), 30 (cress/Adam Gault/OJO Images), 32 (family/Image Source RF/InStock), 32 (couple with keys/Jamie Grill), 32 (mechanic/Musketeer), 36 (mountain restaurant/Richard Elliott), 42 (Metropolitan Museum of Art/Mitchell Funk), 46 (cherry blossom/The Asahi Shimbun), 54 (fisherman/UpperCut Images), 54 (doctor/LWA), 54 (spacewalk 1995/SSPL/NASA), 56 (Cecile Duflot & Francois Lamy/Jean-Francois monier/AFP), 56 (Andy Murray/Clive Brunskill), 56 (wedding/Tom Williams/CQ Roll Call), 57 (car door/Erik Snyder), 58 (wind turbine/Dave Porter Peterborough Uk), 70 (polar bear/Wayne Lynch), 72 (work colleagues/JGI/Jamie Grill), 73 (businessmen/ImagesBazaar), 90 (truffles/John Carey), 90 (chocolatier/Lonely Planet), 95 (sticky notes/Fuse), 96 (bike building/Jesse Grant), 105 (engine assembly/Ulrich Baumgarten), 105 (telephonists/Image Source), 105 (traders/Tim Boyle/Bloomberg), 109 (discussion/Troels Graugaard), 114 (Ben & Jerry/Gareth Davies), 114 (HP logo/Tony Avelar/Bloomberg), 114 (The Wright Brothers 1903/SSPL); Hippo Water Roller Project www.hipporoller.org/Grant Gibbs p.66 (hipporoller); iStockphoto p.94 (recycling bins/Onur Dongel); Kaboura Events/Chris Skeet p.96 (team ice-cream making); Mary Evans Picture Library pp.30 (futuristic city from The Wonder Book of Inventions, Henry Woolley), 30 (city of the future, 'amazing stories', Frank R Paul), 30 (futuristic skyscraper/Interfoto/TV-yesterday); Off Limits Events/Alicia Currie p.96 (Picasso Picture Show); OUP pp.44 (Angkor Wat/Photodisc), 57 (pencils/Photodisc), 59 (on phone/Asia Images RF), 69 (water drop/Corbis), 127 (Liverpool/Corel); Rex Features pp.66 (Lifesaver bottle/), 68 (Dr Joshua Silver/Robert Judges), 129 (car in wall/KPA/Zuma), 134 (car accident/Quirky China News); Shutterstock pp.6 (woman with glasses/Goodluz), 6 (salesman/Goodluz), 32 (student/Gelpi JM), 32 (man in suit/Appear), 32 (woman working/violetblue), 33 (microchip/Shawn Hempel), 54 (American football/Brocreative), 57 (London bus/Chris Jenner), 57 (red poppy/kostrez), 57 (New York taxi/Stuart Monk/Shutterstock.com), 57 (blue mailbox/Myotis), 60 (Hong Kong/leungchopan), 131 (Stonehenge/Albo), 136 (Giant's Causeway/Pecold), 137 (Edinburgh/Shaiith).

Cover images by kind permission: Corbis (Cafe table and chairs/Ron Chapple), Getty Images (Serious businessman/Paul Simcock), (Smiling businesswoman/David Leahy/Juice Images), (Ponte Vasco da Gama, Lisbon/Image Source), (Conference table/Marnie Burkhart).

Illustrations by: Roarr Design pp.9, 47, 69, 80; Fred Van Deelan/The Organisation pp.24, 48, 68, 97, 108; Mark Duffin pp.55, 63, 93.

Welcome to *International Express*

Your guide to the Student's Book Pack

Here are the details of what is in the pack and how the various parts of the course work.

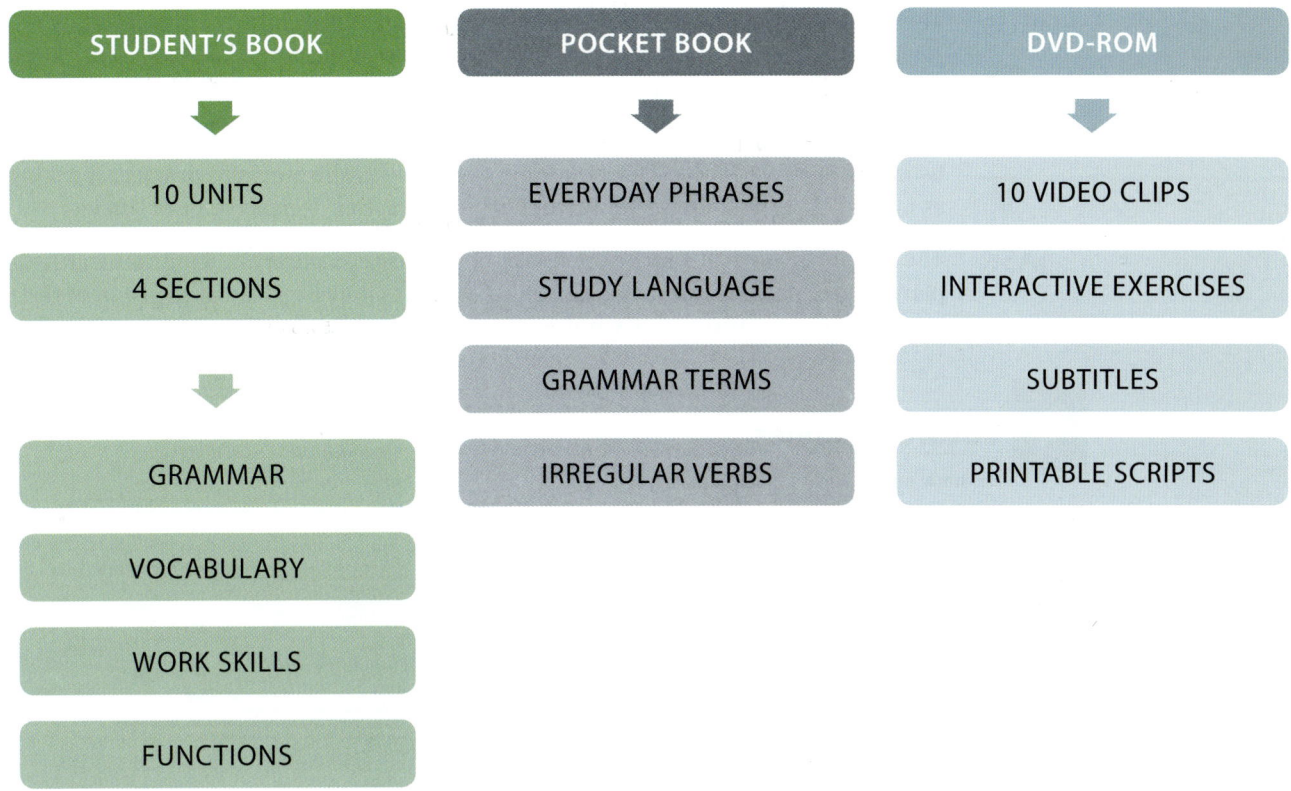

The **Student's Book Pack** contains the Student's Book, the Pocket Book, and the DVD-ROM.

The **Student's Book** has 10 units and each unit has four sections: Grammar, Vocabulary, Work skills, and Functions. One unit is eight pages, and is followed by a Review section of four pages. The Review section can be done in class or for self-study.

The **Pocket Book** contains examples of everyday phrases taken from the Student's Book. This can be used at work or for travel to help remember and use key phrases. There is also a section on Study language that gives examples of useful phrases for the classroom and expressions used in the Student's Book. *Grammar terms* has details about key words and phrases we use to talk about grammar. This is followed by a list of irregular verbs.

The **DVD-ROM** has one video clip for every unit. The topic of the video is linked to the topic of the unit.

There are two sets of exercises which can be done during or after the video. You can move from the video to the exercises without stopping the video. The video will start at the same place when you go back. There are optional subtitles and the script can be printed.

How a unit works

The **Grammar** and **Functions** sections have four stages: Introduction, Focus, Practice, and Task.

INTRODUCTION The language is introduced in a recorded conversation or in a reading text. There are questions to check understanding of the text.

FOCUS The Focus highlights the main areas of the language introduced in the previous stage and asks some questions about how we form and use the language. The notes in the **Review** section help answer these questions.

PRACTICE The Practice stage has activities to practise the language from the Introduction, using the answers to the Focus questions as a guide. The aim is to practise speaking as much as possible. There are further written practice exercises in the **Review**.

TASK The section ends with a more open task to practise speaking and communicating in pairs or groups. More information about the tasks may be given at the back of the book in the **Task and activity notes**.

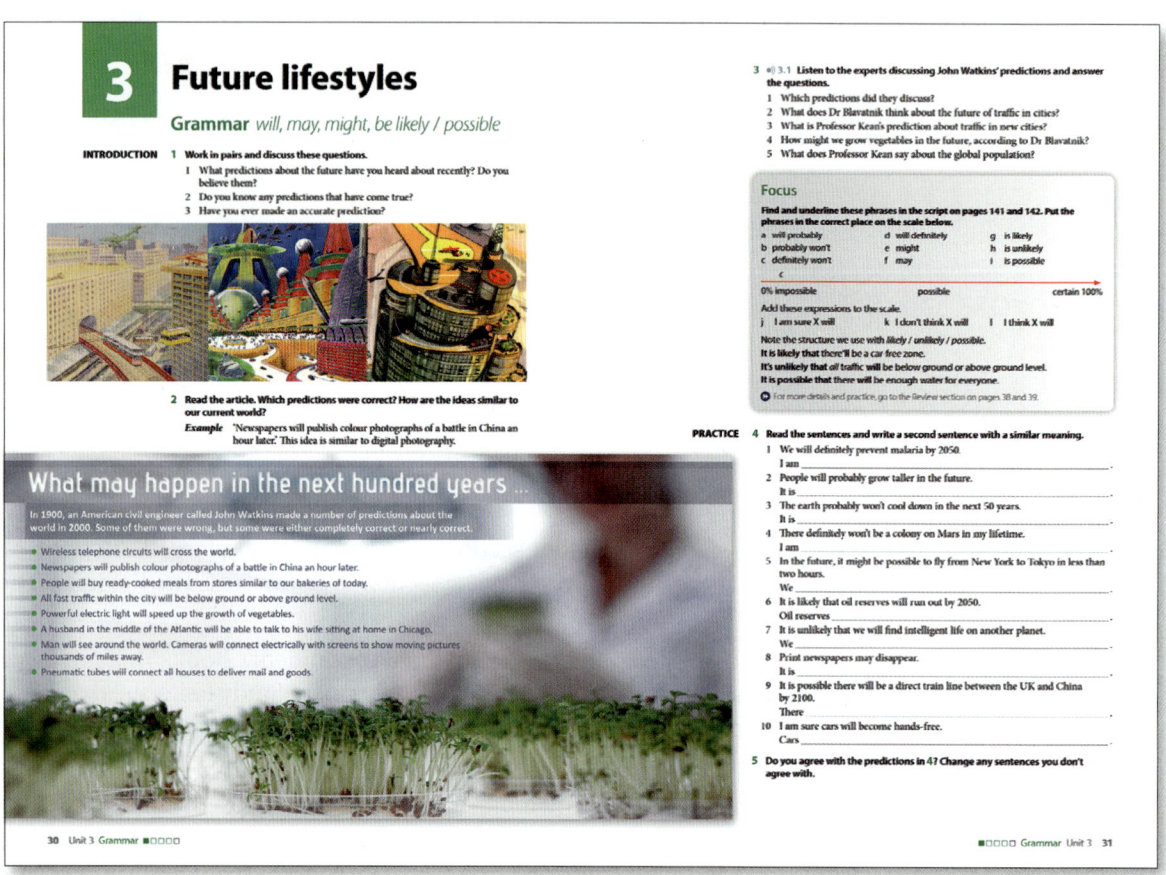

The **Vocabulary** and **Work skills** sections work in a similar way but have a more flexible format which allows for a variety of vocabulary and work skills to be studied and practised. There are further practice activities for both of these sections in the **Review**.

REVIEW There is a **Review** at the end of each unit. It contains notes on the form and use of the language in the Grammar and Functions sections, and practice and review exercises for all four sections. There are listening, reading, and writing exercises which can be done as self-study or in class time.

TASK AND ACTIVITY NOTES This section has notes for the tasks and activities in the unit. For some tasks, there are notes for Student A and Student B on different pages.

SCRIPTS This section has all the scripts for the conversations and listening practice activities.

ANSWER KEY The answers for activities and exercises in the units can be found here.

Contents

	Grammar	Vocabulary	Work skills	Functions
1 p.6	**Making connections** Present Simple and Present Continuous	Social networks and the internet	Writing a professional profile	Networking
2 p.18	**International design** Past Simple; Present Perfect Simple and Present Perfect Continuous	Starting a new business; phrasal verbs	Team meetings	Checking progress; delegating tasks
3 p.30	**Future lifestyles** *will*, *may*, *might*, *be likely / possible*	The speed of change; describing cause and effect	Emails 1: confirming arrangements	Making arrangements
4 p.42	**Heritage** Making comparisons	City descriptions; *-ing* vs *-ed* adjectives	Presentations 1: using visual aids	Giving opinions
5 p.54	**Fashion and function** Modal and related verbs: *have to, must, need to, be allowed to, can*	Colours and colour idioms; prefixes	Telephoning	Giving advice and suggestions
6 p.66	**Using innovation** Past Simple, Past Continuous, Past Perfect	Water footprint; noun formation	Presentations 2: structuring a talk	Describing problems and finding solutions
7 p.78	**Work styles and careers** Zero, 1st, and 2nd Conditional	Money and finance	Emails 2: job applications	Discussing and reaching agreement
8 p.90	**Processes** Passives: Present Simple, Present Continuous, Present Perfect Simple, Past Simple, *will*	Product journey	Time management	Checking understanding and clarifying
9 p.102	**The business of sport** Relative clauses	Describing personal qualities at work	Job interviews	Changing plans
10 p.114	**Great partnerships** 3rd Conditional; *should / shouldn't have*	Changing careers; *-ing* vs infinitive	Teleconferencing and videoconferencing	Catching up

Task and activity notes p.126
Scripts p.139
Answer key p.155

1 Making connections

Grammar Present Simple and Present Continuous

INTRODUCTION

1 Work in pairs and discuss these questions.
   1 How do you keep in touch with friends, colleagues, and family members?
   2 Do you use professional networking sites to look for jobs or recruit people?
   3 How do companies use social media, such as Facebook and Twitter, to sell their products and services?

2 Read the *High Flyer* article. Compare with your ideas in **1** and then answer the questions below.

High Flyer talked to three people about how they stay connected.

Lynn I have friends and family all over the world. I can't talk to them all or meet them very often, so Facebook is a great way to keep in touch. We share our news, our photos, talk about our friends, discuss music and fashion – that sort of thing. I spend about three hours every evening online.

Harry Our company uses LinkedIn, a professional networking site, to recruit staff. We prefer it to more traditional ways of recruitment because it's quicker – and it's free! For example, at the moment we're looking for a new research officer. I posted the advert yesterday and I already have ten excellent CVs and applications. The process took months before we had professional networking.

Keith and Lucie We run a hotel business and our website is our most important marketing tool. On the current site we update information every day so, for example, the restaurant menus are always up to date. People can book a table online as well as a room. We are currently improving the site and plan to have Twitter and Facebook feeds as well as a blog. This will keep people interested in the site as well as promote events, offers, and so on.

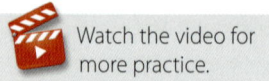 Watch the video for more practice.

   1 How does Lynn keep in touch with her friends and family?
   2 How has LinkedIn changed the way Harry recruits staff?
   3 How do Keith and Lucie plan to use social media to promote their business?

3 ◆)) 1.1 *High Flyer's* John Martin talks to Geoff Walker about his job. Are these statements true or false? Correct the false statements.
   1 Geoff is a sales manager.
   2 He uses social media to market his company's products.
   3 He's not very busy at the moment.
   4 At the moment Geoff is creating a new blog.
   5 About ten people are working on his current project.
   6 Geoff is having problems with his current project.
   7 He usually works a five-day week only.
   8 Geoff doesn't enjoy his job.

Focus

Complete the table with these phrases.

I'm in charge of marketing a new laptop for our company.
I'm sorry, I don't remember your name.
My email address is Pshen (all one word) at pshen dot com.
Would you like to meet my colleague, Diane Smith?
I'm based here in Santiago.

Meeting	Talking about your work
It's Pete Shen, isn't it? Pleased to meet you, Pete.	I'm a … Currently, I'm working on a technology website. Previously, I worked for … a computer manufacturer. Are you familiar with recent developments in hardware?
Introducing another person	
I want you to meet Pete Shen.	
Sharing contact details	
Here's my card.	

▶ For more details and practice, go to the Review section on page 17.

PRACTICE

6 Match 1–6 with responses a–f.

1 Here's my card. ___
2 It's Jamila Hassan, isn't it? ___
3 Eliza, I want you to meet our London Manager, Tim Collins. ___
4 Pleased to meet you. ___
5 Are you familiar with designing e-books? ___
6 Would you like to meet our sales team? ___

a That's right. I'm sorry, I don't remember your name.
b Yes, I am. I've worked on several of them.
c Thank you very much. Let me give you mine.
d Pleased to meet you, Tim.
e Yes, I would. I've only had contact with them by email before.
f And you.

7 Complete the sentences so they are true for you.

1 I'm a _____.
2 I'm in charge of _____.
3 Previously, I _____.
4 Currently, I'm _____.

TASK

8 Work in pairs. You meet at a trade fair. Practise the conversation using these prompts.

A	B
Start conversation. You think you remember B's name.	You know you met A, but you don't know A's name.
Give your name. Explain you met B at a car show last year.	Respond.
Ask B what they do.	Respond. Ask A the same question.
Respond.	Ask A where they are based.
Respond. Ask B the same question.	Respond.
Ask B about their current work / project.	Respond. Ask A same question.
Respond.	Offer your business card.
Thank B for their card. Offer yours.	Thank A. Say goodbye.

Functions Unit 1

Review

Grammar Present Simple and Present Continuous

Form

We form the Present Simple with the infinitive form of the verb. For *he*, *she*, and *it*, we add an *-s* to the end of the verb.
Examples I work for Apple. He works for Microsoft.

We use the auxiliary verb *be* and the *-ing* form of the main verb to form the Present Continuous.
Example We are updating the website.

We put *be* before the subject to form a question.
Example Are you using your laptop?

We put *not* between *be* and the main verb to form the negative.
Example He is not staying in New York.

We usually use the contracted form in spoken English.
Example I'm working on a new project this week.

Use

We use the Present Simple to talk about facts, and habits and routines.
Examples Ottawa is the capital of Canada.
I get up late on Saturdays.

We use the Present Continuous to talk about activities in progress, temporary situations, and trends.
Examples He's writing an email.
She's staying with a friend at the moment.
The number of smartphone users is growing rapidly.

Action and state verbs

Verbs which express an action or activity, e.g. *arrive*, *bring*, *deal with*, *look for*, *manage*, *travel*, *work*, are used in both Simple and Continuous tenses. They are called action verbs.

Verbs which express a state, e.g. *understand*, *know*, *want*, *believe*, *prefer*, *recognize*, *remember*, are not usually used in Continuous tenses. They are called state verbs. Some verbs, e.g. *have*, *see*, *look*, *taste*, *feel*, *think*, are used in both Simple and Continuous tenses, as they can express either an action or a state.

PRACTICE

1 **Complete the facts and trends about social network use with the correct form of these verbs.**

grow   check   send   spend   use

1 More and more people _____ social networks these days.
2 People _____ 20% of their online time looking at social networks.
3 The number of women users _____ faster than men.
4 On average, people aged between 18 and 25 _____ 20 texts a day.
5 Fifty per cent of employers _____ job candidates' profiles on social network pages before an interview.

2 Complete the blog about the Travbuddy social network with the correct form of the verbs in brackets.

I _____¹ (post) this blog to tell you about a website I _____² (use) a lot. Travbuddy.com is a social networking website. It _____³ (specialize) in connecting travellers. The site _____⁴ (allow) users to find travel companions, create travel based blogs, and review bars, restaurants, hotels, and attractions. The website _____⁵ (claim) it is the biggest social networking site for travellers, and it _____⁶ (grow) every week. Users _____⁷ (have) access to millions of travel 'buddies', and thousands of travel reviews and blogs. I _____⁸ (like) the travel and hotel reviews most of all, and this service _____⁹ (expand) at the moment. The site is very user-friendly: I _____¹⁰ (look) at it now and I can see that 'Evan _____¹¹ (travel) to Australia' and 'Abdul _____¹² (want) to travel to Peru'.
I _____¹³ (think) you should check it out.

3 Complete the phone conversation with the correct form of the verbs in brackets.

A Beta Travel. How can I help you?
B I _____¹ (try) to book my holiday online, but I _____² (have) trouble getting a quote.
A Are you online now?
B Yes, I _____³ (look) at the booking page.
A Have you entered the number of people?
B Yes, and I _____⁴ (want) to add one child, but it _____⁵ (only show) two adults.
A Right. Could you give me the name of the hotel?
B OK. Er … Hold on. I _____⁶ (just check). It's Old College Hotel.
A I see. I'm afraid that hotel only _____⁷ (take) adult bookings.

Vocabulary Social networks and the internet

1 Read this text about blogging.

Writing a blog
If you are thinking of starting a blog, here's some simple advice.

Getting started
You can create your own website for your blog, but most people use a blogging site to host their blog. There are thousands of blogging sites on the Internet, two of the most popular are *Blogger* and *WordPress*. First of all, you'll need to create an account. After you've done this, you'll get an address for your blog. Your friends can then access your blog through this address. On your blogging page, you can write text, or upload photos and videos. When you click on the 'publish' button, your content will go live and other people can see it online. It's that simple!

Writing your blog
Style: Blogs are usually quite informal and conversational in style. People like to read them quickly so keep it fairly brief. Use short sentences and short paragraphs as these are quicker to read. Lists are a popular way of presenting information quickly.

Create a dialogue: Remember that blogging is interactive. It's about creating a dialogue with your readers or other blogs. Try to include links to other websites and blogs in your posts. People find these interesting and it helps you to join a wider blogging community. Also post comments on other people's blogs; they may then look at your own blog.

Updating your blog: Update your blog on a regular basis; once a week is quite good for a blog. When you plan your schedule, be realistic about how much time you will have available to write your blog.

Blogging content: Most importantly, post interesting content! If your blog is boring, no one will want to read it. Write about subjects that you're passionate about; no one likes to read complaints!

Blogging for business
Blogging is a great way to build relationships with potential customers. Here are a few tips: Firstly, don't update your blog too frequently, as it will seem like spam. Also avoid posting material that seems like advertising; readers hate this and they'll stop reading your blog. See them as guests on your site, not customers.

2 Are the statements about the text in **1** true or false? Correct the false statements.
1. Most people create a website for their blog.
2. A blogging site will give you an individual address for your blog.
3. You can't upload videos onto your blog.
4. A blog is often quite formal.
5. A blog is like a conversation.
6. You should post links to your blog on other people's sites.
7. You should update your blog every day.
8. You should write about what interests you.
9. Businesses shouldn't post advertising on their blogs.

3 Complete the sentences with these words.

access   chat   click   downloaded   link   log in   posted   update   uploaded

1. When you _____ to the website, you need to enter your username and password.
2. I've _____ my holiday photos onto my Facebook page so you can all see them.
3. I can _____ my email using my smartphone.
4. If you _____ this link, it will take you to our home page.
5. I _____ some songs from iTunes and put them on my mobile.
6. They _____ the website every hour so it always has the latest news.
7. She's _____ some comments on her blog about the concert.
8. You can _____ your Flickr photo album to your blog so people can see your pictures.
9. If you join our website, you can _____ with friends online or meet new people.

Work skills Writing a professional profile

1 Read the professional profile. Answer the questions below.

Chris Goddard

Freelance coach and consultant specializing in cross-cultural relations between China and Europe

Now based in London, Chris has worked in the Greater China region for more than nine years. He used this experience to found 'Uncrossed Wires' in 2005. He believes in the importance of understanding cultural differences and runs a number of training courses for companies and organizations in Europe and in China. He also offers consultancy services in Human Resources. In his free time, he likes to travel and play squash.

1. Where does Chris live now?
2. What is the name of his company?
3. What kind of training does he provide?
4. What other services does he offer?
5. What are his interests?

2 Write your future professional profile.
1. Make notes on what you think your job and life will be like in ten years' time. What position will you have? What skills? What interests?
2. Use the notes to write a professional profile for the year 'now plus ten'.

Functions Networking

We use these phrases when we meet people at a conference or networking event.
Examples It's Aziz, isn't it?
I'm sorry, I don't remember your name.
Nice / Pleased to meet you, Corinne.
We met last year at the Virtual Reality conference.
It's nice to meet you again.

We use these phrases to introduce another person.
Examples I want you to meet Pete Shen. / Would you like to meet Mr Yamada?

We use these phrases to talk about our work.
Examples I'm based in Chile.
I'm in charge of designing the company website.
Previously, I worked for (+ company).
Currently, I'm working on (+ project).
I deal with reviews of laptops and tablets.
Are you familiar with …? Yes, I am / No, I'm not.

We use these phrases to share our contact details.
Examples Here's my card.
Give me your email and I'll save it on my phone.
My email address is Collins (all one word) at tcollins dot com.

PRACTICE

1 Choose the correct words to complete the conversations.
1 A What do you do as the production manager?
   B Well, I deal *about / with* problems in the factory and things like that.
2 A Where did you work before you joined BMW?
   B *Eventually / Previously* I worked for Mercedes.
3 A Do you often come to China?
   B Yes, because *currently / recently* I'm working on a project in Beijing.
4 A Would you like *meeting / to meet* our new office manager?
   B Yes, I would. Can you introduce us, please?
5 A Let's talk again. *Give / Say* me your email and I'll save it on my phone.
   B Sure. Here's my card. It has my email and my phone number.

2 ◁)) 1.5 Listen to three conversations. What industry do the people work in?
1 Chizuko _____   2 Julienne _____   3 Nikolai _____

3 ◁)) 1.5 Complete the missing words in the extracts. Listen again and check.
1 Adriana   I want you t_____ m_____ Chizuko Honda. Chizuko, this is Felipe Diaz.
   Felipe   P_____ t_____ meet you, Chizuko.
   Chizuko   Nice to meet you too, Felipe.
   Adriana   Chizuko is i_____ c_____ of our hotels in Osaka.
2 Brian   Excuse me. It's Julienne Blanc, i_____ i_____? We met last year at the WA Forum.
   Julienne That's right. I'm so sorry, I d_____ r_____ your name.
   Brian   Brian. Brian Smith.
   Julienne Nice to m_____ you a_____, Brian.
   Brian   Are you working here in New York now?
   Julienne No, I'm not. I'm b_____ i_____ Washington.
3 Chloe   Are you f_____ w_____ our software, Nikolai?
   Nikolai   No, I'm not.
   Chloe   In that case, let's talk again. Here's m_____ c_____.
   Nikolai   Thank you. Here's mine.

2 International design

Grammar Past Simple; Present Perfect Simple and Present Perfect Continuous

INTRODUCTION

1 Work in pairs. Look at the buildings in the article in **2**. Discuss which ones you like. What do you think they are used for?

2 Read about the person who designed the buildings. Answer the questions below.

Inspiring designs

Zaha Hadid has designed some of the world's most famous and unusual modern buildings: the Aquatic Centre for the London 2012 Olympics, the Guangzhou Opera House in China, and the BMW Central Building in Germany. Zaha was born in Baghdad in 1950. She received a degree in mathematics from the American University of Beirut and then moved to the UK. She has lived in London since 1972.

She set up her own architectural office in 1980, and has been working there ever since. In 2004, she became the first woman to receive the Pritzker Award prize, and in 2010 and 2011, she won the Stirling Prize for architecture.

She is not just an architect. She has also been designing products for some time, including a range of unusual sofas and shelving units, called 'Dune Formations'. The idea for the design came from the Sumerian deserts which she visited as a teenager.

Recently, she has been working on projects in Korea, China, Italy, and France. But perhaps the most exciting of all is the Central Bank of Iraq, her first project in her native country.

1 What does Zaha Hadid do?
2 Where was she born?
3 How long has she lived in London?
4 How long has she had her own business?
5 How many times has she won the Stirling Prize?
6 What inspired her 'Dune Formations' design?
7 What has she been doing recently?

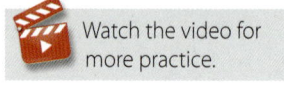 Watch the video for more practice.

3 Which architects or designers (e.g. fashion, furniture, jewellery, etc.) do you like? What do you know about their backgrounds?

Work skills Team meetings

1 **Work in pairs and discuss these questions.**
1. Do you ever go to team meetings? Who is at the meetings? What do you talk about? Where do you usually have the meetings? How long do they usually last?
2. What makes a team meeting successful or unsuccessful? Think of examples.

2 **Work in pairs. Look at the tips for the chair of a team meeting. Which do you think are the five most essential things for the chair to do?**

1. Have a clear agenda. Email this to everyone before the meeting.
2. Keep to time. Don't spend too long on one agenda point.
3. Keep the atmosphere light and friendly.
4. Agree action points for each item on the agenda. Summarize these at the end.
5. Make sure everyone has the opportunity to speak.
6. Allow time for informal conversation. This is important for team-building.
7. If a team member needs help, ask for volunteers, or offer help yourself.
8. Make sure everyone understands issues. Ask for more details if necessary.

3 **2.3 Listen to the extracts from a weekly team meeting. Are the statements true or false?**
1. Everyone is at the meeting.
2. The plans for the launch are on time.
3. The launch is over budget.
4. Carl and Sara are going to meet to discuss the budget.
5. Liza is going to speak at the sales conference.
6. The meeting has lasted 30 minutes.
7. Koichi is going to email suggestions to everyone this week.
8. The next meeting will be in the same place.

4 **2.3 Complete the sentences used by the chair of the meeting with these words. Listen again and check.**

discuss   move on   item   help   specific   sum up   fill us in   make

1. Pieter can't _____ the meeting today.
2. The first _____ on the agenda is the product launch.
3. Would you like me to _____?
4. Let's _____ to the next point.
5. Could you be a bit more _____?
6. Would you like to _____ on what's happening with that?
7. Does anyone have anything else they want to _____?
8. To _____, we've agreed that Sara and I will meet to discuss the budget for the launch, Liza is going to …

5 Which of the tips in **2** does the chair of the meeting follow?

6 **Work in groups. Have a 'team meeting' to discuss ideas for improving the class's progress on this course. Take turns to be the chair. The chair introduces the next agenda point and sums up at the end.**
- Before the meeting, prepare an agenda (i.e. each person gives a brief progress update and suggests one idea for improving progress in English).
- Agree action points for each suggestion made.

Functions Checking progress; delegating tasks

INTRODUCTION

1 Read the email and answer the questions.
1 What is the purpose of the meeting?
2 What kind of company is this?
3 What season are they working on?
4 What are 'mannequins'?

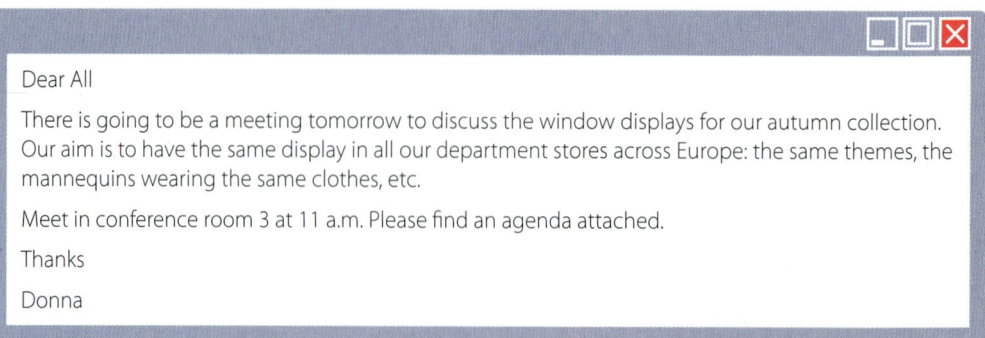

Dear All

There is going to be a meeting tomorrow to discuss the window displays for our autumn collection. Our aim is to have the same display in all our department stores across Europe: the same themes, the mannequins wearing the same clothes, etc.

Meet in conference room 3 at 11 a.m. Please find an agenda attached.

Thanks

Donna

2 ◆) 2.4 Listen to the first part of the meeting referred to in **1**. Find three mistakes in the artist's sketch of the window display.

3 ◆) 2.4 Choose the correct options to complete the sentences. Listen again and check.
1 Have we ordered the bikes *still / yet*?
2 Britta, *I / I'd* like you to handle that.
3 Leave it *on / with* me.
4 *I'd / I'm* rather not because I have a lot of other work.

4 ◆) 2.5 Listen to the second part of the meeting. Complete the notes.

Colin will arrange a meeting with _____¹ suppliers at the beginning of _____².
Last year, the _____³ of the display was wrong. Britta will fix this.
The _____⁴ for the display is on maternity leave. _____⁵ knows another one: Sven Olsen.

5 ◆) 2.5 Complete the sentences with these words. Listen again and check.

able   covered   handle   leave

1 Yes, I can _____ that.
2 I won't be _____ to do that because I'll be in New York.
3 Have we _____ everything?
4 Can I _____ this with you?

24 Unit 2 Functions

Focus

Complete the table with the phrases from 3 and 5.

Checking progress	Delegating
How are we doing with the autumn collection …?	Who's responsible for the lighting …? Is anyone free to organize the mannequins?
Agreeing to do something	**Saying you can't do something**
Yes, I can do that.	I'm not free, I'm afraid.

▶ For more details and practice, go to the Review section on page 29.

PRACTICE

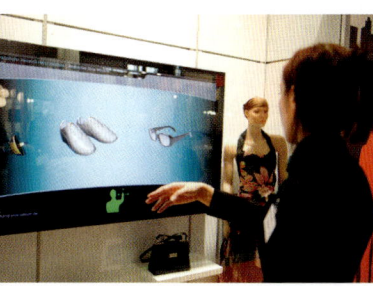

6 Complete the conversation with these phrases

I'd like you to   Have we covered   How are we doing   I can do
Is anyone free   I won't be able to do that   Leave it with me

Morgan   _____¹ with the video for our window display?
Flavia   Everything's going well. We recorded it last week. We should finish editing it next month. Does that sound OK to you?
Morgan   Yes, that's fine. _____² to show the video to our Managing Director tomorrow?
Flavia   Sorry, _____³ because I have an all-day meeting.
Morgan   What about Robert? Can he do it?
Flavia   I'll ask him today. _____⁴. I'll find someone.
Morgan   Thanks. We also need someone to make the final payment for the video production company. _____⁵ handle that too, if it's OK.
Flavia   Yes, _____⁶ that.
Morgan   Thanks. _____⁷ everything?
Flavia   Yes, that's it. …

7 Rewrite the sentences using the words in brackets.

Example   Can anyone do this job for me? (free)
            Is anyone free to do this job for me?

1   I can do that job for you. (handle)
2   I'm busy. (free)
3   Who's in charge of recruitment? (responsible)
4   Louise, will you organize this job for me? (leave)
5   I don't want to go to the meeting because I have too much work. (rather not)

TASK

8 Work in groups of four. Student A, go to page 126. Student B, go to page 131. Student C, go to page 135. Student D, go to page 136.
You are going to organize a window display for a department store. Hold the meeting using the agenda below.

1   Apologies
2   Theme of display?
3   Mannequins – Appearance? Target customer?
4   Clothing – Which items of clothing? Brands? Talk to main supplier(s)?
5   Accessories, sportswear – need to agree what appears in display with local store managers
6   A video – What to show? – get a price quote from production company
7   Summary

Review

Grammar Past Simple; Present Perfect Simple and Present Perfect Continuous

Form

Past Simple	verb + -ed*	I started my company in 2007.
		He didn't go to university.
		Where did she grow up?
Present Perfect Simple	have/has + past participle	We've bought a new car.
		I haven't seen him for ages.
		Have you been to a fashion show before?
Present Perfect Continuous	have/has + -ing form of the verb	I've been working on this project for three years.

* For a list of irregular verbs, see Pocket Book pages 40–43.

Use

Past Simple

We use the Past Simple to talk about finished actions and situations in the past.
Example   I lived in Shanghai from 2008 to 2012.

Present Perfect Simple

We use the Present Perfect Simple to talk about situations that link the past with the present in the following ways.
We talk about situations that began in the past and continue to the present.
Examples   She's been an architect since 1994.
She's been an architect for more than 10 years.

We use *for* to talk about periods of time and *since* to talk about the point when a situation started.
We talk about past actions that are relevant to the present.
Example   She has designed five office buildings.
(*We are looking for someone with experience in office design.*)

The actions may be finished or not depending on the sentence.
Examples   She has designed five office buildings. (*The buildings are complete.*)
She has completed most of the design for a sixth office. (*The building is not complete.*)

If we specify the time, we use the Past Simple.
Example   She designed six office buildings last year.

We use the Present Perfect Continuous to talk about situations that began in the past and continue to the present. The focus is on the activity and the period of time rather than the result.
Example   I've been trying to get through to David all morning. (*It's taking a long time.*)

PRACTICE

1 Choose the correct verb forms to complete the sentences.
1 I *have grown / grew* up in Chicago, but I *didn't go / haven't been* back there since my brother's wedding.
2 My parents *emigrated / have emigrated* to Chicago in the 1960s.
3 My brother *lived / has lived* there all his life: he's still there now.
4 He *opened / has opened* his first pizza shop in 1990.
5 In the early days, he *didn't employ / hasn't employed* any staff.
6 Since then, he *opened / has opened* ten pizza shops across the city.
7 He *opened / has opened* his most recent shop last year.
8 He *gave / has given* work to more than 500 people over the years.
9 He *didn't have / hasn't had* a holiday for five years, but yesterday he *booked / has booked* a world cruise for next summer.

2 Write the questions for each of the sentences in 1.
1 Where *did you grow up* ?
2 When _____?
3 How long _____?
4 When _____?
5 How many _____?
6 How many _____?
7 When _____?
8 How many _____?
9 How often _____ in the last ten years?

3 Complete the conversation using the verbs next to each line.

A *Have you heard* ¹ the news about Manuel?   hear
B No, what _____²?   happen
A He _____³ the company.   leave
B Really! When _____ this _____⁴?   happen
A He _____⁵ his notice yesterday.   give
B That's a shock. He _____⁶ here for years.   be
A I know. I _____⁷ him since he first started.   know
B When _____ you _____⁸?   find out
A Rene _____⁹ me at lunch today. Apparently he _____¹⁰   tell, speak
   to Manuel yesterday.
B What _____ he _____¹¹?   say
A He _____¹² a new job. He _____¹³ the interview last week   find, have
   and they _____¹⁴ him the job already.   offer
B That's great news for Manuel.

Vocabulary Starting a new business; phrasal verbs

1 Match 1–8 with a–h.

1 set up   ___   a the TV
2 put together   ___   b new staff
3 carry out   ___   c a problem
4 find out   ___   d a child
5 sort out   ___   e research
6 look after   ___   f new information
7 take on   ___   g a report
8 turn on   ___   h a new company

Review Unit 2

2 Replace the words in *italics* in the sentences with these phrasal verbs. Change the form of the verb if necessary.

look into   point out   put me off   sort out   take over   turn off   turn up   turn it down

1 She *arrived* / _____ late for the meeting.
2 Can you *shut down* / _____ the computer?
3 I'm *investigating* / _____ the complaints from our customers.
4 She *discouraged me from* / _____ seeing the film. She said it was awful!
5 A large multinational *bought* / _____ her company.
6 We made them an offer but they *rejected it* / _____ .
7 He managed to *solve* / _____ the problem with the printer.
8 She *drew my attention to* / _____ a few mistakes in the report.

3 2.6 Listen to the conversation and answer the questions.

1 What did Mila discuss with a financial advisor?
2 What is the problem with Mila's business plan?
3 Has Mila done any research into other websites?
4 What does Mila need to do before her next meeting?
5 What problem does she have with her web designer?
6 Who is Claudia meeting? What is she going to do while she waits?

4 2.6 Complete the sentences with these phrasal verbs. Listen again and check.

break it down   carry out   looked into   pointed out
put together   put you off   sort out   turns up

1 I need to _____ more research into existing fashion websites.
2 You've already _____ the competition.
3 She _____ that my idea is easy to copy.
4 Don't let that _____ . I thought your idea was great.
5 I need to _____ a marketing plan.
6 She wants me to _____ into markets.
7 I also need to _____ a few problems with our web designer.
8 He always _____ half an hour late!

Work skills Team meetings

1 Match 1–8 with a–h to make sentences from a team meeting.

1 I'm afraid Junko can't   ___
2 The first item on   ___
3 Would you like   ___
4 Does anyone have anything else ___
5 Could you be   ___
6 Let's move on   ___
7 So to sum up, we've   ___
8 Can you fill us in   ___

a me to help?
b to the next point.
c they want to discuss?
d on what's happening with the marketing campaign?
e the agenda is the sales conference.
f make the meeting today.
g a bit more specific?
h agreed that Tom is going to write a report.

2 2.7 Listen to the beginning of a team meeting. Answer the questions.

1 Is there anyone who can't attend the meeting? If so, who?
2 What two things is Jay working on?
3 Why did they choose Radio 6 and Jazz FM for their adverts?
4 What has Jay done recently for the radio campaign?
5 Why is he confident that the writers are good?
6 What is Virginia working on?

Functions Checking progress; delegating tasks

In meetings, we use these phrases to check progress of projects, etc.
Examples How are we doing with (project)?
Have we covered everything?
Have we done (job / task) yet?

We use these phrases when we want to delegate tasks.
Examples Can you deal with (task)?
Who's going to look after (task)?
Who's responsible for (+ noun or verb -*ing*)?
I'd like you to handle that. / Can I leave this with you?
Is anyone free to (do a job)?

We use these phrases to agree to do something.
Examples Yes, I can do that. / Yes, we can handle that.
Leave it with me.

We use these phrases to say we can't do something.
Examples I'm not free, I'm afraid.
I won't be able to do that because … / I'd rather not because …

PRACTICE

1 Put the words in the right order to complete the conversations.

1. A (*go / free / to / anyone / is*) _____ to the conference next week?
   B Yes, Antonio is. Ask him.
2. A Lukas, can you meet our visitors at the airport, please?
   B (*that / I / yes / do / can*) _____ .
3. A (*doing / are / with / we / how*) _____ the new product range?
   B Everything's fine. We'll get final approval from Head Office next week.
4. A Otto, can you put the data on the website today?
   B Sorry, (*to / I / be / that / able / do / won't*) _____ because I don't have all the figures yet.
5. A I think that's the end of the meeting. (*everything / covered / we / have*) _____ ?
   B Yes, that's it. We can finish there.
6. A Eric, can you organize the shifts in the factory for the next six months?
   B (*handle / can / yes / that / I*) _____ .

2 ◁) 2.8 Listen to four conversations. Tick ✓ if the people can do the job. Cross ✗ if they can't do the job.

1 ☐   2 ☐   3 ☐   4 ☐

3 ◁) 2.8 Complete the sentences with a word in each gap. Listen again and check.

1. a Have we paid the staff bonuses _____?
   b Can I _____ this with you, Barry?
2. a Who's going to _____ after the lighting for the photo shoot tomorrow? Mia?
   b I'd _____ not because I have a doctor's appointment in the afternoon.
3. a Gordon, I'd like you to _____ that. Tomorrow?
   b No, I'm not free, I'm _____ .
4. a Who's responsible _____ organizing the cars?
   b _____ it with me.

3 Future lifestyles

Grammar *will, may, might, be likely / possible*

INTRODUCTION

1 Work in pairs and discuss these questions.

1. What predictions about the future have you heard about recently? Do you believe them?
2. Do you know any predictions that have come true?
3. Have you ever made an accurate prediction?

2 Read the article. Which predictions were correct? How are the ideas similar to our current world?

Example 'Newspapers will publish colour photographs of a battle in China an hour later.' This idea is similar to digital photography.

What may happen in the next hundred years ...

In 1900, an American civil engineer called John Watkins made a number of predictions about the world in 2000. Some of them were wrong, but some were either completely correct or nearly correct.

- Wireless telephone circuits will cross the world.
- Newspapers will publish colour photographs of a battle in China an hour later.
- People will buy ready-cooked meals from stores similar to our bakeries of today.
- All fast traffic within the city will be below ground or above ground level.
- Powerful electric light will speed up the growth of vegetables.
- A husband in the middle of the Atlantic will be able to talk to his wife sitting at home in Chicago.
- Man will see around the world. Cameras will connect electrically with screens to show moving pictures thousands of miles away.
- Pneumatic tubes will connect all houses to deliver mail and goods.

3 🔊 **3.1** Listen to the experts discussing John Watkins' predictions and answer the questions.
1 Which predictions did they discuss?
2 What does Dr Blavatnik think about the future of traffic in cities?
3 What is Professor Kean's prediction about traffic in new cities?
4 How might we grow vegetables in the future, according to Dr Blavatnik?
5 What does Professor Kean say about the global population?

> **Focus**
>
> **Find and underline these phrases in the script on pages 141 and 142. Put the phrases in the correct place on the scale below.**
>
> a will probably   d will definitely   g is likely
> b probably won't   e might   h is unlikely
> c definitely won't   f may   i is possible
>
>   c
> ──▶
> 0% impossible   possible   certain 100%
>
> Add these expressions to the scale.
> j I am sure X will   k I don't think X will   l I think X will
>
> Note the structure we use with *likely / unlikely / possible*.
> **It is likely that** there'll be a car-free zone.
> **It's unlikely that** *all* traffic **will** be below ground or above ground level.
> **It is possible that** there **will** be enough water for everyone.
>
> ⏩ For more details and practice, go to the Review section on pages 38 and 39.

PRACTICE

4 Read the sentences and write a second sentence with a similar meaning.
1 We will definitely prevent malaria by 2050.
  I am _____.
2 People will probably grow taller in the future.
  It is _____.
3 The earth probably won't cool down in the next 50 years.
  It is _____.
4 There definitely won't be a colony on Mars in my lifetime.
  I am _____.
5 In the future, it might be possible to fly from New York to Tokyo in less than two hours.
  We _____.
6 It is likely that oil reserves will run out by 2050.
  Oil reserves _____.
7 It is unlikely that we will find intelligent life on another planet.
  We _____.
8 Print newspapers may disappear.
  It is _____.
9 It is possible there will be a direct train line between the UK and China by 2100.
  There _____.
10 I am sure cars will become hands-free.
  Cars _____.

5 Do you agree with the predictions in **4**? Change any sentences you don't agree with.

6 ◉ **3.2** Listen to three young professionals talk about their future. Make a note of their answers to the questions in the table.

	Yolanda	Dmitri	Haruka
1 Will you buy your own house / apartment?	*probably won't*		
2 Will you have more than one child?			
3 Will you work until you are 70?			

7 Work in pairs. Take turns to ask your partner about how they see their future.

TASK

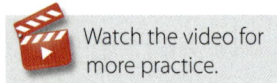
Watch the video for more practice.

8 Choose five questions from the list to ask other people in the class. Make a note of people's answers in the table below.

In the next hundred years, do you think …?
- people will stop commuting – they will live and work in the same building
- children will learn online – school will only be for learning social skills
- travel to other countries will be limited to top businesspeople and celebrities
- most people will live in cities
- all cities will have free wireless connectivity
- food will be produced in factories – the countryside will be used only for leisure activities
- travel using carbon-based transport will be banned

Name				
Question 1				
Question 2				
Question 3				
Question 4				
Question 5				

32   Unit 3 Grammar ■□□□□

Vocabulary The speed of change; describing cause and effect

1 Work in pairs and discuss these questions.
   1 In what ways has computer technology changed our lives? Make a list.
   2 Do you think the world is becoming more competitive? Why / Why not?

2 Read the text and answer the questions below.

The power of numbers

There is an Indian legend that goes like this: once upon a time, a king challenged a pilgrim to a game of chess. The pilgrim agreed, but on one condition: if the king lost, he would put a single grain of rice on the first chess square and then double the amount on every square after that. The king lost and then discovered the price he had to pay: 1 grain on the first square, 2 on the second, 4 on the third, 8 on the fourth, and so on. By the 64th square, the amount came to more than 18,000,000,000,000,000,000 grains of rice!

A modern example of this type of growth is Moore's Law. This law says that the power of computer microchips doubles every 18 months. We can see the effects of this if we compare the space shuttle with a smartphone. The computer on the first space shuttle could process 400,000 instructions per second and had a memory of 424 kilobytes. A modern smartphone is over 35,000 times quicker and has over 33,000,000 times more memory! These increases in computing power have caused scientific discovery to speed up. It took the Human Genome Project 13 years, from 1990 to 2003, to analyse the entire human genome*. Due to faster computers, scientists can now do this in a week. In the next decades, computers will equal the power of the human brain. This may result in the development of computers that are more intelligent than humans. The possible consequences of this are profound.

The increasing speed of scientific discovery is also partly the result of larger social trends. In the 1960s in the UK, about 5% of young people went to university. Nowadays, 40% of people in the UK do a degree, whilst in Finland the number has reached 80%. Between 2000 and 2010, the number of students studying in universities abroad rose by 75%. Because of the increase in university students, more people now do research at a postgraduate level. This has created greater competition between research departments for funding. As a result, there is more pressure on scientists to publish their findings quickly. This new research leads to other new discoveries and, as a consequence, new technologies are developed more rapidly.

The speed of change is hard to cope with because it means we need to keep learning and adapting. But we'd better get used to it: it's not going to slow down!

*genome = the complete set of genes in a cell or living thing

1 Why did the king have to give the pilgrim so much rice?
2 What is Moore's Law?
3 Which has more memory: the computer on the first space shuttle or a smartphone?
4 Why is it now quicker to analyse human genes?
5 How many people now go to university in the UK and in Finland?
6 Why is research now published more quickly?

3 Look at the phrases in *italics* in the sentences used to talk about cause and effect. Underline the cause in each sentence and circle the effect.
1 *Because of* the fall in sales, (we will need to cut our sales team).
2 We closed down our factory in England. *As a consequence*, we have managed to lower our production costs significantly.
3 Belinda's quit her job *because* she wants to start her own company.
4 *Due to* the rising price of copper, our manufacturing costs have increased.
5 The new law *has led to* a reduction in crime.
6 The marketing campaign *resulted in* a 15% increase in sales.
7 The fall in share prices in 2008 *was the result of* the banking crisis.
8 The factory *will cause* more pollution in the surrounding area.
9 We've recently spent more money on advertising; *as a result*, sales of our new smartphone have risen.
10 The development of the business park *will create* hundreds of jobs in the area.

4 ◉ 3.3 Listen to four people talking about changing trends. What topics are they talking about?

Speaker 1 _____
Speaker 2 _____
Speaker 3 _____
Speaker 4 _____

5 ◉ 3.3 Complete the sentences with these phrases. Sometimes more than one phrase is possible. Listen again and compare your answers with the phrases used in the recording.

as a consequence   because of   the result of   lead to   as a result   due to   cause   result in

1 _____ the growing popularity of 3-D television, I think TV will have a bigger impact upon sport.
2 There will be more sporting events in Asia and Africa. _____ this, I think we'll see a lot more sportspeople coming from these countries.
3 Forty-seven per cent of Swedish households now only have one person living in them. _____, one of the big problems will be social isolation.
4 This may also _____ a rise in property prices.
5 This growing trend is _____ economic changes.
6 For the developing nations, this will _____ many social changes.
7 People want to access books through digital devices, such as a Kindle or a tablet. _____, the way we publish books is changing.
8 Digital publishing will _____ major changes to the way we work.

6 Work in groups. Do you agree with the speakers in **5**? What other future trends can you think of? What do you think the consequences of these trends will be? Consider the following areas.

- technology
- food
- transport
- work
- lifestyle and entertainment
- housing and living conditions

34 Unit 3 Vocabulary

Work skills Emails 1: confirming arrangements

1 **Work in pairs and discuss these questions.**
   1 How often do you send / receive emails in English? What do you find difficult about writing emails in another language?
   2 What is the difference between emails you write to work colleagues and to friends? Do you use different kinds of language?

2 **Work in pairs. Read the three emails and answer the questions.**
   1 Where is Nell Hart going?
   2 When is she arriving?
   3 Who is she meeting for dinner?
   4 Which of the emails is
      a from a colleague to a colleague who they don't know very well? ___
      b from a company to a client / customer? ___
      c from a friend to a friend? ___

A

Dear Ms Hart

I am writing to confirm[1] the arrangements for your flights from London Heathrow to Singapore. We have booked you on the 10 a.m. flight on Monday 1 October. *Please find your e-ticket attached*[2]. *Please be sure to print this out*[3] and take it with you to the airport. Your return flight is on Friday 5 October at 8 p.m. You can check in online 24 hours before your flight.

Could you please confirm that[4] you do not require our taxi pickup from the airport?

Thank you for booking with BizTravUK.

Kind regards,

R Smith

Booking Agent

B

Dear Yi Ling

Thank you for making the arrangements at the Singapore office for me at such short notice. *I'd like to confirm that*[5] I'll be arriving late afternoon your time. *Can you just confirm that*[6] someone will be at the airport to meet me?

I've attached an agenda for the meeting on Tuesday[7]. *Please can you look at it*[8] and let me know if there's anything you want to add?

I'm looking forward to meeting you again.

Best wishes,

Nell Hart

Director International Operations

C

Hey Tom!

Great news that you can meet me in Singapore! What an amazing coincidence that I'm coming out for work while you're out there. My hotel looks lovely (*check out the attachment*[9])!

Wednesday evening sounds fine[10] for meeting up, but 7 p.m. is a bit early. Is 8 p.m. OK with you? *Let me know if that suits*[11]. BTW I didn't catch the name of the restaurant on the phone. *Can you text it to me*[12]? Thanks!

See you next week.

Bye for now,

Nell

3 **Work in pairs. Match the numbered phrases in the emails in 2 with the categories below. Which phrases are more formal?**
   a Giving confirmation: ___, ___, ___
   b Asking for confirmation: ___, ___, ___
   c Referring to attachments: ___, ___, ___
   d Requesting an action: ___, ___, ___

4 **Work in pairs. Student A, go to page 131. Student B, go to page 135.**

Functions Making arrangements

INTRODUCTION

1 Work in groups. When you make arrangements to meet colleagues or friends, which of these methods do you prefer? Why?

emailing   talking face-to-face   talking on the phone
texting / instant messaging

2 ◉ 3.4 Work in pairs. Listen to a conversation between two managers, Dave Warner and Elke Christen. Answer the questions.
1 What are their companies going to do?
2 What industry do they work in?
3 Which countries are their companies based in?

3 ◉ 3.4 Complete these notes from the meeting. Listen again and check.

Arrange a _____¹-day visit to Switzerland.
Begin with a dinner where the _____² can get to meet each other.
Venue for the dinner will be a restaurant in _____³.
Proposed date for the dinner: _____⁴.

4 Work in groups. Elke and Dave are going to call members of their team to check the dates for the visit. Do you think this will be easy? What problems might they have?

5 ◉ 3.5 Listen to Elke and Dave calling members of their team. Write the days the people are free.

1 Reto _____   3 Cheryl _____
2 Tony _____   4 Anna _____

6 ◉ 3.5 Listen again and complete the extracts from the conversations.

1 **Elke** We're trying to arrange a meeting with the US managers and the Swiss managers, here in Switzerland. _____¹ on 30th August?
   Reto The 30th? Hmm ... I'm busy then because I'm in Geneva _____². I can make the 31st though.
   Elke OK, thanks. I can't confirm the date now because I need to speak to the _____³. I'll get back to you.

2 **Tony** When were you thinking of?
   Dave Is August 30th _____¹ you?
   Tony August 30th? Yeah, that should be fine. I just need to check _____². I'll get back to you _____³, OK?
   Dave Great. Thanks, Tony.

3 **Cheryl** I'm afraid that August is no good for me because I'm away _____¹.
   Dave I'm sorry, I forgot.
   Cheryl Why don't we meet _____²? Er ... Is September 4th good for you?
   Dave September 4th? Hmm, I need to check that with Elke in Zurich.
   Cheryl September is best for me.
   Dave I'll try and change _____³. As soon as I know, I'll let you know.

36 Unit 3 Functions

4 Elke I'm calling _____¹.
Anna Yes, I read your email.
Elke Reto suggested August 31st. Does that sound OK to you?
Anna I can't make August 31st. It's my daughter's _____².
Elke How about the next week? Is September 3rd good for you?
Anna That suits _____³.
Elke Great. Let's _____⁴ in September 3rd.

7 Work in pairs. Everyone in **6** suggests a different time. How would you resolve this situation?

Focus

Match phrases 1–4 with functions a–d.

1 I'm busy then because I'm in Geneva all day.
2 Is August 30th convenient for you?
3 As soon as I know, I'll let you know.
4 That suits me fine.

a Agreeing to a date / time
b Saying a date / time is not convenient
c Suggesting a date / time
d Waiting on a decision

Look again at the conversations in 6. Find one more phrase for a–d above. Compare your answers with a partner. Do you have the same phrases?

▶ For more details and practice, go to the Review section on page 41.

PRACTICE

8 Complete the conversation with these phrases.

as soon as   busy then   can't make   convenient for you
don't we meet on pencil in   sounds good to

A We want to have a dinner to welcome the new members of the team. Is Friday the 10th _____¹?
B The 10th? Sorry, I'm _____² because I'm visiting the factory in Budapest. Why _____³ Thursday?
A I _____⁴ Thursday because I have visitors at my house.
B The following week then. Would you rather meet on Wednesday or Thursday?
A Wednesday, I think. I may need to go to watch my daughter's basketball match at school. _____⁵ I know, I'll let you know.
B OK, but let's _____⁶ Wednesday for now.
A That _____⁷ me.

9 Work in pairs. Take turns to say the sentences and respond, using a phrase from the Focus section.

1 Let's choose a time for our next English class. Why don't we meet on Saturday at 12.00?
2 I can't make the dinner at your house on Friday night.
3 We need to arrange a job interview with you. Is Monday morning convenient for you?
4 I want you and John to come to the meeting. John thinks he's free on the 4th of October, but he's not sure.
5 You can see the dentist at 9 a.m., 1 p.m., or 5 p.m. What time would suit you best?
6 Some people are interested in buying your flat and they want to come and see it. Is next Sunday good for you?

TASK **10** Work in groups of three or four. Go to page 138.

Review

Grammar *will, may, might, be likely / possible*

Form

will future	subject + will / won't + verb	The population will continue to grow.
		There won't be enough food for everyone.
		Will we write letters in the future?
will + definitely / probably	subject + will + definitely / probably + verb	We will probably / definitely find life forms on other planets.
might	subject + might (not) + verb	The climate might change.
may	subject + may (not) + verb	Some areas may suffer from drought.
be likely / unlikely / possible	it + be + likely / possible / unlikely + will + verb	It is likely that oil will run out soon.

We change *will* to *will not / won't* to form the negative. We often put *definitely* or *probably* before *won't*, but after *will*.
Examples We probably / definitely won't find life forms on other planets.
　　　　　　We will probably find life forms on other planets.

We put *I am sure / I think / I don't think* before *will*.
Example   I am sure it will rain tomorrow.

We often use *It is …* with *likely / unlikely / possible*.
Examples **It is likely that** I'll be late for the meeting tomorrow.
　　　　　　It's unlikely that James **will** be able to come to the annual meeting.

Use

We use *will* to make predictions about the future.
We use *might, may, be likely / possible / unlikely* to describe the degree of possibility of something happening in the future.
We use *I am sure / I think / I don't think* to indicate how certain we are about a future event.

Use	Examples
Certain	The use of smartphones **will** (**definitely**) increase. **I am sure** the use of smartphones **will** (**definitely**) increase.
Likely	The cost of mobile technology **will probably** fall. It**'s likely** that in the future we**'ll** import more phones than we export. **I think** the use of smartphones **will** increase.
Possible	Tablets **might** replace textbooks. Food **may** become more expensive. It **is possible** that everyone **will** speak English.
Unlikely	It**'s unlikely** that Earth **will** be hit by a meteorite. People **probably won't** choose to have holidays in space. **I don't think** the use of smartphones **will** increase.
Impossible	People **definitely won't** live on Mars.

PRACTICE

1 Complete the sentences according to the degree of possibility next to each line.

1	Cities like São Paolo _____ continue to grow.	certain
2	There _____ be no more oil by 2050.	possible
3	I _____ we _____ find another planet similar to Earth.	likely
4	Dogs _____ learn to talk.	impossible
5	The population of India _____ fall in the next five years.	unlikely
6	People _____ do most of their shopping online.	possible
7	The internet _____ not disappear.	certain
8	We _____ find a cheap solution for producing energy.	unlikely
9	The average lifespan _____ exceed 120 years.	impossible
10	Robots _____ do more of the jobs that humans currently do.	likely

2 Find and correct the mistakes in the sentences. You may need to change the word order, the form of the verb, or change adjectives for adverbs (or adverbs for adjectives).
1 There will be definitely more people living in the cities.
2 I suppose it might happen, but I'm not surely.
3 It's possibly, but I think it's unlikely.
4 I think it's more likely that the number of people living in cities is increasing.
5 Pollution from cars might be increase.
6 I sure we will need to control population growth.

3 Read the predictions about the future of communication. Write a sentence expressing your opinion about how possible the predictions are.
1 Most people in the world will speak English as a second language.
2 Most people will study English digitally, not in the classroom.
3 Chinese will become the most common language of business.
4 Only ten main languages will continue to exist.
5 More communication will be digital than spoken.

Vocabulary The speed of change; describing cause and effect

1 Choose the correct words to complete the sentences.
1 *Because / Due to / As a result* the fall in unemployment, it is now easier to get a job.
2 The rise in oil prices has *caused / led / resulted* in higher manufacturing and transportation costs.
3 She moved back to New Zealand *as a result / because / due* she wanted to be close to her family.
4 The invention of the World Wide Web *created / led / resulted* to a revolution in the way people communicate.
5 Orders have increased dramatically over the past year. *As a consequence / Because of / Due to*, we plan to open a new factory in June.
6 The good end-of-year results *caused / resulted / led* the company's share price to rise.
7 He had to leave his job *a consequence / the result / because* of illness.
8 The discovery was *caused / due to / the result* of years of hard work by the research team.

2 Join the sentences together using the cause and effect words in brackets. Make any changes to the sentences and words in brackets that are necessary.

1 There was a build-up of gas. There was an explosion. (cause)
   The build-up of gas caused an explosion.

2 He's bought a new laptop. His old laptop is broken. (because)
   _____

3 There's been a rise in orders. We need to take on more staff. (as a result)
   _____

4 There was heavy snow last night. The road is closed today. (due to)
   _____

5 There is increased demand for natural gas. There has been a rise in gas prices. (lead to)
   _____

6 She has to wear glasses. She has poor eyesight. (because of)
   _____

7 There was a decision to close the factory. There were many job losses. (result in)
   _____

8 He's been eating a lot of junk food. He has put on weight. (as a consequence)
   _____

Work skills Emails 1: confirming arrangements

1 Complete the email with these phrases.

I've attached   Can you just confirm   if that's OK with you
to seeing you   Best wishes   you want to add

Hi Jerry

Concerning our phone conversation just now, it sounds like we may have a serious problem. I think we'd better get the team together in Paris as soon as possible. _____¹ that you can make a meeting tomorrow in Paris? I'd prefer to meet early afternoon _____². _____³ the agenda for the meeting. I've put down the main points. Can you let me know if there's anything _____⁴?
Look forward _____⁵ tomorrow.
_____⁶,

Nico

2 Use Jerry's notes to write an email to Nico in Paris.

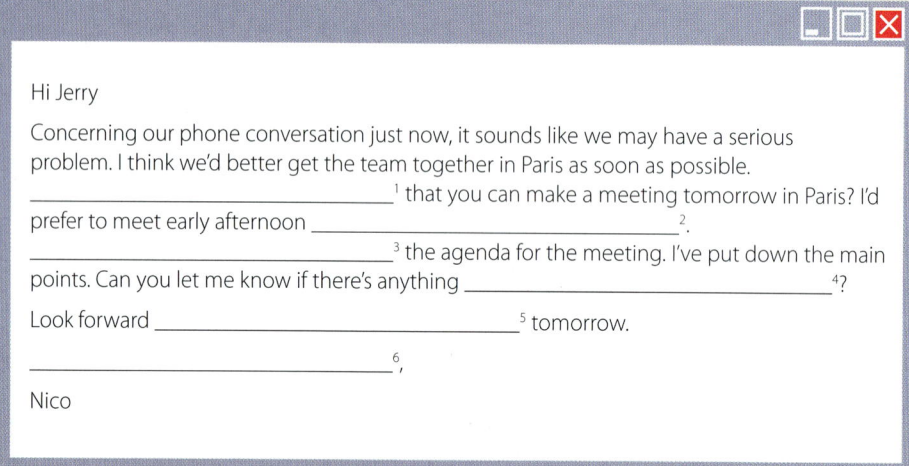

- Confirm that I can attend the meeting in Paris.
- Tell them my flight number and arrival time.
- Check someone will meet me at airport.
- Request details of meeting room and time of meeting.
- Attach new agenda with additional points.

Functions Making arrangements

When making arrangements, we use these phrases to suggest a time to meet.
Examples Are you free on (date)?
Does (date / day / time) sound good to you?
Is (date / day / time) convenient / good for you?
Why don't we meet (*in* + month / *on* + date)?

We use these phrases to agree a time.
Examples I can make (date / day / time).
That should be / suits me fine.

We use these phrases to say a time is not convenient for us.
Examples I can't make (day / date / time).
I'm afraid that (day / date / time) is no good for me.
I'm busy then.

We use these phrases when we are waiting on a decision about a time to meet.
Examples As soon as I know, I'll let you know.
I can't confirm the date / time right now.
I'll get back to you tomorrow.
Let's pencil in (3rd September).

PRACTICE

1 Choose the correct words to complete the sentences.
1 They want to meet tomorrow? That *must / should* be fine.
2 Is the day after tomorrow good *for / with* you?
3 I need to check the day with Simon. As soon *as / when* I know, I'll let you know.
4 Is 19th July convenient *by / for* you?
5 Let's pencil *in / on* 4th December.
6 We need to change the day of the meeting. I can't *make / take* next Thursday.
7 Monday morning suits *it / me* fine. I'll see you then.

2 Rewrite the sentences using the words in brackets.
1 We don't know if 16th May is OK at the moment. (confirm)
___
2 I won't be able to meet tomorrow afternoon. (afraid)
___
3 An 8 a.m. meeting on Wednesday is OK for me. (make)
___
4 How about meeting on 18th May? (don't)
___
5 She'll give you her answer next week. (back)
___
6 Is 7 p.m. in the Jasmine Garden restaurant OK? (sound)
___
7 I'm working all day tomorrow. (busy)
___
8 How about lunchtime on 15th October? (free)
___

3 ◆)) **3.6 Listen to six conversations. Are the people agreeing a time, saying it's not convenient, or waiting on a decision? Tick ✓ the correct column.**

Conversation	1	2	3	4	5	6
Agreeing						
Saying not convenient						
Waiting on a decision						

4 Heritage

Grammar Making comparisons

INTRODUCTION

1 Work in pairs and discuss these questions.
1 Which art museums do you know of?
2 Which art museums have you visited or would like to visit?

2 ◆)) 4.1 Listen to an art expert, Jacques Martin, talk about three of the world's most popular art museums. Complete the information below.

National Gallery
Location	London
Opened	_____¹
Size	46,396 m²
Paintings	2,300
Famous painting	*Sunflowers* by Van Gogh
Visitors	_____² million
Tickets	free
Popular exhibition	Leonardo da Vinci: 333,897 visitors

Musée du Louvre
Location	Paris
Opened	1793
Size	_____³
Paintings	7,500
Famous painting	_____⁴ by Leonardo da Vinci
Visitors	8.8 million
Tickets	€_____⁵
Popular exhibition	Rembrandt: 225,000 visitors

Metropolitan Museum of Art
Location	New York
Opened	1870
Size	190,000 m²
Paintings	_____⁶ European paintings 13,000 works of modern art
Famous painting	*The Great Wave* by Hokusai
Visitors	6 million
Tickets	$25
Popular exhibition	_____⁷: 661,509 visitors

3 ◆)) 4.2 Listen and complete the sentences.
1 The National is the _____ museum.
2 It opened in 1753 and is just _____ than the Louvre.
3 The Louvre is _____ than the Met, which charges $25.
4 The _____ painting of all is the *Mona Lisa* by Leonardo da Vinci.
5 The Louvre has _____ transport connections.
6 But this wasn't _____ the Met's fashion exhibition by Alexander McQueen.
7 Surprisingly, this was _____ than the Louvre's Rembrandt show.
8 The Louvre's Rembrandt show was the _____ of the three.

Focus

Use the sentences in 3 to complete the rules with the following.

more / less   -er   -est   most / least

One-syllable adjectives

We add _____ to the end of the adjective to make the comparative.
We add _____ to the end of the adjective to make the superlative.

Two-syllable and three-syllable adjectives

We put _____ before the adjective to make the comparative.
We put _____ before the adjective to make the superlative.

Two-syllable adjectives ending in -y

We change the -y to -i and add -er / -est to the end of the adjective.

Irregular adjectives

good	better	best
bad	worse	worst
far	further	furthest

We use *as* + adjective + *as* to show that things are the same or equal.
The National is **as good as** the Louvre.
We use *not as* + adjective + *as* to show that things are not the same or equal.
The Met is **not as old as** the Louvre.

▶ For more details and practice, go to the Review section on pages 50 and 51.

PRACTICE

4 Complete the second sentence so that it has the same meaning as the first sentence.

1 The Rembrandt painting is worth more than the Picasso or the Van Gogh.
   The Rembrandt is _____ valuable painting.
2 The Hermitage Museum isn't as big as the Prado Museum.
   The Prado is _____ than the Hermitage.
3 This landscape is bigger than that portrait.
   That portrait is _____ than this landscape.
4 This Van Gogh is older than the Picasso.
   The Picasso isn't _____ as this Van Gogh.
5 We saw more paintings than sculptures.
   We didn't see _____ sculptures.
6 The Uffizi Gallery opened 200 years before the Prado Museum.
   The Uffizi Gallery is _____ than the Prado Museum.
7 I've never seen such a beautiful painting.
   It's the _____ painting I've ever seen.
8 **A** I think Seurat was a better painter than Monet.
   B I don't think so. Seurat isn't _____ as Monet.
9 This exhibition isn't as interesting as last year's.
   Last year's exhibition was _____ than this year's.
10 The entrance fee for the Prado is more than the Hermitage or the Uffizi.
   The Hermitage is _____ expensive than the Prado.

5 Work in pairs. Make comparisons about the three museums in **2**. Take turns to make a second sentence with the same meaning.

Example   **A** The Met is a lot bigger than the National.
            B The National is a lot smaller than the Met.

Watch the video for more practice.

6 🔊 **4.3** Listen and put the adjectives in the correct group.

~~interesting~~   dirty   educational   relaxing   exciting   dangerous
beautiful   independent   expensive   international   enjoyable   professional

1st syllable stress	2nd syllable stress	3rd syllable stress
interesting		

7 Work in pairs. Ask and answer questions about places you have visited or lived. Use your own ideas or an appropriate adjective from **6**.

Example   **A** Where is the most interesting place you've visited?
            B Egypt is the most interesting place I've visited recently.

TASK 8 Work in pairs. You are organizing a trip of a lifetime with your partner. Look at the article on temples in Asia. Compare the temples and choose which one you are going to visit. Give reasons for your decision using *-er*, *more*, *-est*, *most*, and *(not) as … as*.

Example   We've decided to visit Kinkaku-ji because it is the most beautiful. It's more …

High Flyer Special Feature

Asia is home to some of the most amazing temples in the world. Here are three of our favourites.

Tiger's Nest Monastery, Bhutan

The Tiger's Nest or Taktsang was built in 1692. It is one of the most famous temples in Bhutan. The temple is at the top of a 1200-metre cliff and it takes between two and three hours to walk there. Visitors need special permission to visit and should go with a guide.

Visitors to Bhutan pay a minimum of $250 per day in high season.

Kinkaku-ji, Kyoto

Kinkaku-ji is a Zen temple built in 1397. One of the buildings is the Golden Pavilion, a three-storey building surrounded by a lake and beautiful gardens. The top two floors of the pavilion are covered in gold leaf. The building was built originally as a villa for the shogun Ashikaga Yoshimitsu. Today the temple and gardens are open to the public.

The entrance fee is $4 and the temple is 40 minutes from Kyoto station by bus.

Ankor Wat, Cambodia

Ankor Wat is the most famous temple in the largest archaeological site in the world. The site covers a 400-kilometre area and contains an amazing number of temples and ancient buildings.

A one-day pass is $20 and a guide is about $20.

It is 20-minutes' drive from the nearest town, Siem Reap. It takes four hours to get to Siem Reap from the capital, Phnom Penh.

Vocabulary City descriptions; -ing vs -ed adjectives

1 Work in pairs. Read the text about the Japanese city Kyoto and make notes under these headings.

Geography   Climate   Business / Industry
Places to visit   Places to stay   Food

City profile: Kyoto, Japan

If you're **interested** in Japan, then you must visit Kyoto. Along with Tokyo, it's one of the most cosmopolitan and **fascinating** cities in Japan. A mixture of the traditional and the modern, you'll find ancient temples, lively bars, and wonderful restaurants. If you go, you won't be **disappointed**. The local people are always **pleased** to see visitors, and the food is **amazing**!

Geography and history

Kyoto is in the western part of Japan's main island Honshu. It is surrounded by three mountains and the Kamogawa river passes through the centre of the city. For most of Japanese history, Kyoto was the official capital where the Japanese emperor lived. But Kyoto isn't just a city of tourism. Many people are **surprised** to learn that Kyoto is also an important centre for information technology and education. The electronic games company Nintendo is one of many IT companies that have their headquarters in the city, and Kyoto University is one of the top universities in the world.

When to go

Kyoto has a sub-tropical climate, with mild winters and hot and humid summers. The most popular time to visit is autumn, when the leaves change colour and the temple gardens look **stunning**. But be warned! This time of year is very popular, so if you're **annoyed** by large crowds, go another time when it is less busy.

What to see

Kyoto has so many **interesting** places to visit, including 17 World Heritage sites. Highlights include:
- Temples: the most famous temple in Kyoto is Kinkaku-ji ('The Golden Temple').
- Castles: Nijo Castle has a 'nightingale floor' – a wooden floor that squeaks to warn the shogun of possible assassins.
- Geishas: in Gion, the traditional geisha district, you can still see trainee geishas, called 'maiko', walking down the street in their wooden shoes.
- Bamboo forests: if you go to Arashiyama in the north of the city, you can walk through forests of giant bamboo.

What to eat

If you're feeling **tired** from looking at so many temples, stop and try the incredible food on offer in Kyoto. A famous kind of food is kaiseki ryori, which has many small dishes presented in the most beautiful way. Shojin ryori is based on the vegetarian food eaten by Buddhist monks. It contains tofu in a pot, which sounds **boring**, but is actually very tasty.

Where to stay

There are hundreds of hotels in the city centre. If you want a **surprising** experience, you could stay in a capsule hotel where you sleep inside a small space set into a wall. If you want a more relaxing place to stay, why not stay in a ryokan (a traditional Japanese inn)? You'll sleep well and eat the most delicious food.

2 Match the adjectives in blue in the text to these words with a similar meaning.

1	attracted to	_interested_	7	weary	_____
2	extremely interesting	_____	8	fantastic	_____
3	unusual	_____	9	unhappy	_____
4	irritated	_____	10	intriguing	_____
5	beautiful	_____	11	happy	_____
6	not interesting	_____	12	astonished	_____

3 Work in pairs and answer these questions about the adjectives in blue in the text.
1 Which of the adjectives do we use
   a to describe how we feel about something?
      _____
   b to describe something that causes the feelings?
      _____
2 What do you notice about the endings of the adjectives?

4 Complete the sentences by adding *-ing* or *-ed* to the adjectives.
1 I was really disappoint___ by the hotel. It wasn't like the advert at all.
2 This guidebook is fascinat___. You must read it.
3 I hate it when the trains are delayed. It's so annoy___.
4 I'm interest___ in Chinese history – I'm hoping to visit Beijing next year.
5 The cherry blossom in Yoshino is stunn___ in spring.
6 We've been walking for hours. I'm really tir___.
7 The food in that restaurant was amaz___. We must go back.
8 I was surpris___ by her reaction. She seemed very pleased.

5 Work in pairs. Ask and answer the questions.
1 When were you last surprised / annoyed / disappointed / pleased? Why?
2 What do you find interesting / fascinating / annoying? Why?
3 What makes you feel relaxed / tired / bored? Why?
Example **A** When were you last surprised?
          B I was surprised when I got a promotion. I wasn't expecting it.

6 Which of these adjectives from the text in **1** can you use to describe the things below? You can use more than one adjective to describe some of the things.

ancient   cosmopolitan   delicious   famous   humid
lively   modern   popular   traditional

1 _____ dance / dish / music
2 _____ area / city
3 _____ castle / palace / temple
4 _____ artist / painting / scientist
5 _____ climate / weather
6 _____ area / bar / party
7 _____ dinner / dish / food
8 _____ architecture / building / shopping centre
9 _____ destination / resort / venue

7 Work in pairs. Use the adjectives you have studied to describe one of the places below.

your home town   the town / city where you live now   a holiday destination

8 Write a profile of your place from **7**. Use the city profile in **1** as a guide.

Work skills Presentations 1: using visual aids

1 Work in pairs. Match these visual aids used in presentations with 1–4.

slide with prompt words   pie chart   table   line graph

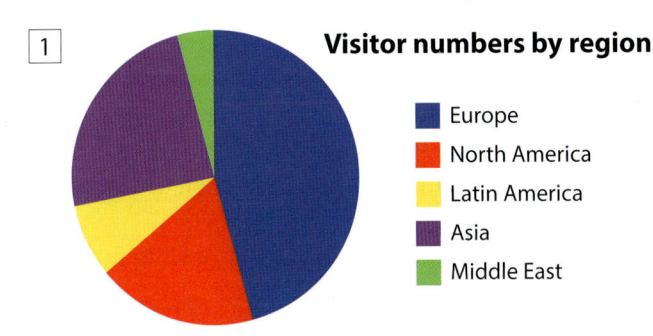

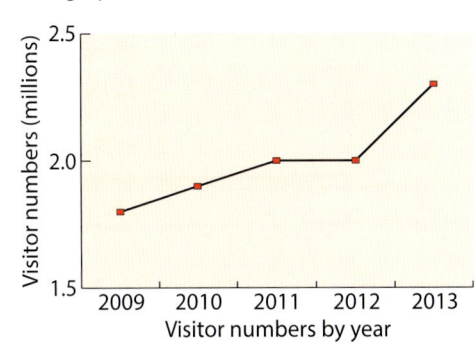

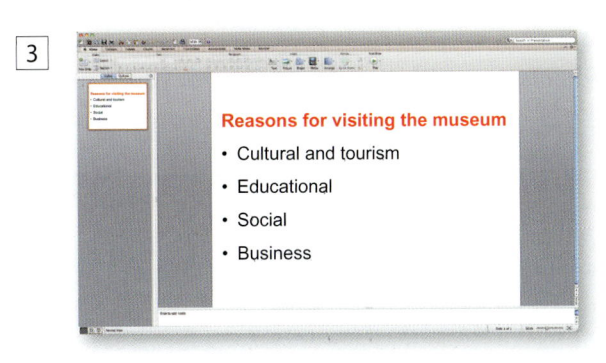

1 Visitor numbers by region
- Europe
- North America
- Latin America
- Asia
- Middle East

2 Visitor numbers (millions) / Visitor numbers by year (2009–2013)

3 Reasons for visiting the museum
- Cultural and tourism
- Educational
- Social
- Business

4

Ticket type	Price
Adult	$25
Student	$15
Child / Senior citizen	$10
Family pass (2 Adults + 2 Children)	$40
Annual pass (Adult / Student)	$60
Annual pass (Child / Senior citizen)	$30

2 Which visual aid in **1** would you use
- a to introduce / summarize a topic? ___
- b to show trends? ___
- c to present facts and figures? ___
- d to show market / regional share of a product or service? ___

3 ◊) 4.4 Listen to three extracts from a presentation about museum visitor numbers. Which visual aids from **1** does the presenter use in each extract?

1 _____ 2 _____ 3 _____

4 ◊) 4.4 Listen again. Complete the sentences with these words.

describes   indicates   represent   look at   see   shows

1 This graph _____ our visitor numbers in the past five years.
2 The horizontal axis shows the year and the vertical axis _____ visitor numbers.
3 As you can _____ from the way the line rises, we appear to be doing very well.
4 These pie charts _____ the main nationalities of our visitors five years ago compared to today.
5 If you _____ the blue segment, you can see the percentage of visitors from Europe.
6 This _____ our pricing structure.

5 Work in pairs. Look at the tips for using visual aids on page 138.
1 Which of the tips does the presenter in **3** follow or not follow?
2 Which of the tips do you agree with? Do you have any other tips for presenters?

6 Work in groups. Choose a museum or tourist attraction that you know well.
1 Decide on three or four visual aids to use in a presentation about this place for lottery funding to market the attraction.
2 Draw a simple drawing of the visuals. Give your presentation to the funding group.

Functions Giving opinions

INTRODUCTION

1 ◉ 4.5 Impact Africa Tours arranges adventure holidays. They are currently planning a safari in Kenya. Listen to the first part of the meeting and complete the information about the tour.

Name: *Kenya Safari* Months: _____ 2
Length: _____ 1 Cost: _____ 3

2 ◉ 4.5 Listen again. Complete the reasons that people give for 1–3.
   1 From a financial point of view, it needs to be two weeks. People won't pay a lot of money for _____ .
   2 I'm afraid I completely disagree. We can't do the tour from April to June because it _____ then.
   3 $6,000? I'm sorry, but I don't agree. Last year, our Botswana tour was $6,000. We cancelled it because _____ .

3 When you book a holiday, what is the most important thing for you?
   the cost   the length of the trip   the time of year   the weather

4 ◉ 4.6 Listen to the second part of the meeting and tick ✓ the three World Heritage Sites on the map.

5 ◉ 4.6 In the meeting, the team are arranging the route across Kenya. Listen again. Draw a line to mark the route on the map.

6 ◉ 4.6 Choose the correct option. Listen again and check.
   1 We can start in Mombasa and also visit the *city / island* of Lamu. Lamu is one World Heritage Site. What are your views?
   2 I'm not sure about that. Lamu is a beautiful place for *diving / sightseeing*, but that's not really a safari holiday.
   3 Hmm. I can see where you're coming from, Sumiko. Let's think about this. You also need to *drive / fly* from Mombasa to Nairobi.
   4 Definitely. There are *tigers / zebras*, hippos, and flamingos in the Great Rift Valley. It's beautiful.
   5 In my view, the *balloon / cycle* ride should be an extra thing. People pay more money if they want to do it.

Focus

Look at script 4.5 on page 144. Find and underline these phrases.

Asking for opinions
What do you think about …? What's your opinion of that?

Giving opinions
From a financial point of view, … I think we should …
Personally, I think … In my opinion, we should …

Agreeing
I completely agree. Yes, that's a good point. I agree.

Disagreeing
I'm afraid I completely disagree. I'm sorry, but I don't agree.

Recognizing someone's point of view
I see what you mean. I take your point, but …

Look again at the sentences in 6. Find five phrases to add to the groups above.

>> For more details and practice, go to the Review section on page 53.

PRACTICE

7 4.7 Complete the conversation with these phrases. Listen and check.

from a marketing   I completely   I see where Bradley is
I think we should   that's a good   what do you think about

Clive Bradley is thinking of organizing a new package of trips for people over 55. _____¹ that, Sumiko?

Sumiko _____² point of view, it's a good idea. There are particular websites where we can advertise the trips.

Mona _____³ coming from, but I don't think it's a good idea. Our customers enjoy travelling with people of all ages: young and old.

Clive Yes, _____⁴ agree. Our customer feedback tells us that they like the mix of people.

Sumiko I don't know. Personally, _____⁵ do some research on the idea. Maybe there's a new market of older travellers out there for us.

Clive Yes, _____⁶ point. I agree. Are you able to do the research?

Sumiko Sure, leave it with me.

8 Work in pairs. Read the comments and complete the best response (a or b) with your own opinion.

1 The best way to learn English is to read lots of books in the language.
   a I see what you mean. Personally, _____.
   b I'm afraid I (completely) disagree because _____.
2 The best form of exercise is jogging and running.
   a Definitely, I _____.
   b I'm sorry, but I don't agree because _____.
3 I think people should only work three days a week.
   a I completely agree. From my point of view, _____.
   b I'm not sure about that because _____.
4 Working from home is a waste of time. People work harder in the office.
   a Yes, I agree, that's a good point. I _____.
   b I take your point, but _____.

TASK

9 Work in groups of four. You work for a tour company. You are going to arrange a holiday to Britain and Ireland. Student A, go to page 127. Student B, go to page 131. Student C, go to page 136. Student D, go to page 137.

Review

Grammar Making comparisons

Form

Type of adjective	Example	Comparative	Superlative
Regular one syllable	cheap big	cheaper bigger	the cheapest the biggest
two or three syllables	expensive famous	more / less expensive more / less famous	the most / least expensive the most / least famous
two syllables ending in -y	busy	busier	the busiest
Irregular	good bad far	better worse further / farther	the best the worst the furthest / farthest

Use

We use *than* after a comparative adjective.
Example   The British Museum is **older than** the National Gallery.

(not) as … as shows something is (or isn't) the same or equal.
Example   Travelling by train is**n't as expensive as** flying.

a little / a bit / slightly show a small difference.
Example   Coffee is **slightly more** expensive than tea.

a lot / much / far show a big difference.
Example   Houses are **much more expensive** in the centre of the city.

Comparatives can be used with noun phrases as well as adjectives.
Examples   There are **far fewer** people living in the countryside today **than** a hundred years ago.
There were not **as many** visitors to the UK this year **as** there were last year.
The British Museum has **more** visitors **than** the New York Met.

PRACTICE   **1**   Look at this information about famous buildings.

Building	Place	Built	Height	Visitors per year	Claim to fame
Taj Mahal	Agra, India	1630s	171 m	3 million	_____ [1] example of Mughal architecture in the world
Big Ben	London, UK	1858	96 m	not open	_____ [2] 4-faced chiming clock in the world
Burj Khalifa	Dubai, UAE	2010	830 m	1.5 million	_____ [3] man-made structure in the world
Sydney Opera House	Sydney, Australia	1973	65 m	7 million	_____ [4] venue for performing arts in the world
Eiffel Tower	Paris, France	1889	320 m	7.1 million	_____ [5] (paid) monument in the world
Colosseum	Rome, Italy	80 AD	48 m	3.9 million	_____ [6] work of Roman engineering in the world

Use the information on page 50 to write sentences comparing the places. Write two sentences for each pair as in the example.

Example   Big Ben / Eiffel Tower (old)
Big Ben is older than the Eiffel Tower.
The Eiffel Tower isn't as old as Big Ben.

1 Eiffel Tower / Big Ben (tall)
_____
2 Taj Mahal / Sydney Opera House (old)
_____
3 Colosseum / Taj Mahal (old)
_____
4 Eiffel Tower / Sydney Opera House (have / visitors)
_____
5 Burj Khalifa / Eiffel Tower (tall)
_____
6 Taj Mahal / Colosseum (have / visitors)
_____
7 Burj Khalifa / Sydney Opera House (modern)
_____
8 Colosseum / Big Ben (short)
_____

2 Where appropriate, modify the sentences you wrote in **1** using *a little*, *a bit*, *slightly*, *a lot*, *much*, *far*, etc.

Example   Big Ben is slightly / a little older than the Eiffel Tower.

3 Complete the gaps in the final column with the superlative form of one of these adjectives.

famous   fine   great   large   tall   visited

4 Use the information in the chart to write a short article on 'Facts about the most famous buildings in the world'.

_____
_____
_____
_____
_____
_____
_____

Vocabulary City descriptions; *-ing* vs *-ed* adjectives

1 ◆)) 4.8 Listen to six short conversations. How does the second speaker feel? Match feelings a–f to conversations 1–6.

a annoyed ___
b disappointed ___
c interested ___
d pleased ___
e surprised ___
f tired ___

Review Unit 4   51

2 Complete the sentences by adding -ing or -ed to the adjectives.

1. I'm really pleas___ with the decision. We made the right choice
2. The view of the city from the top of the skyscraper is amaz___!
3. I'm not a fan of musicals. I think they're a bit bor___.
4. She looked a bit annoy___ when I told her I couldn't come to the meeting.
5. We were surpris___ that he turned down the job. He seemed very interested.
6. The flowers are beautiful. Your garden looks stunn___.
7. I've been working at the computer all day. My eyes are really tir___.
8. The lecture was really interest___. I learnt a lot.

3 Choose the correct adjectives.

1. The area by the river has a lot of bars and clubs. It's very *delicious / humid / lively* at night.
2. Picasso is one of Spain's most *ancient / famous / traditional* artists.
3. Summer in Beijing is very *cosmopolitan / delicious / humid*. You need to use air conditioning.
4. We went to see a folk band on Saturday. They all played *lively / popular / traditional* instruments from the Basque country.
5. We went to a Thai restaurant for dinner. The food was *delicious / famous / humid*.
6. Singapore is a(n) *ancient / cosmopolitan / popular* city with a mixture of many different cultures.
7. Egypt is famous for its *ancient / delicious / traditional* temples and pyramids which are over 4,000 years old.
8. France is a *cosmopolitan / popular / traditional* destination for Chinese tourists – more than half a million Chinese people went there last year.

Work skills Presentations 1: using visual aids

1 Which visual aid a–d is the best to use in a presentation to answer these questions?

1. How have the sales figures changed in the last five years? ___
2. What percentage of sales comes from different markets? ___
3. What are the four main points I must remember? ___
4. What is the height, length, and weight of each item? ___

a line graph
b table
c slide with prompt words
d pie chart

2 Complete the extracts from a presentation using these words.

indicate   look   shows   see

1. This graph _____ the effect of our increase in admission charges last year.
2. As you can _____, visitor numbers fell quite a lot initially.
3. However, on the next screen, you can _____ a steady increase.
4. Let's now _____ more closely at this increase.
5. I'd like you to _____ at this pie chart from before the price increase.
6. The chart _____ that more than 50% of our visitors were aged 30 or over.
7. Now _____ carefully at this next pie chart and you can see that there is a big increase in younger visitors aged 18 and under.
8. The pie charts clearly _____ the success of our new family ticket which we introduced at the same time as the price increase.

Functions Giving opinions

We use these phrases to ask people for their opinions.
Examples What's your view? / What's your opinion of that?
What do you think about …?

We use these phrases to give our opinions.
Examples From my / a financial point of view, it's a good idea.
In my opinion, we should do one tour in January …
In my view, that's not a good idea.
(Personally) I think we should do some research on the idea.

We use these phrases to agree with someone.
Examples I completely agree. / Definitely.
Yes, that's a good point. I agree.

We use these phrases to disagree with someone.
Examples I'm afraid I completely disagree. / I'm sorry, but I don't agree.
I'm not sure about that.

We use these phrases to show we recognize someone's point of view.
Examples I can see where you're coming from. / I see you what you mean.
I take your point, but …

PRACTICE

1 Complete the words in the conversations.

1 A I think we s_____ combine a tour of Kenya with a tour of Tanzania.
   B Yes, d_____. I think that's a great idea.
2 A We could expand our business by organizing tours to Asia. What's your v_____?
   B I'm not s_____ about that, but it's an interesting suggestion.
3 A I'm not sure about a trip with Impact Tours. They're very expensive.
   B P_____, I think it's a good idea to book with Impact Tours. They're a good company.
4 A What do you t_____ about inviting some journalists to do one of our tours for free?
   B From an advertising point of v_____, it's an excellent idea.
5 A We need to arrange holidays just for younger people, in their 20s. They like to travel with people of the same age. What's your o_____ of that?
   B I take your p_____, but we don't have a lot of customers aged 20–29.

2 ◆)) 4.9 Listen to six conversations. Tick ✓ the people who agree with the suggestions made. Cross ✗ the people who disagree.

1 Olga ☐   3 Gloria ☐   5 Wulfram ☐
2 Tony ☐   4 Satoko ☐   6 Andrew ☐

3 ◆)) 4.9 Choose the correct words to complete the sentences. Listen again and check.

1 A 10% pay rise? I'm sorry but *I'm not / I don't* agree. That's too much money.
2 I see what you *mean / say*. Online advertising is the best way of reaching new customers.
3 I'm afraid I *complete / completely* disagree. The German factory produces very high-quality products. We shouldn't close it.
4 *In / On* my view, that's not a good idea. There are security problems with an outside cleaning company.
5 Yes, *that's / what's* a good point. I know a perfect manager for the Middle East: Nasrin in the Jordan office.
6 Yes, I can see where you're coming *from / to*. Which are the best management consultants to contact?

5 Fashion and function

Grammar Modal and related verbs: *have to, must, need to, be allowed to, can*

INTRODUCTION

1 What do you wear at work? Are there any rules about what you can or cannot wear?

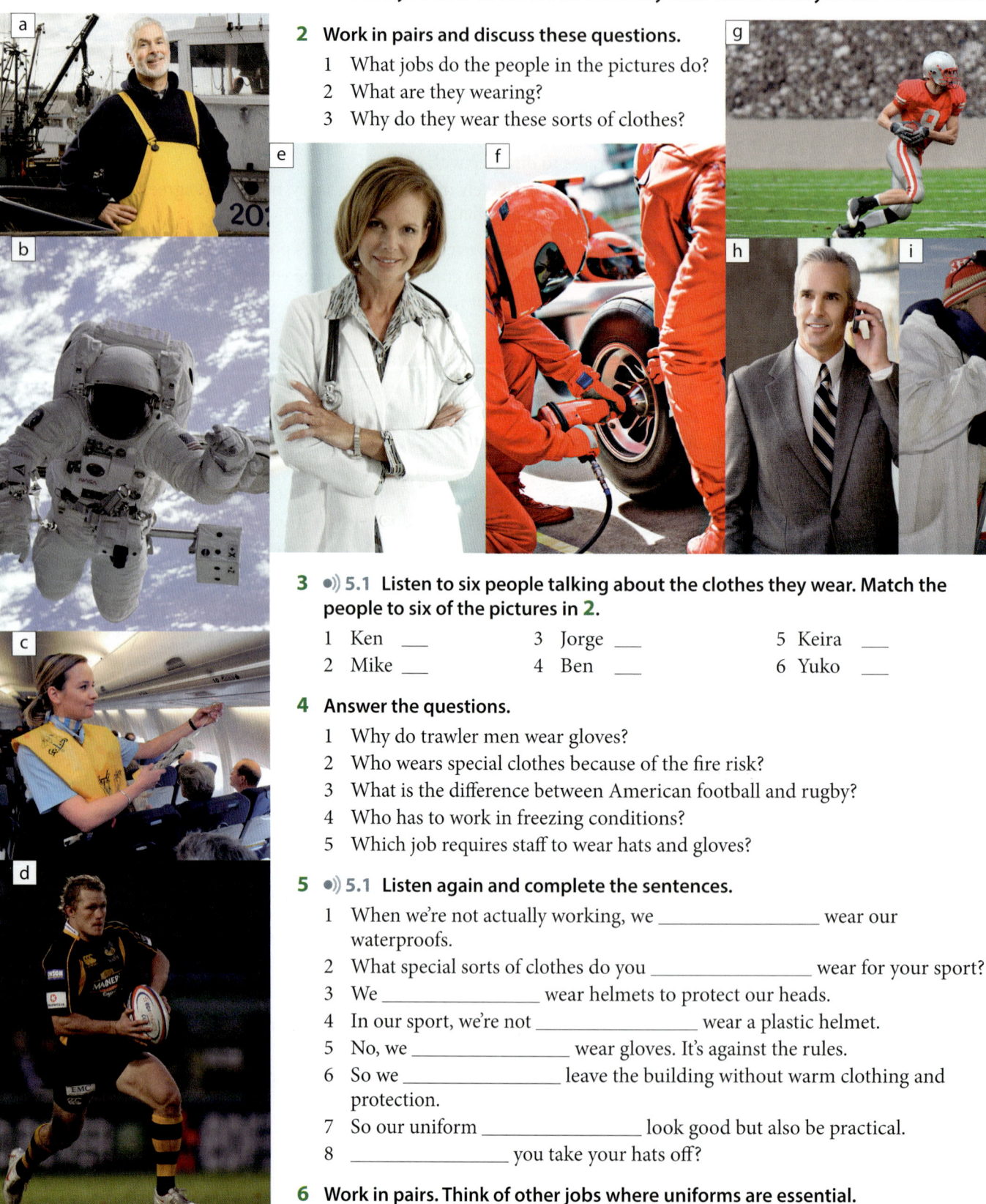

2 Work in pairs and discuss these questions.
   1 What jobs do the people in the pictures do?
   2 What are they wearing?
   3 Why do they wear these sorts of clothes?

3 ») 5.1 Listen to six people talking about the clothes they wear. Match the people to six of the pictures in **2**.
   1 Ken ___   3 Jorge ___   5 Keira ___
   2 Mike ___ 4 Ben ___   6 Yuko ___

4 Answer the questions.
   1 Why do trawler men wear gloves?
   2 Who wears special clothes because of the fire risk?
   3 What is the difference between American football and rugby?
   4 Who has to work in freezing conditions?
   5 Which job requires staff to wear hats and gloves?

5 ») 5.1 Listen again and complete the sentences.
   1 When we're not actually working, we _____ wear our waterproofs.
   2 What special sorts of clothes do you _____ wear for your sport?
   3 We _____ wear helmets to protect our heads.
   4 In our sport, we're not _____ wear a plastic helmet.
   5 No, we _____ wear gloves. It's against the rules.
   6 So we _____ leave the building without warm clothing and protection.
   7 So our uniform _____ look good but also be practical.
   8 _____ you take your hats off?

6 Work in pairs. Think of other jobs where uniforms are essential. Why is the uniform necessary? Would you like to do that job?

54 Unit 5 Grammar

Focus

Match these headings to the groups.

It's not permitted   It's necessary   It's permitted   It's not necessary

	have to, must, need to
	mustn't, not be allowed to, can't
	don't have to, don't need to
	can, be allowed to

▶▶ For more details and practice, go to the Review section on pages 62 and 63.

PRACTICE

7 Where would you see these signs and notices? What do they mean?

Example   1 – construction site
You must wear a hard hat in this area.

8 Check the meaning of the signs with a partner.

Example   **A** Do I have to wear a hard hat in this area?
B Yes. You mustn't enter this area without a hard hat.

9 Work in pairs. Describe the rules for the following in your country.

alcohol	driving	smoking
identity cards	public transport	going to the cinema

10 Read the article and answer the questions below.

The 'grammar' of clothes

Someone once said that there are only two things that make humans different from animals: we speak languages and we wear clothes. Some people think that wearing clothes is also a language. Like a language, there are rules and conventions. Rules are things you have to do and things that you mustn't do. Conventions are things that you don't have to do, but which are advisable and expected.

Recently, a government minister in France caused a stir when she wore denim jeans to a cabinet meeting at the presidential palace in Paris. Opponents of Cecile Duflot, head of the Green Party, were shocked: 'It is expected that you wear a suit or a dress. We must all show respect to our institutions.' Supporters of Ms Duflot responded: 'She doesn't have to follow all the formal rules of the past. She just has to be good at her job.'

In sport, players at the Wimbledon tennis championships have to wear kit that is mainly white. There mustn't be more than 5 per cent other colours on their clothes. They are allowed to have corporate logos, but they shouldn't be too big. It would be difficult to imagine a player at Wimbledon wearing orange or purple!

At social events in many countries the conventions of dress are very strict. In certain restaurants men have to wear ties, at weddings you shouldn't wear the same colour dress as the bride, and at bars in the USA there is often a sign: 'All guests must wear shirts'.

1. According to the writer, what are the two things that make humans different from animals?
2. What is the difference between 'rules' and 'conventions'?
3. Find four examples of rules or conventions in the article.

11 Work in pairs. What do you think of the rules and conventions described in the article in **10**? Are there similar rules and conventions in your country?

Watch the video for more practice.

12 Work in groups. Choose one of the areas below. Discuss the rules and conventions for what to wear in the situations.

Where you work
A job interview
A normal day at work
Attending an international conference

Social occasions
A night at the opera or theatre
An evening out with friends
A wedding (as bride / bridegroom and as guest)

TASK 13 Work in pairs. You are going to discuss rules regarding various social issues. Student A, read the rules on page 128. Student B, read the rules on page 132. Compare the rules and decide which ones are the best.

56 Unit 5 Grammar

Vocabulary Colours and colour idioms; prefixes

1 **Work in pairs and discuss these questions.**
   1 What is your favourite colour? Why?
   2 What colour clothes do you like / dislike wearing? Why?
   3 Do you consider any colours to be lucky or unlucky?

2 **Complete the colour-related phrases using the correct colour on the right.**

   1 A company 'in the _____' owes money. — black
   2 Electrical equipment in the house, like fridges and washing machines are called '_____ goods'. — green / white
   3 When something happens 'out of the _____', it is unexpected. — red
   4 Getting a '_____ light' means that you can start a project. — black
   5 Someone who 'sees _____' is very angry. — blue
   6 Some people call having interesting and new ideas '_____ sky thinking'. — grey / red
   7 '_____ Monday' was the day the stock markets crashed. — blue
   8 A company 'in the _____' has more money than it owes.
   9 The amount of corporation tax companies should pay is a '_____ area'.

3 **Think of some colour idioms in your culture. How can you explain them in English?**

4 ◉) 5.2 **Listen to the descriptions of different colours. Number the colours in the order you hear them.**

   yellow ☐   red ☐   black ☐   green ☐   blue ☐

5 ◉) 5.2 **Work in pairs. Add prefixes to make the negative form of these words and add them to the table. Listen again and check.**

   ~~qualified~~   legal   visible   usual   happy
   responsible   lucky   known   possible   satisfied

un-	in-	im-	il-	ir-	dis-
					disqualified

6 **Work in pairs. Add the negative form of these words to the table in 5. Use a dictionary to help you and check the meaning.**

   efficient   capable   moral   perfect   regular   relevant
   tidy   organized   similar   honest   legible   logical

7 Work in pairs and answer the questions.

1 Look at the words in the columns for *im-*, *il-*, and *ir-* in **5**. What letter do the words that follow these negative prefixes begin with?
_____

2 *un-* and *in-* are the most common negative prefixes for adjectives. Can you think of some more examples?
_____

3 *dis-* is often used with nouns and verbs. Can you think of some examples?
_____

8 Complete the sentences with the correct words from the table in **5**. There is one word from each column.

1 In the UK, it is _____ to drive whilst holding a mobile phone. You'll receive a fine if you do it.
2 I don't trust him, I think he's _____. He looked like he was lying.
3 Her comment seemed totally _____. It had nothing to do with the subject we were discussing.
4 I think it is _____ to kill animals for meat. That's why I'm a vegetarian.
5 Have you ever been to her flat? It's really messy. She's very _____.
6 Our system of working is very _____. It is expensive and takes too long. We need to make improvements.

9 Work in pairs. Look at the prefixes and the examples. Match the prefixes with the definitions a–f.

1 *e-*	email, e-commerce, e-business	___
2 *ex-*	ex-wife, ex-president, ex-partner	___
3 *co-*	cooperate, co-pilot, co-produce	___
4 *anti-*	anti-war, anti-smoking, anti-bullying	___
5 *eco-*	eco-friendly, ecotourism, eco-warrior	___
6 *cyber-*	cybercafé, cyberspace, cybercrime	___

a previous / former
b electronic
c opposed to
d together / with
e related to the environment
f connected with computers

10 Complete the sentences with correct words from **9**.

1 The company wanted to be more _____ so it reduced its carbon emissions and use of electricity.
2 The biggest threat to global internet security is _____.
3 The _____ campaign aims to stop people smoking in any public area.
4 The Italian and Chinese manufacturing companies will _____ a new motorcycle.
5 The _____ of the United States wrote a book about his time in office at the White House.
6 _____ companies such as iTunes and Amazon are changing the way we buy things.

Work skills Telephoning

1 How often do you need to use English on the telephone? What for? Are there any situations you find difficult?

2 Work in pairs. Look at these phrases used in telephone conversations. Match phrases 1–8 with phrases a–h that have the same meaning.

1 Could I speak to …, please? ___
2 Please hold the line. ___
3 Thanks for getting back to me. ___
4 Can I take a message? ___
5 Can I call you back later today? ___
6 I'm afraid she's on another call. ___
7 Your phone's cutting out. ___
8 I'm sorry, I didn't catch that. ___

a Can you repeat that?
b Would you like to leave a message?
c Thanks for calling me back.
d You're breaking up.
e Can I give you a call later?
f Could you hold on a moment?
g Her line's busy at the moment.
h Can you put me through to …?

3 Match the phrases in 2 with these stages of a telephone call.

1 Offering to take a message ___ ___
2 Saying someone is busy ___ ___
3 Telling someone that the mobile reception is bad ___ ___
4 Asking to speak to someone ___ ___
5 Asking someone to wait ___ ___
6 Asking someone to repeat what they said ___ ___
7 Thanking someone for returning your call ___ ___
8 Asking someone if you can call them later ___ ___

4 ◉ 5.3 Listen to two telephone conversations and answer the questions.
1 a Why is Paolo phoning Fashion World?
  b What is his mobile number?
2 a Why did Simone call Paolo?
  b Where is Simone calling from?

5 ◉ 5.3 Listen again. Tick ✓ the phrases in 2 that you hear.

6 Work in pairs (A and B). Use the phrases in 2 to role-play these two telephone conversations. The numbers show the order of the conversations.

Call	A	B
1	**You are the caller.** 1 Ask to speak to Dita Vacek. 3 Agree to wait. 5 Ask the receptionist to ask Dita to call you. Give your mobile number.	**You are the receptionist.** 2 Ask A to wait while you connect them to Dita. 4 Dita's line is busy. Offer to take a message. 6 Check the mobile number.
2	**You are speaking on a mobile.** 2 Thank Dita for returning your call. Say why you called. 4 Repeat what you said in 2. 6 Tell Dita to call your landline. Give her the number.	**You are Dita.** 1 Return A's call. Apologize for being busy earlier. 3 Ask A to repeat. Their mobile reception is bad. 5 The line is still bad. Offer to call A back.

7 Think of a telephone call you might make in your job / life. Write down the details of the conversation as in 6. Then work in pairs and role-play your conversations.

Functions Giving advice and suggestions

INTRODUCTION

1 Complete the guide for business travellers to Hong Kong with the missing questions a–e.

   a We have a big meeting in Hong Kong and we know it'll be hot. Do you think we should wear summer clothes?
   b I don't know when the best time is to do a sales tour of Hong Kong. What do you recommend?
   c I'm going to meet my Hong Kong business partner for the first time. I'm not sure about meeting and greeting. Do you have any advice?
   d My whole team is going to Hong Kong for a conference, but I'm worried about the price of accommodation. What do you think I should do?
   e I have a free day in Hong Kong on my next trip and I'd like to do some sightseeing. Do you have any suggestions?

The business traveller's guide to ... Hong Kong

Last week, we asked you to send us your questions about travelling in Hong Kong. Here is a selection, with replies from our expert on the ground, Jessica Ling.

Q1 ___: You shouldn't go at Chinese New Year because everything is closed. I'd also avoid September because it's the typhoon season. That causes a lot of delays and cancellations of flights. The rest of the year is no problem.

Q2 ___: No! You should definitely take formal clothes: suit and tie for men and the equivalent for women.

Q3 ___: People shake hands. One thing you should be careful about is business cards. People present them in two hands, with the text facing the visitor. Take the card in both hands.

Q4 ___: How about going to Sheung Wan? It's a district with lots of old buildings and some incredible markets too. Why don't you ask one of your Hong Kong contacts to show you around?

Q5 ___: Have you considered the Bishop Lei International House? It's in the heart of Central (that's the main business district in Hong Kong) and it has very reasonable prices. You'd better book it early though.

2 Work in pairs. Guess the missing information in these comments about visiting Hong Kong.
   1 In Hong Kong, _____ is fast, modern, clean, and cheap.
   2 _____ are also very cheap in Hong Kong and you don't need to tip the drivers.
   3 Do you know that you can hire a _____ and do a 15-minute flight over Hong Kong? It costs about $850.
   4 Why don't you do a short course before you go? Then you can learn some _____ _____, like 'I'm lost'!
   5 There are some _____ _____ in the IMC mall by the harbour.
   6 One thing you could do is visit Victoria _____. It's a lovely green space in the centre of the city.

3 ◆)) 5.4 Jessica Ling is doing a podcast on Hong Kong. She's talking to a business traveller, Ian Hill. Listen and check your answers to **2**.

4 ◆)) 5.4 Listen again. Match responses a–f to comments 1–6 in **2**.
   a Great. Thanks for the advice.   ___
   b I'm not keen on shopping, actually.   ___
   c Yes, that sounds like a good idea.   ___
   d Good idea. I like the sound of that.   ___
   e I'd rather not go on the underground …   ___
   f That's an interesting idea, but it's quite expensive. ___

Focus

Complete the table with phrases from 1.

Asking for advice and suggestions	Giving advice and suggestions
Do you think we should …?	You shouldn't …
What do you recommend?	I'd also avoid …
_____	_____
_____	_____
_____	_____
	_____
	You'd better …

Look again at the responses in 4. Put them in the correct group.

Accepting ideas: ___ ___ ___
Rejecting ideas: ___ ___ ___

⏵⏵ For more details and practice, go to the Review section on page 65.

PRACTICE

5 Work in pairs. Put the words in the right order to make questions. Then think of a suitable response.

1. from your country / do you recommend / what books or magazines?
2. tomorrow / we should wear / do you think / gloves and a scarf?
3. I should go / for a coffee / do you think / after class / where?
4. for learning / any advice / English vocabulary / do you have?
5. from your country / for a typical gift / any suggestions / do you have?

6 ◉) 5.5 Choose the correct words to complete the conversations. Listen and check.

1. **A** One thing you should *be / take* careful about is travelling on the underground – there are lots of pickpockets!
   B Oh, right. Thanks *for / of* the tip.
2. **A** How about *go / going* to the Olympic Swimming Pool? It also has a gym.
   B That *makes / sounds* like a good idea.
3. **A** Let's see. I'm not keen *about / on* spicy food.
   B Then you'd better *no / not* have the red curry – it's incredibly hot!
4. **A** If you like history, you should *definite / definitely* go to the City Museum. There's a fascinating Roman exhibition there at the moment.
   B That's *a / the* good idea.
5. **A** Have you considered *get / getting* a coach? You can get there in about five hours.
   B I think *I'd / I'm* rather get the train than the coach. I don't like buses.
6. **A** Personally, *I'd / I'll* avoid the area round the park because it's very touristy.
   B Oh, I don't like the sound *by / of* that.

7 Work in pairs. Take turns to be A and B.

A You are planning to visit B's town / city. Call B to ask for advice and suggestions for using the transport system. Ask at least five questions. Decide which ideas to accept or reject.

B Answer A's questions. Give advice and suggestions.

TASK

8 Work in pairs. Write a guide for visitors to your country, with questions and answers like in 1. Use these headings to help you.

| Transport | Places to stay | Prices and money | Places to visit and relax |
| Work clothes | Places to eat | Some warnings | Shopping and souvenirs |

Review

Modal and related verbs *have to, must, need to, be allowed to, can*

Form

The ending of the modal verbs *must* and *can* is the same for all persons.
Example I / He / They must wear a tie.

The third person 's' is used for the non-modals *have to* and *need to*.
Examples I have to / He has to be there at 11.00.
I need / He needs to get up early.

To make the negative, we add *not* or *-n't* to modals.
Example You cannot / can't see him today.

We put modals before the subject to make questions.
Example Can I go home early?

To make questions and negatives with *have to* and *need to*, we use the auxiliary verb *do*.
Examples Does he have to wear a jacket?
You don't need to wait for me.

Use

It's necessary	All guests must wear a tie. You need to show ID. You have to wear a jacket.
It's not permitted	You mustn't smoke in the seminar room. You're not allowed to bring guests. You can't bring any pets into the building.
It's not necessary	You don't have to wear a suit to the conference sessions. You don't need to make notes.
It's permitted	Guests are allowed to use the swimming pool until 10 p.m. You can smoke in the garden if you want.

PRACTICE   **1** Read the email. Choose the correct verbs.

From: Elisa Cheng
To: Stephen Halts
Subject: Colombia trip

Hi Stephen

Here are some last-minute reminders about your trip to Colombia. You *have to / can*[1] get to the airport at least two hours before your flight. I've arranged for a taxi to pick you up at 7 a.m. so you *don't need to / mustn't*[2] worry about getting to the airport. But you *must / mustn't*[3] remember to set your alarm clock!

You are *allowed to / expected to*[4] take a maximum of 10 kg in luggage. I think it's OK, as you *mustn't / don't need to*[5] take all the conference papers with you because there'll be copies for you at the conference. However, you *need to / can't*[6] take a backup copy of your presentation with you, just in case.

You *can / need*[7] to check in online 24 hours before the flight if you want, but you *mustn't / don't have to*[8] if you don't want to. By the way, I'm sure you know this, but you *don't need to / are not allowed to*[9] smoke anywhere in the terminal building.

Have a good trip. And don't forget – you *must / mustn't*[10] bring me back some coffee!

Best

Elisa

2 Rewrite the sentences where necessary so they are true for the place where you work or study.

1 You need to show ID to get in.
2 You have to wear a suit.
3 You don't have to be on time.
4 You have to call your manager if you are going to be late.
5 You mustn't use your computer for personal emails.
6 You can't make personal phone calls in work time.
7 You are allowed to bring your children to work.
8 You don't need to wear a uniform.
9 You don't have to bring in your own lunch because there is a cafeteria.
10 You need to bring your own coffee because the coffee they serve is awful!

3 Write the question forms for each of the sentences in **2**.

Example 1 Do you need to show ID to get in?

4 Look at these signs and notices. What are the rules and conventions?

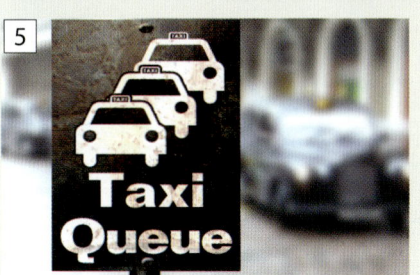

Example 1 You mustn't smoke.

Vocabulary Colours and colour idioms; prefixes

1 Match these adjectives with the prefixes below to make negative forms.

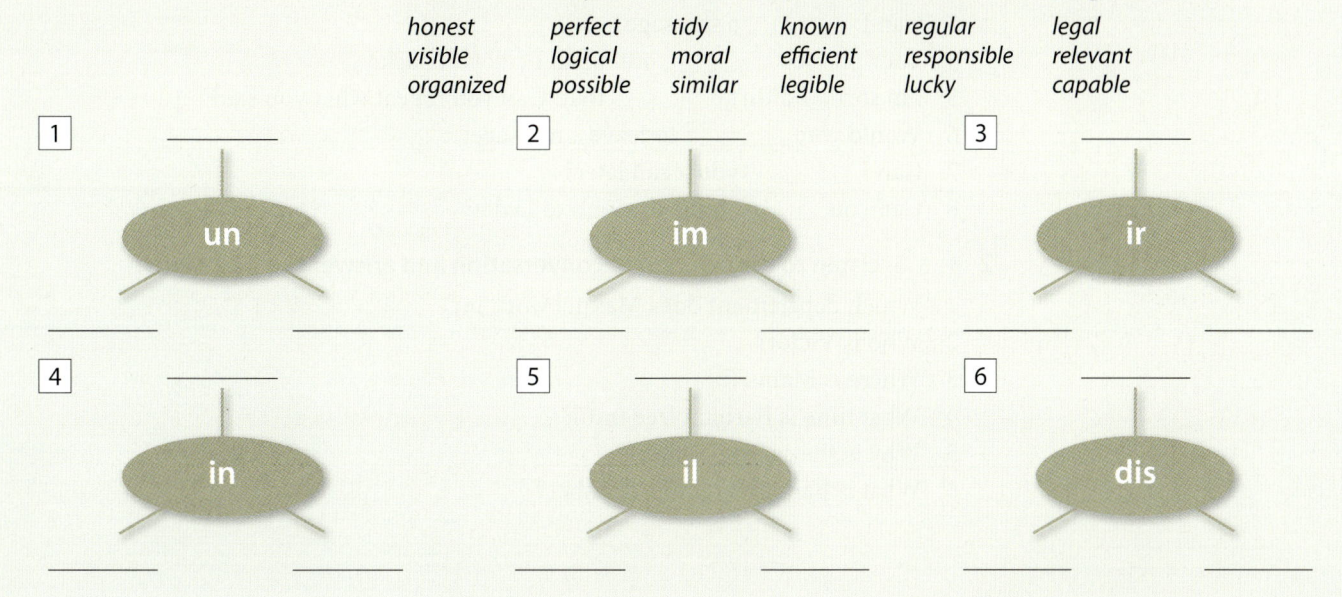

honest   perfect   tidy   known   regular   legal
visible   logical   moral   efficient responsible relevant
organized possible similar legible   lucky   capable

1 un
2 im
3 ir
4 in
5 il
6 dis

2 Complete the sentences with the negative form of one of the words in **1**. There is one word from each group.
1 His handwriting is terrible. It's completely _____ .
2 Bacteria are so small that they are _____ , unless you look through a microscope.
3 It will be _____ to finish this work on time. It can't be done!
4 He's quite _____ and wastes a lot of time. I think he needs to improve his time management skills.
5 They were _____ not to win the match. They were the better team, but the referee made some bad decisions.
6 Her behaviour was completely _____ . She can't be trusted to look after the children again.

3 Complete the words in the sentences with these prefixes.
e- ex- co- anti- eco- cyber
1 I try to use _____friendly products that don't damage the environment.
2 The pilot handed over control of the plane to her _____pilot.
3 She's quite _____smoking. She won't let anyone smoke in her house.
4 I saw my _____wife at the supermarket. She told me she'd got engaged again.
5 Computer viruses and _____crime cost businesses billions of dollars every year.
6 We're investing more in _____commerce. We now sell a lot of products online.

4 Complete the idioms with a colour.
1 His comments made me see _____ . They were so rude!
2 On _____ Monday in October 1987, stock markets around the world crashed.
3 My new flat contains _____ goods in the kitchen, but it has no furniture.
4 I spent too much last month. My bank account is now in the _____ .
5 The announcement came out of the _____ . None of us was expecting it.
6 We've been given the _____ light to build a new warehouse.

Work skills Telephoning

1 Complete the telephone phrases with these words.

take put hold getting give cutting catch like

1 Please _____ the line.
2 Thanks for _____ back to me.
3 Can I _____ a message?
4 Your phone's _____ out. Shall I call you back?
5 I'm sorry, I didn't _____ that. Can you repeat what you said?
6 Would you _____ to leave a message?
7 Can I _____ you a call later?
8 Can you _____ me through to Lydia?

2 ◆)) 5.6 Listen to the telephone conversation and answer the questions.
1 Which department does Manuel work in?
2 Who is Victor?
3 Where is Manuel?
4 What time is Barbara free until?
5 Why is she calling Manuel?
6 What is Barbara's mobile number?

Functions Giving advice and suggestions

We use these phrases to ask for advice and suggestions.
Examples What do you recommend?
Do you have any advice / suggestions?
What do you think I should do? / Do you think we should …?

We use these phrases to give advice and suggestions.
Examples You should definitely … / How about (+ -*ing*)?
Why don't you (do)? / Have you considered (+ -*ing* / noun)?
You shouldn't … / You'd better (not) …
I'd also avoid … because …
One thing you should be careful about is …

We use these phrases to accept ideas.
Examples Thanks for the advice / tip.
That sounds like a good idea. / Good idea. I like the sound of that.

We use these phrases to reject ideas.
Examples I'm not keen on (+ -*ing* / noun), (actually).
I'd rather not (do). / That's an interesting idea, but …

PRACTICE **1** Complete the missing words in the web article.

Do you have any a_____¹ for surviving a long-haul flight? I'm moving with my family from Germany to New Zealand. It's our first long-haul flight. Do you have any s_____² for travelling with kids?

One thing you should be c_____³ about is the time when you fly. At peak times, flights are very busy. Fly at other times, and your plane may be half empty.

H_____⁴ about taking a stopover? If you have to take a connecting flight, stay one or two nights in the country where the planes change. Singapore is popular for this.

I'd also a_____⁵ bringing a lot of hand luggage on the plane. If you have to put things under the seat in front, you have less space for your legs.

You s_____⁶ drink plenty of water during the flight. Many people feel dehydrated at the end of a flight.

Have you c_____⁷ packing your own food? Some kids don't like aeroplane food and they'll be hungry.

You'd b_____⁸ recharge all your batteries for tablets and games, etc. before you fly.

Finally, w_____⁹ don't you take your kids to the playground if there is one? If they are tired before the flight, they will sleep on the plane!

2 Put the words in the right order to complete the responses to the suggestions in the web article.

1 A stopover in Singapore? Good idea. (*the / sound / that / like / of / I*)
_____.

2 (*not / on / I'm / keen / travelling*) _____ without hand luggage, actually. I need my bag!

3 I'll drink lots of water. (*tip / thanks / the / for*) _____.

4 (*not / pack / rather / I'd*) _____ my own food because I have a lot of other things to prepare!

5 Going to a play area (*good / idea / is / but / a*) _____ one of my kids is a baby. He's not going there!

3 Is the traveller in **2** accepting (*A*) or rejecting (*R*) the suggestions?
1 ___   2 ___   3 ___   4 ___   5 ___

Review Unit 5

6 Using innovation

Grammar Past Simple, Past Continuous, Past Perfect

INTRODUCTION

1 **Work in pairs and discuss these questions.**
   1 How many uses for water can you think of?
   2 In which countries is there a shortage of clean drinking water?

2 **Read the water facts. How can the developed world help solve these problems?**

   People need 25 litres per person per day, including two litres for drinking.
   1.1 billion people live more than a kilometre from their water source and use just five litres of unsafe water a day.
   Women in some countries carry 20-kg water buckets for three hours a day.

3 **Look at the pictures in the article. What do you think the ideas are?**

4 **Read the article about two designs and answer the questions below.**

Hippo Water Roller

In the early 1990s, two South African engineers, Pettie Petzer and Johan Jonker, invented the Hippo Water Roller. As engineers, they had seen the problems people in Africa faced carrying water buckets. They decided they wanted to help, so they started to work on various ideas. While they were working on a design for a wheelbarrow, they realized that the wheel was the most expensive part. So they had the idea to put water in the wheel itself, not in a container on top. The Hippo Water Roller was born.

Lifesaver Bottle

Michael Pritchard was watching the television when he saw the news about the Asian Tsunami in 2004. For days and weeks after the tsunami, people had to travel many miles to find safe drinking water. Four months later, he saw the same thing in the USA. After Hurricane Katrina had struck, it took five days to get fresh water to people. Michael decided to do something and designed a bottle with its own filter system. People had tried to produce filtered water before, but in Michael's design the holes in the filter were small enough to remove all bacteria and viruses, making the water completely clean and safe.

Watch the video for more practice.

1 Who invented the Hippo Water Roller?
2 Who did they want to help?
3 What was different about their design?
4 When did Michael Pritchard hear about the Asian Tsunami?
5 How was Hurricane Katrina similar to the Asian Tsunami?
6 What was special about Michael's bottle design?

5 What do you think of the designs? Do you know of any other designs that help people in the developing world?

> **Focus**
>
> **Read the example sentences and answer the questions.**
>
> While they **were working** on a design for a wheelbarrow, they realized that the wheel was the most expensive part.
>
> Michael Pritchard was watching the television when he **saw** the news about the Asian Tsunami in 2004.
>
> After Hurricane Katrina **had struck**, it took five days to get fresh water to people.
>
> **Which of the verbs in bold describe**
>
> 1 an event which was completed in the past?
> 2 an event that was in progress at a time in the past?
> 3 an event in the past which happened before another event in the past?
>
> **Match the descriptions 1–3 with the correct tense.**
>
> a Past Continuous ___
> b Past Perfect Simple ___
> c Past Simple ___
>
> **Find more examples of these tenses in the article in 4.**
>
> ▸▸ For more details and practice, go to the Review section on pages 74 and 75.

PRACTICE

6 ◉) **6.1** Listen to a story about a girl called Lila. Are these statements true or false? Correct the false statements.
1 Lila got up at 6 a.m. every day to collect water.
2 Lila's mother had done the same thing when Lila was younger.
3 Lila was bitten by a snake while she was walking home.
4 Lila told her teacher that she had fallen over.
5 This was the first time that Lila had been late for lessons.
6 After she had talked to her mother, she found out about an organization that could help.
7 By the end of the following year, there was a new well in Lila's village.

7 Write questions for the statements in **6**.

Example   What did Lila do every morning? / What time did Lila get up every day?

8 Work in pairs. Ask and answer the questions in **7**. Use the statements in **6**.

9 Complete the sentences with the correct form of the verbs in brackets.
1 He _____ (watch) television when he had an idea.
2 He couldn't work any longer because he _____ (lose) his eyesight.
3 While they were working in Ghana, they _____ (have) the idea of designing a new kind of water carrier.
4 By the time she was 16, she _____ (carry) more than 100,000 litres of water to her village.
5 Children were getting sick all the time till they _____ (install) a water well in the village.
6 The team _____ (work) in India for six months before they realized that eyesight was a big problem.
7 Two girls had both been bitten by a snake while they _____ (walk) to the river.
8 He was shocked when I told him I _____ (find) the solution.

10 Read the article on another invention and answer the questions below.

Seeing the future

Currently, there is one optician for every one million people in sub-Saharan Africa.

Josh Silver is a professor of physics at Oxford University. In 1985, Silver was discussing optical lenses with a colleague when he had a moment of inspiration. His idea was to make a pair of glasses which didn't need to be fitted by an optician. The glasses could be adjusted by the wearer to correct their own vision.

Silver developed this idea and so far around 40,000 pairs of his glasses have been distributed in over 20 countries. He has also managed to design the glasses so they are affordable. His target is one dollar per pair.

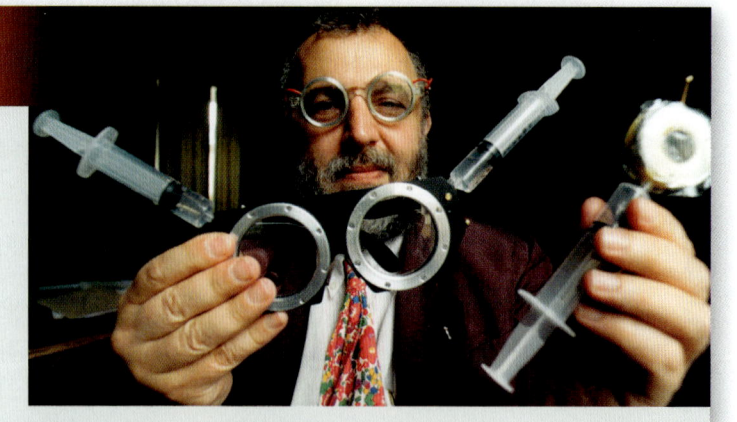

While he was working on an early project in Ghana, Silver met Henry Adjei-Mensah. Henry was a tailor who had been forced to retire because he could no longer see to thread the needle of his sewing machine. Henry had retired 20 years before he really needed to and was only 35 when he stopped. When Henry tried the glasses, after he had adjusted them, he was able to thread his needle and go straight back to work.

1. When did Josh Silver have the idea for the adjustable glasses?
2. What was the main feature of the glasses?
3. How many glasses have been made so far?
4. When did Silver meet Henry Adjei-Mensah?
5. What was Henry's problem?
6. How did Silver's glasses help Henry?

TASK 11 Work in pairs. Read about two other projects for the developing world and share the main ideas with your partner. Student A, see below. Student B, go to page 132.

Student A
Read the text and match the underlined items with the numbers in the picture. Then tell Student B about the PlayPump® story.

The PlayPump®

The inventor of the original play pump was Ronnie Stuiver. A businessman, Trevor Field, and his colleague, Paul Ristic, licensed the idea from Stuiver in 1990. After they had done some more work on the initial design, the partners came up with the concept of the current PlayPump® Water System. It is a children's merry-go-round with a pump, a storage tank, and tap. There is a pipe which connects the merry-go-round and pump with the water underground. The spinning motion of the merry-go-round pumps water from a hole in the ground to the tank, about 7 m above ground.

So far, 1,000 systems have been installed in South Africa, Lesotho, Mozambique, Swaziland, and Zambia. Communities do not pay for the pump systems – all installations are donated. The company's goal is to give 10 million people access to fresh drinking water.

Vocabulary Water footprint; noun formation

1 **Work in pairs and discuss these questions.**
   1 How much water do you use each day? Make a list of when you use water.
   2 Are you careful about how much water you use? If so, how do you control the amount of water you use?

2 **Read the text about water and answer the questions below.**

What's your water-footprint?

How much water do you think is in an espresso? According to Professor Tony Allan, a typical espresso contains 140 litres of water! In his book *Virtual Water*, he says that we are not aware of 90% of the water we use, as it is 'hidden' water used in the production of the food and goods we buy. So it takes 140 litres to grow, produce, package, and ship the beans you use to make your morning espresso. Professor Allan calls this water 'virtual water'. Since the appearance of his book, many people are taking his ideas very seriously.

Water consumption varies greatly by country. In wealthy countries, people use about 150 litres a day for washing and drinking. However, if you include the 'virtual water' in their food and clothes, the figure jumps to 5,000 litres per day for a meat eater. There is a significant reduction if you are a vegetarian: the figure falls to 2,700 litres per day. A huge amount of water is used in beef production.

Due to the growth of cities and rising populations, water is becoming a more valuable resource. In the next few decades, water will become a major issue for the world. Part of the solution may come through improvements in agricultural performance, through the use of better fertilizers, pesticides, etc. In recent years, agricultural production in Europe has increased from 3 tonnes of food per hectare to 10 tonnes. But we also need to improve the management of our water supply. This can happen through more waste-water recycling (e.g. reusing water from your bath) or the development of better methods of desalination (= the removal of salt from water) – we can then use more sea water in agriculture.

In the meantime, what can the individual do? Well, have you thought about taking a shower instead of a bath, fixing your leaky taps, or eating hamburgers less often? These actions may seem like a drop in the ocean, but every drop helps!

- Beef 15,500 litres per kg
- Pork 4,800 litres per kg
- Cheese 5,000 litres per kg
- Milk 1,000 litres per litre of milk
- Egg 200 litres per egg
- Rice 3,400 litres per kg
- Cotton T-shirt 2,700 litres per T-shirt
- Paper 10 litres per A4 sheet

1 How much water is in an espresso? Why?
2 What is 'virtual water'?
3 How much water do people in wealthy countries use for washing and drinking?
4 Why do vegetarians use less water than meat eaters?
5 Why is demand for water increasing?
6 What are some of the ways that we can manage our water supply more effectively?
7 What can the individual do to reduce their water consumption?

3 Make these verbs into nouns by adding the correct suffix: -ment, -tion, -ance, or -al. Make any other spelling changes that are necessary. Put the nouns in the correct group in the table. Use the text in 2 and a dictionary to help you.

~~consume~~   perform   produce   improve   remove
develop   manage   solve   appear   reduce

-ment	-tion	-ance	-al
	consumption		

4 Work in pairs. Make these words into nouns and add them to the table in 3. Check the meaning and spelling in a dictionary.

agree   appraise   assist   define   disappear   explore   explain   encourage
guide   refuse   resist   pay   satisfy   deny   survive   invest

5 6.2 Work in pairs. Mark the stress on the words in the table in 3. What do you notice about the stress pattern of the words that end -tion? Listen and check.

Example   consumption

6 Complete the sentences with nouns you made in 3 and 4.
1 He expressed his _____ with the results of the survey. He was very pleased.
2 We accept _____ by cash or credit card.
3 Our office gives _____ to students, concerning jobs and work opportunities.
4 Meryl Streep's _____ in that movie was amazing. She won an Oscar for it.
5 Governments need to work together to find a _____ to the problem of global warming.
6 There has been significant _____ in his work. It's much better.
7 I saw him steal the money, so his _____ of the charge against him is unbelievable.
8 The _____ of this species of flower is threatened. We need to introduce measures to protect it.

7 Work in groups and discuss these questions. Think of several points for each question.
1 Do you think that humans have been responsible for the disappearance of many species of animal? If so, which?
2 How have people in your country reduced energy consumption in the last ten years?
3 Should government officials accept payments from private companies for advice or consultancy work? Why / Why not?
4 Has the development of the motor car been a positive or negative thing for humanity? Why?
5 How can wealthy countries contribute to the improvement of living conditions in developing countries?

8 Work in groups. Think of four discussion questions similar to the ones in 7. Use one of the nouns from 3 and 4 in each question. Give your questions to another group to discuss.

70   Unit 6   Vocabulary

Work skills Presentations 2: structuring a talk

1 **Work in pairs. Think about presentations that you have seen or given. Discuss these questions.**
   1 What was good or bad about the presentations?
   2 What is a good structure for a presentation?

2 **Work in pairs. Look at these tips for effective presentations. Choose the five tips which you think are the most important.**
   1 Make sure your presentation has a clear beginning, middle, and end.
   2 The start is the most important part: get your audience interested!
   3 'Signpost' each part of the presentation (in other words, clearly say when one section begins and ends).
   4 Give a summary at the end, and recap your point at the end of each stage.
   5 Make eye contact with your audience.
   6 Don't just read out the words on the screen.
   7 Try to interact with the audience (e.g. ask them questions).
   8 Give an opportunity for questions at the end.
   9 Give the audience a handout.
   10 Smile and relax. It's important to appear confident.

3 ◉ 6.3 **Listen to extracts from a presentation and answer the questions.**
   1 What is the subject of the presentation?
   2 What are the three main sections about?
   3 What is the main conclusion?

4 ◉ 6.3 **Listen again. Tick ✓ the tips in 2 that the presenter follows.**

5 ◉ 6.3 **Look at these phrases from the presentation in 3. Which phrases are used at the beginning, the middle, and the end of the presentation? Put them in the correct group in the table. Listen again and check.**

I've divided my talk into three sections …   Today, I'm going to talk to you about …
That brings me to the end of my talk.   Now let's move on to the second section …
Good morning everyone and thank you for coming.   Does anyone have any questions?
Let's begin with …   My next point deals with …   Thank you for listening.   So to sum up …
My name is …   I'd like to leave you with one last point to think about …

beginning	middle	end
I've divided my talk into three sections …		

6 **Work in pairs. Think of a problem facing the organization where you work or the city or country where you live. Plan the outline of a short presentation using the structure below. Decide on your 'audience' first.**
   - Introduction
   - Body (e.g. problem – solution – how to implement it)
   - Conclusion

7 **Work in pairs. Practise your presentation. Then give your presentation to the class.**

Functions Describing problems and finding solutions

INTRODUCTION

1 Work in groups. What sort of problems do people have with computers or other electronic devices? Have you ever had problems with any of these?

battery   internet   mouse   printer   password
screen   speakers   update   website   (anti)virus

2 🔊 6.4 Tariq Antar is visiting some clients to give a presentation. Listen to four conversations. Tick ✓ the things in **1** that Tariq has problems with.

3 🔊 6.4 Work in pairs. Match the solutions a–d with the problems 1–4 that Tariq has. Listen again and check.

1 the internet   ___
2 the speakers   ___
3 an update   ___
4 the mouse   ___

a Restart the computer.
b Use a completely different device.
c Wait and do nothing.
d Replace with a new version of the same device.

4 Look at sentences 1–5 from the script. Which verbs in **bold** do we use to talk about problems and solutions when

a we think something is possibly true?   ___ ___ ___
b we think something is definitely true?   ___
c we think something is definitely not true? ___

1 That **must** be the problem. If the servers aren't working, it's impossible to connect to the internet.
2 It **could** be the speakers. Have you tried using the other ones?
3 Yes, that **might** fix the problem. Fingers crossed!
4 I'm not sure what the problem is. It **may** be the battery.
5 It **can't** be the battery because I put a new one in this morning.

5 Complete the phrases with these words. Check your answers in the script on page 147.

before   caused   working   fault   like   need   try   solution   wrong

1 The internet isn't _____ .
2 How long has it been _____ that?
3 There's a _____ with the sound.
4 Have you noticed it _____ ?
5 What do you think _____ it?
6 Why don't we _____ restarting your computer?
7 Something's _____ with the mouse.
8 What we _____ to do is change the mouse.
9 One _____ is to use the touch pad on your laptop.

Focus

Complete the table with phrases from 5.

Describing problems	Asking about problems	Discussing solutions
It keeps (on) …	What happened?	It looks like a problem with … Have you tried …?

▶ For more details and practice, go to the Review section on page 77.

PRACTICE

6 ◆) **6.5** Listen to four conversations. Number the problems (a–d) in the order they are mentioned (1–4).

   a a drinks machine ___   c a mobile ___

   b a car ___   d a website ___

7 ◆) **6.5** Complete the extracts with the phrases. Listen again and check.

1 *have you noticed   it keeps making   what you need*

   A I'm worried about my jeep. _____ a strange noise when I drive over 70 kilometres per hour.

   B _____ it before?

   A No, I haven't.

   B _____ to do is take it to the garage as soon as possible.

2 *how long has it been   something's wrong   why don't we put*

   A _____ with the coffee machine. It isn't giving any money back.

   B _____ like that?

   A It started yesterday.

   B _____ a notice on it saying 'Exact money only – no change given'?

3 *isn't working   a problem with   tried using*

   A What's wrong?

   B I want to buy some plane tickets, but there's _____ the website. I can't pay with my credit card.

   A Have you _____ a different one?

   B Yes, I have. It won't accept any of my cards.

   A Maybe there's a problem with the site. Perhaps their payment processing _____ at the moment. Wait half an hour and then try again.

4 *do you think   happened   looks like*

   A I heard a noise. What _____?

   B My mobile was recharging and it suddenly exploded!

   A Oh, yeah. I see the smoke. What _____ caused it?

   B I'm not sure. Can you look at it?

   A Hmmm … it _____ a problem with the charger.

8 Work in pairs. Think of possible responses to these comments.

1 My computer keeps crashing. *It might be a problem with the automatic updates.*

2 There's no hot water in my home. Even the shower's cold!

3 My credit card doesn't work when I travel to other countries.

4 A window in the office is broken.

5 I can't get any lunch because the office canteen is closed all week.

6 It's impossible to find a parking space for my car when I go to work.

TASK

9 Work in pairs. Help each other find a solution to a problem. Student A, go to page 128. Student B, go to page 132.

Review

Grammar Past Simple, Past Continuous, Past Perfect

Form

Past Simple	subject + verb -ed	The engineers invented a new system for transporting water.
		At first they didn't understand the problem.
		Did they find the solution immediately? No, they didn't.
Past Continuous	subject + was / were + verb -ing	Ten years ago, people were walking long distances to find water.
		Many people weren't drinking clean water.
		Where were they getting the water from?
Past Perfect	subject + had + past participle	They had tried various designs before they found the one that worked.
		They hadn't realized how simple the solution was.
		Had anyone thought of the idea before? No, they hadn't.

We put *when* before the Past Simple clause and *while* before the Past Continuous clause.
Examples She was walking home **when** she dropped her bucket.
While she was walking home, she dropped her bucket.

Use

Past Simple

We use the Past Simple to talk about a completed event in the past or a sequence of past events.
Example We packed our bags, left the camp, and walked to the river.

Past Continuous

We use the Past Continuous to talk about a background event or state in progress at the time of the main past event.
Example We were sailing up the river when we saw a man in the water.

Past Perfect

We use the Past Perfect to talk about an event in the past which happened before another event in the past.
Example Luckily, we had already set up our tents before the rain started.

PRACTICE

1 Match 1–5 with a–e to make complete sentences.

1 He was doing research in Oxford ___
2 He moved to Spain ___
3 When he got to the meeting ___
4 She saw an article about an old friend ___
5 She had spent a long time training ___

a while she was reading the newspaper.
b it had already started.
c after he had learnt some Spanish.
d before she did her first marathon.
e when he had the idea for his first book.

2 Choose the correct verb forms to complete the sentences.

1 Chris and Jo *studied / were studying* at university when they *decided / had decided* to 'do something different'. They *were both failing / had both failed* their mid-term exams, and *were feeling / had felt* depressed about the future.
2 One day, they *watched / were watching* a programme about the River Ganges in India. They *never saw / had never seen* anything like it before. They *found / were finding* it very interesting and *decided / were deciding* to go there.
3 So they *left / had left* their homes in Oxford and *flew / were flying* to India.
4 After they *were / had been* in India for a few weeks, they *travelled / had travelled* to the Himalayas.
5 They *started / were starting* on foot. But while they *carried / were carrying* their equipment down the mountain, they *met / were meeting* someone who *wanted / had wanted* to sell a rickshaw. So they *bought / were buying* it.
6 When they *got / were getting* to the river, they *decided / were deciding* to sell the rickshaw. After they *were selling / had sold* it, they *bought / had bought* a row boat and *floated / were floating* down the river.
7 One day, they *floated / were floating* down the river when they *saw / were seeing* a crocodile. It *came / had come* very near to the boat, but it *didn't attack / hadn't attacked* them.
8 By the time they *reached / were reaching* the end of their journey, they *were having / had had* many adventures.
9 They *experienced / had experienced* a river and a culture in a way that *was never being done / had never been done* before.
10 They *didn't go / hadn't gone* back to university.

3 Complete the article with the correct form of the verbs in brackets.

The perfect time to achieve

Is there an ideal time in your life to achieve great things? We all know about the young computer and social-networking entrepreneurs like Mark Zuckerberg and Dustin Muscovitz. They _____¹ (study) at college when they _____² (establish) Facebook. The man who _____³ (invent) the cathode ray TV, Philo Farnsworth, was also in his 20s when he _____⁴ (come up with) the idea that _____⁵ (lead) to the modern television. He _____⁶ (have) the idea when he _____⁷ (plough) a field. He _____⁸ (imagine) all the furrows as lines on a screen. He _____⁹ (already invent) an earlier version when he was just 15.

So the age of achievement for inventors seems to be young: 20s or 30s. We might think political achievers are usually older. However, when Barack Obama _____¹⁰ (become) President of the USA in 2008 at the age of 47, there _____¹¹ (be) eight previous presidents in their 40s, including Bill Clinton and John F Kennedy.

What about the world of sport? Surely you have to be young to achieve anything? Not really. Think about the marathon runner, Fauja Singh. He was 89 years old when he _____¹² (run) his first marathon. He _____¹³ (start) running at the age of 63 when most of his friends _____¹⁴ (think of) retirement. He _____¹⁵ (retire) from marathon running at the age of 101. By that time, he _____¹⁶ (run) nine marathons with a personal best of 5 hours and 40 minutes.

So what's the message from all this? There is no 'perfect time to achieve'. You can achieve great things in whatever field you want, whatever age you are.

Vocabulary Water footprint; noun formation

1 Use a suffix to make these verbs into nouns.

1 improve _____
2 deny _____
3 assist _____
4 remove _____
5 perform _____
6 produce _____
7 explain _____
8 develop _____
9 define _____
10 appear _____
11 satisfy _____
12 reduce _____

2 Complete the sentences with the nouns in 1.

1 I didn't know the meaning of the word, so I looked up its _____ in the dictionary.
2 The filter will ensure the _____ of all bacteria from the water.
3 She demanded an _____ for his recent strange behaviour.
4 These measures will achieve a significant _____ in costs. We should save about $400,000.
5 We will begin _____ of the new mobiles in June. They'll go on sale in August.
6 We were shocked at his _____. He hadn't washed and looked tired and dirty.
7 The government provided _____ to the earthquake victims.
8 Customer _____ has been 100% this year. We've had no complaints about our service.
9 We've made an _____ to the design – it works better now.
10 During your appraisal, your manager will discuss your _____ during the year.
11 Our research department is working on the _____ of a new kind of electric engine. We hope to have the new design ready next year.
12 The company has issued a _____ of the accusations. It claims they are completely false.

Work skills Presentations 2: structuring a talk

Match 1–8 with a–h to make phrases from a presentation.

1 I've divided my talk ___
2 Good morning, everyone, and ___
3 Now let's move ___
4 Does anyone have ___
5 Today, I'm going to talk ___
6 My first point deals with ___
7 To sum up, we've ___
8 That brings me ___

a any questions?
b about some of our recent research.
c to my last point today.
d on to the second point in my talk.
e the findings of our latest research.
f into three sections.
g thank you for coming.
h looked at the research and discussed possible solutions.

Functions Describing problems and finding solutions

We use these phrases to describe problems.
Examples   It keeps (on) (+ -ing) …
Something's wrong with / There's a problem with the (+ noun).
The … isn't / aren't working (properly).

We use these phrases to ask for more details about problems.
Examples   Have you noticed it before?
How long has it been like that?
What do you think caused it?
What happened?

We use these phrases to discuss solutions.
Examples   Have you tried / Why don't you try (+ -ing)?
It looks like a problem with …
What we need to do is (+ verb) …
One solution is to (+ verb) …

PRACTICE

1 Complete the conversations with these questions.

Have you noticed it before? *Have you tried asking Michelle?*
How long has it been like that? *What do you think caused it?*
Why don't you try offering two meals for the price of one?

1 A I was so disappointed. My watch stopped working and I had to throw it away.
   B _____
   A I wore it when I went swimming and I think water got inside.
2 A I need someone to welcome our visitors, but no one is free tomorrow.
   B _____
   A Good idea. I forgot about her!
3 A That's strange. A red light is flashing on this machine.
   B _____
   A No, never. This is the first time.
4 A The restaurant is not getting any customers.
   B _____
   A We could lose a lot of money by doing that.
5 A My office door doesn't close properly.
   B _____
   A Since I've worked here – about two months!

2 Match comments 1–4 with responses a–d.

1 There's a problem with the electronic message boards in the station. They aren't giving us any information. ___
2 Why is everyone in the street outside the office? What happened? ___
3 The GPS isn't working properly. It doesn't know where we are. ___
4 My laptop keeps on making this strange noise. ___

a What we need to do is switch if off and on again. It sometimes helps you get a signal.
b It looks like a problem with the hard disk. I think you need a new computer.
c Something's wrong with the fire alarm. We can't go back inside until they fix it.
d It's because the servers are down. Don't worry, we'll tell you what's happening with the trains.

7 Work styles and careers

Grammar Zero, 1st, and 2nd Conditional

INTRODUCTION

1 Work in pairs and discuss these questions.
1. How would you describe yourself at work: a good team player, calm, helpful?
2. What career plans do you have? How certain are they?

2 🔊 7.1 Listen to Matt and Grace, two professionals in their early 30s, talk about themselves at work. Tick ✓ the statements which are true for Matt and/or Grace.

	Matt	Grace
1 If my boss asks me to work at the weekend, I always say 'Yes'.	☐	☐
2 If it's one of my team's birthday, I buy them a birthday card.	☐	☐
3 If I'm behind schedule, I don't panic.	☐	☐
4 If another employee has performance issues, I try to help them.	☐	☐
5 If someone does a great job, I tell them.	☐	☐
6 If there's a tough decision to make, I don't avoid responsibility.	☐	☐

3 Work in pairs. Take turns to ask your partner which statements in **2** are true for them.

4 🔊 7.2 Matt and Grace talk about the next stage of their careers. Listen and answer the questions.
1. Is Matt likely to be promoted soon?
2. Would he like to work abroad?
3. How likely is he to stay in his present job?
4. Would Grace like to change jobs?
5. What would she like to do?
6. Does she like her job and company?

5 🔊 7.2 Listen again and complete the sentences.

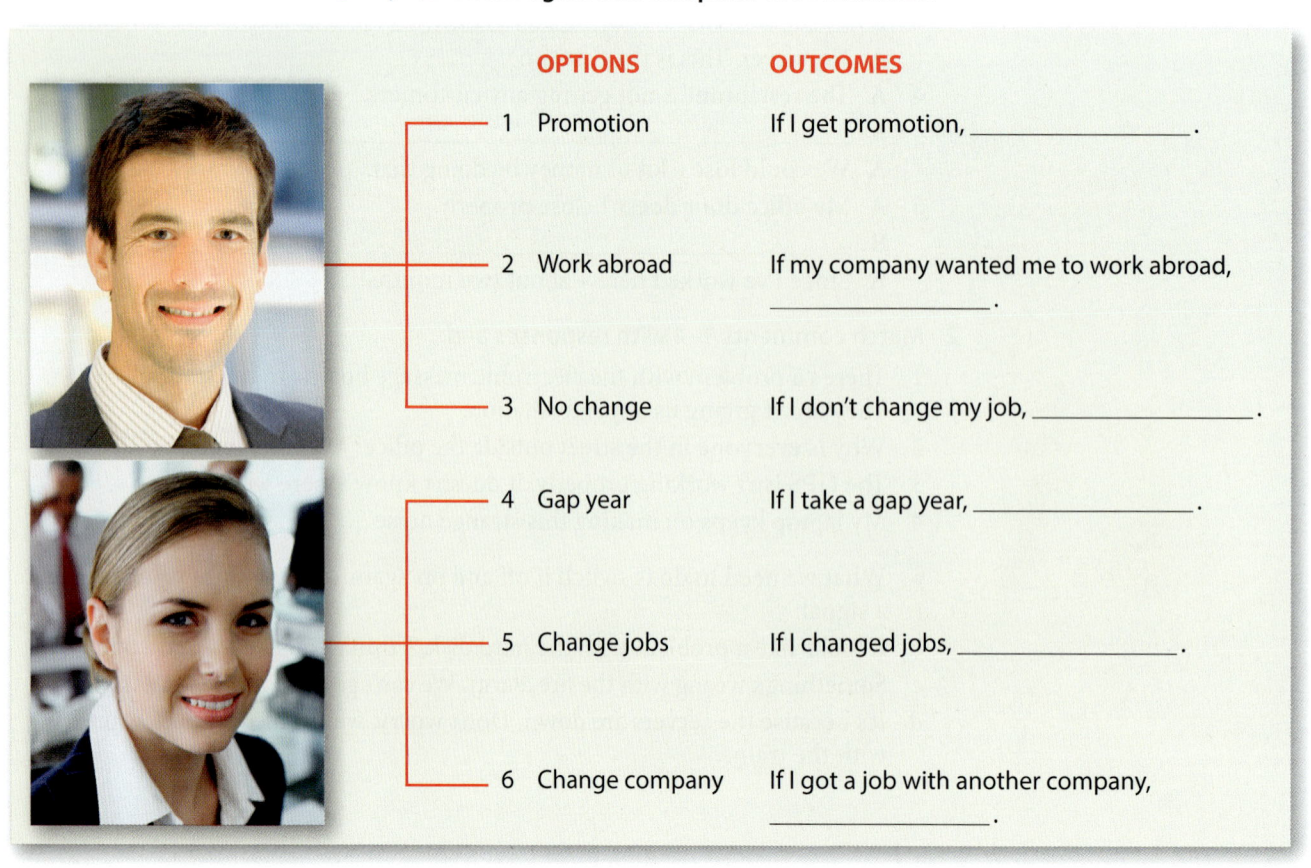

	OPTIONS	OUTCOMES
1	Promotion	If I get promotion, _____.
2	Work abroad	If my company wanted me to work abroad, _____.
3	No change	If I don't change my job, _____.
4	Gap year	If I take a gap year, _____.
5	Change jobs	If I changed jobs, _____.
6	Change company	If I got a job with another company, _____.

Focus

Read the sentences in 2 and 5 again. Complete the rules with the words in *italics*.

Past Simple   Present Simple   will + infinitive

We form the Zero Conditional with *if* + _____ , Present Simple.

We form the 1st Conditional with *if* + Present Simple, _____ .

We form the 2nd Conditional with *if* + _____ , *would* + infinitive.

likely   true   unlikely

We use the Zero Conditional to talk about things that are generally _____ .

We use the 1st Conditional to talk about future outcomes based on _____ or possible conditions.

We use the 2nd Conditional to talk about future outcomes based on _____ or imaginary conditions.

⏵ For more details and practice, go to the Review section on pages 86 and 87.

PRACTICE

6 Complete the sentences with your own ideas. Use the appropriate verb form for the Zero Conditional.
1. If I have to give a presentation, _____ .
2. If I'm behind schedule, _____ .
3. If there is a problem between two members of my team, _____ .
4. If I feel exhausted, _____ .
5. If a customer complains about a product, _____ .
6. If my computer crashes, _____ .
7. If I can't get to work because of the weather, _____ .
8. If my boss is in a bad mood, _____ .

7 Complete the sentences with the appropriate form of the verbs in brackets.
1. If someone _____ (offer) you a better paid job, what will you do?
2. If you had one extra qualification, what _____ (it be)?
3. If your boss _____ (give) you more work to do next month, what will you do?
4. If you saw an interesting job vacancy, what _____ (you do)?
5. If you _____ (move) into a completely different area of business, what would it be?
6. If you stay in your present organization, where _____ (you be) this time next year?
7. If you _____ (can) ask anyone advice about your future, who would you to talk to?
8. If you get the opportunity to work in another country, what _____ (you do)?

8 Work in pairs. Ask and answer the questions in 7.

9 Work in pairs. Play the 'Futures' game. Read the rules before you start. You need a coin and two counters.

Example   If I was offered a job by another company, I would ask them for more details.

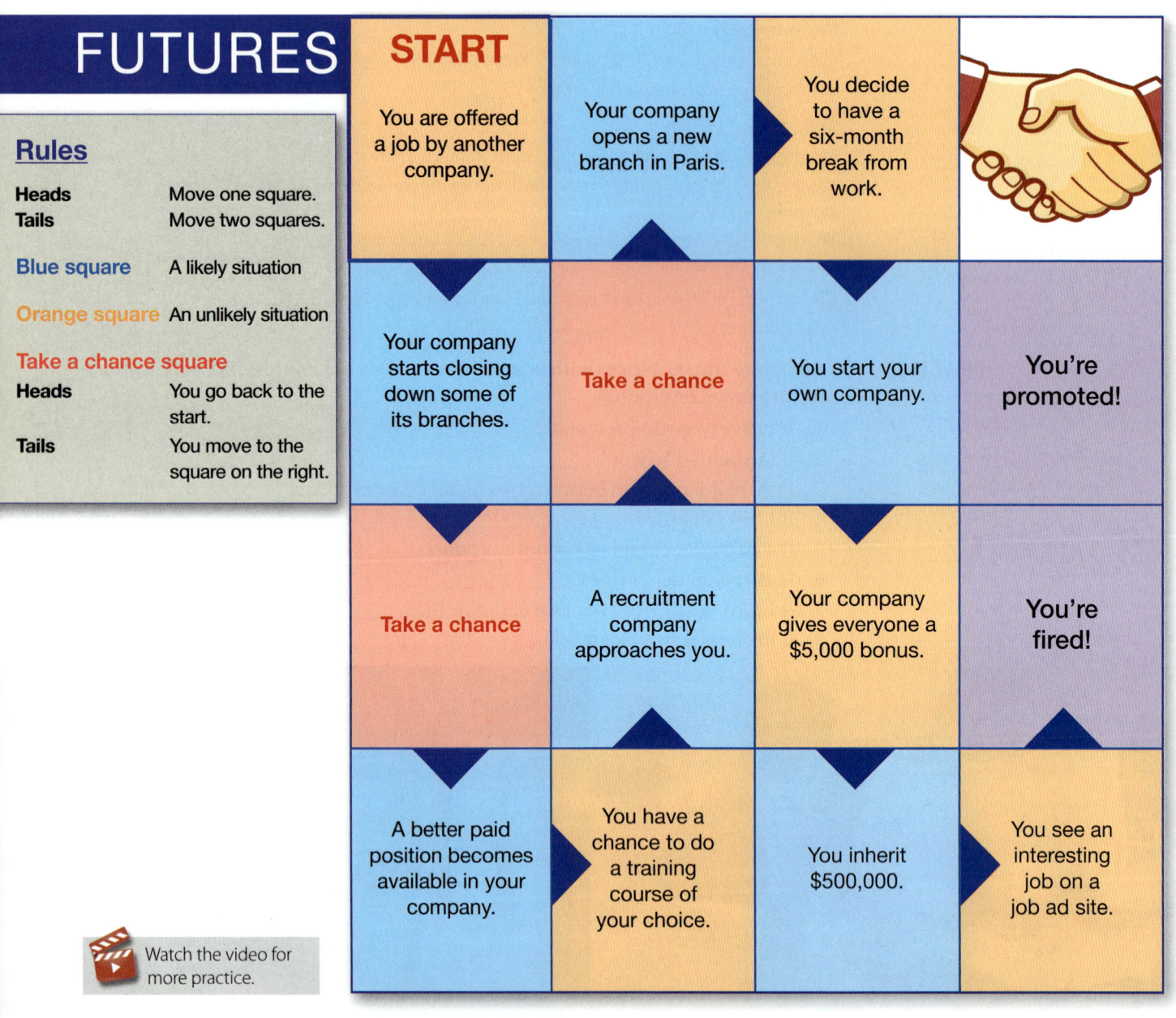

FUTURES

Rules

Heads	Move one square.
Tails	Move two squares.
Blue square	A likely situation
Orange square	An unlikely situation
Take a chance square	
Heads	You go back to the start.
Tails	You move to the square on the right.

Game board squares:

- START
- You are offered a job by another company.
- Your company opens a new branch in Paris.
- You decide to have a six-month break from work.
- Your company starts closing down some of its branches.
- Take a chance
- You start your own company.
- You're promoted!
- Take a chance
- A recruitment company approaches you.
- Your company gives everyone a $5,000 bonus.
- You're fired!
- A better paid position becomes available in your company.
- You have a chance to do a training course of your choice.
- You inherit $500,000.
- You see an interesting job on a job ad site.

Watch the video for more practice.

TASK 10 Work in pairs. Read the letter below. Take turns to role-play the HR Manager. Interview other people using the questionnaire to find out what they will do.

Dear Colleague

As you know, our rivals, ABC Leisure Ltd, made an offer to buy our company. We are negotiating at the moment and it is very likely that the deal will go ahead. If it does, we will become part of ABC Leisure Ltd. This will lead to changes for all of us.

The attached questionnaire is to help us plan for the future. We value your opinion. Please note the questionnaire is anonymous, so be as honest as you can.

Ted Harrison
HR Manager

Questionnaire

1. If we become part of ABC Leisure Ltd, everyone will need to reapply for their jobs. In these circumstances, will you want to continue to work for us?
2. If the deal didn't happen, we would need to reduce our costs. Would you be prepared to take a significant pay cut?
3. If we become part of ABC Leisure, we will close our present offices and move to their headquarters in central London, a one-hour commute from here. Will this be an advantage or a disadvantage for you?
4. ABC Leisure has many branches in other countries. If they offered you a position in another country, would you be prepared to take it?

Vocabulary Money and finance

1 Work in pairs. Which of these financial products or services do you use? Do you use any others?

- online banking
- telephone banking
- a pension
- a mortgage
- loans
- home / car / life insurance

2 🔊 **7.3** Listen to the conversation between a customer and a telephone banking advisor. Answer the questions.

1. How much money does the man want to pay each month for his rent?
2. When does he want to pay the money each month?
3. Why is he surprised?
4. How much money did he take out of his account from an ATM?
5. What bill has he just paid?
6. How much money did he put in his account yesterday?

3 🔊 **7.3** Complete the sentences with these words. Listen again and check.

| direct debit | balance | standing order | withdraw |
| deposited | transfer | debits | account number |

1. I'd like to set up a _____ to pay my rent each month.
2. My _____ is 61757275.
3. I'd like to _____ £800 on the first day of each month.
4. Can I check the _____ on my account?
5. When did I last _____ money from my account?
6. Do you pay your credit card by _____?
7. The credit card company _____ my account automatically on the 17th of each month.
8. I _____ £500 in my account yesterday.

4 Work in pairs. What is the difference between these phrases? Use a dictionary to help you.

1. to lend money to someone / to borrow money from someone
2. to deposit money / to withdraw money
3. a standing order / a direct debit
4. to debit an account / to credit an account
5. to open a bank account / to close a bank account
6. to be in credit / to be overdrawn

5 Match the verbs 1–6 with the nouns / noun phrases a–f to make collocations.

1. set up ___
2. pay by ___
3. deposit ___
4. enter ___
5. transfer ___
6. withdraw ___

a. credit card
b. your PIN
c. £350 from an ATM
d. money to another account
e. a standing order
f. £100 in your account

6 Work in pairs. Discuss these questions.

1. Do you have a credit card? What do you use it for?
2. How do you pay your bills? Do you have any direct debits or standing orders?
3. How often do you withdraw money from ATMs?
4. Do you use online banking to transfer money?
5. Have you ever forgotten your PIN?
6. Is it easy to open a bank account? What do you need to do?

7 Match the words 1–5 with the meanings a–e.

1 inflation ___
2 outgoings ___
3 savings ___
4 shares ___
5 interest ___

a money that you have kept to use in the future
b the money that you regularly spend to pay bills
c the rate at which the price of food, services, etc. increases by each year
d one of the equal parts of a company you can buy as a way of investing money
e the extra money that you pay or receive when you borrow or invest money

8 Read the text about saving money. Are the statements below true or false?

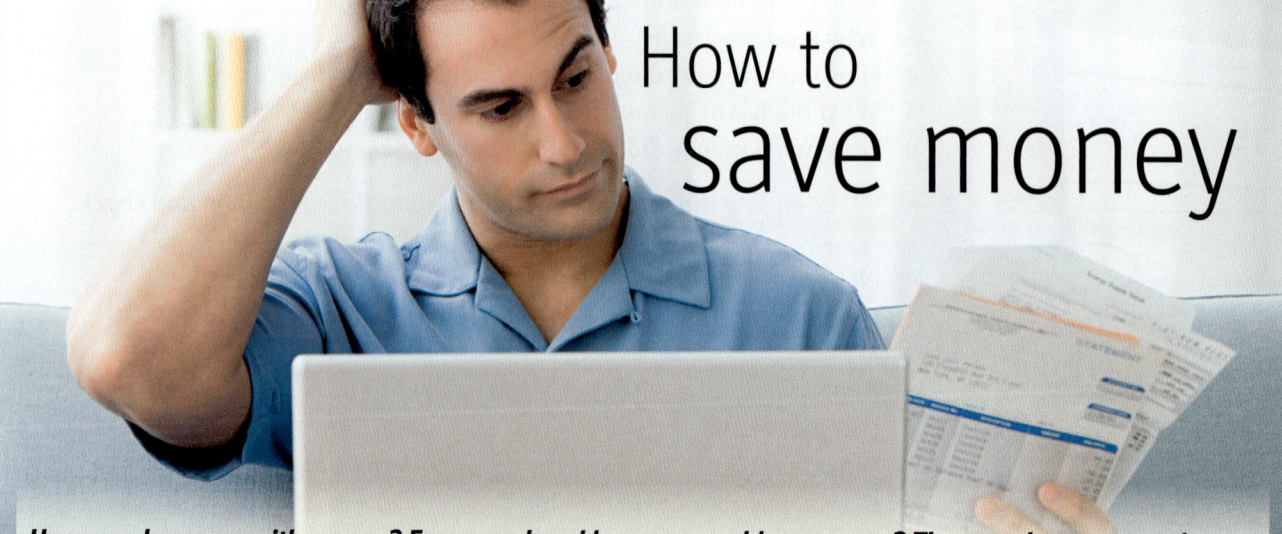

How to save money

How good are you with money? Ever wondered how you could save more? Then read our suggestions for making your money go further.

Make a shopping list: A large part of our monthly outgoings goes on food shopping, so think about what you spend. Plan a few meals ahead, make a shopping list, and only buy what you really need. Also never go food shopping when you're hungry. You'll buy a lot more!

Don't automatically renew insurance: It may be convenient to automatically renew your home or car insurance each year, but it's wise to shop around. You can save a lot of money by changing company each year.

Don't leave large amounts of money in the bank: Banks in the UK currently pay about 2–3% interest on a savings account. Inflation is currently about 3–4%. This means that at the end of the year, your savings are either worth the same or are 1% less valuable. Look into other forms of investment like shares, property, or even antiques. The stock exchange is risky, but so is doing nothing.

Cancel your gym membership: Are you a member of a gym but almost never go? Well, why not cancel that standing order to the gym? You'll save yourself £40 or £50 a month. Use the money to buy yourself a nice bike and then cycle to work instead. That way, you also save on bus or train fares.

Always pay off your credit card debt: Credit cards are great as long as you pay off your balance each month. If you can't, then consider taking out a loan instead. A typical bank loan charges 6–7% interest. Credit cards charge about 14–16%. Do the maths!

Make your own coffee: Do you buy one or two coffees every day? How much do you spend? Two coffees a day in the UK cost you about £3.60. That comes to £1,316 a year. Save yourself some money. Make your own!

1 Go shopping when you're hungry, so you can see what you really want.
2 You should look at other companies before you renew insurance.
3 Leaving money in a savings account may not increase its value.
4 Gyms are an expensive way of staying fit.
5 Credit cards charge higher interest rates than bank loans.
6 You'll save money if you make your own coffee.

9 Work in groups. Do you agree with the suggestions in 8? Why / Why not? Think of three more suggestions for how to save money. When you have finished, tell the rest of the class your ideas.

Idris & Banks is recruiting for its new Shanghai office. We are looking for an IT Consultant to join our research and analysis team. Candidates must have the ability to design, test, install, and monitor new systems. Experience in a similar role essential. Knowledge of Mandarin desirable. Applications with CV to:

Petra James, HR Department,
Ref: *HR/2015PJ.*
Email: *pjames@idrisbanks.com*

Work skills Emails 2: job applications

1 Read the job advertisement. What is the job? What skills and experience are required?

2 Read the email below in reply to the job advertisement in **1**. Find these sentences in the email.
   a a description of the applicant's experience (two sentences) ___ ___
   b the reason for the email ___
   c her availability for interview ___
   d an explanation of why she is interested in the position ___
   e a description of some of her skills ___

To: pjames@idrisbanks.com
From: lisapeng@mail.com
Subject: Shanghai position
Attachment: CV

Dear Ms James

I am writing in response to your advertisement for an IT Consultant in your Shanghai office (as seen on *The Monitor* website, Ref: HR/2015PJ)[1]. The position sounds very exciting and is exactly the challenge I am looking for[2].

As requested, please find attached my CV. You will see that I have several years' experience in IT in both the UK and the US, and that I am currently working with a large Chinese bank based in London[3]. I am a senior IT Analyst in the commodities market, specializing in the copper and gold markets[4]. I am fluent in both Mandarin and English[5].

If you would like to interview me, I am available most days with prior notice[6].

I look forward to hearing from you.

Kind regards

Lisa Peng

---

3 How is the email in **2** different to an email you would send to a colleague in your department?

4 Match the headings 1–7 from a CV with the statements a–g.

   1 Contact details   ___   a Prof W Hastings, MIT
   2 Personal statement   ___   b Email: lisapeng@mail.com
   3 Education   ___   c Fluent in English and Mandarin
   4 Professional experience   ___   d Badminton, scuba diving, cookery, chess.
   5 Other professional skills ___   e An enthusiastic professional with five years'
   6 Interests   ___   experience in analysing financial markets.
   7 Referees   ___   f 2008–2011 Degree in Computer Science, MIT
                                          g 2013–2014 IT Systems Manager, SBS London

5 Write statements of your own for the headings in **4**.

6 Work in pairs.
   1 Write a job advertisement like the advert in **1** for a job you know. Include one thing that is essential and one that is desirable.
   2 Exchange the job advertisement with another pair. Write a short CV and an email applying for the job that the other pair has given you.

Functions Discussing and reaching agreement

INTRODUCTION

1 Work in pairs. Look at the types of training courses and answer the questions.

Customer relations	First aid	Interview techniques	IT
Negotiating	Planning	Sales techniques	Telephone skills
Writing contracts	Management / Leadership training		

1 Have you ever done one of these courses? What was it like?
2 Which course do you think is most / least useful for you? Why?

2 Work in pairs. Read the email from Georgios. Answer the questions.
1 What does Georgios' company do?
2 What questions do you think Martina asked in her email?
3 What do you think is going to happen next?

Dear Martina

Thank you for your email regarding First Aid courses for AGS Plastics. We would be delighted to arrange these for you.

What we can offer you is a complete training package. We can also offer you a discount of 10% if the training courses involve more than 50 people. However, please note that we cannot offer this discount unless all your factories are in the EU.

If you would like to discuss this further, we would be very happy to arrange a meeting at your offices at a time convenient for you.

Best regards

Georgios

SG & J Health and Safety Consultants Ltd

---

3 Find phrases in the email in 2 which mean:
1 We can provide … _____
2 We can give you a reduction in the price … _____
3 This special price is only available if … _____

4 ◆)) 7.4 Georgios meets Martina at her company. Listen to three extracts from the meeting. Correct the false information in the sentences.
1 None of Martina's employees has training in first aid.
2 Martina requests refresher courses where people return every two years to improve their skills.
3 Martina's factories had seven accidents last month.
4 Georgios will organize a government inspection of the factory.
5 The courses will be completed in one month.
6 Georgios offers Martina a final discount of 50%.

5 ◆)) 7.4 Work in pairs. Complete the sentences with these words. Listen again and check.

deal   fine   important   main   propose   return   sorry

1 What's the most _____ thing for you?
2 What I _____ is a package of a beginner course plus refresher courses.
3 That would be _____ for us.
4 What are your _____ concerns?
5 I'm _____, but that's not possible.
6 In _____, would you consider a further discount?
7 It's a _____!

6 Work in pairs. Do you think the discussion between Martina and Georgios was a success? Why / Why not?

> **Focus**
>
> **Put the phrases from 5 in the correct groups.**
>
> **Asking about requirements**
> What's your priority here?
> _____
> _____
>
> **Putting forward a proposal**
> We can offer you a discount of 10% …
> _____
>
> **Negotiating**
> We cannot offer this discount unless all your factories are in the EU.
> _____
>
> **Agreeing to a proposal / request**
> We can agree to that.
> _____
> _____
>
> **Rejecting a proposal / request**
> I'm afraid that wouldn't be possible.
> _____
>
> ▶ For more details and practice, go to the Review section on page 89.

PRACTICE

7 ◆)) **7.5** Listen to six conversations. Do the people agree to (*A*) or reject (*R*) the proposal / request?

1 ___ 2 ___ 3 ___ 4 ___ 5 ___ 6 ___

8 ◆)) **7.5** Work in pairs. Complete the extracts with the missing words. Listen again and check.

1 A I have to go to the bank tomorrow. Can you do my morning shift and I'll do your afternoon one?
  B OK. _____ _____, can we change our shifts this weekend so you work on Saturday and I work on Sunday?

2 A We can deliver 500 chairs to your furniture shop by the end of next month.
  B It's _____ _____!

3 A We would like you to start construction of the research centre on 1st May and to finish the work by September next year.
  B I'm _____ _____ such a short timetable wouldn't be possible.

4 A What we propose is a temporary contract of three months, followed by a possible permanent contract.
  B That _____ _____ fine for us.

5 A We cannot do this project _____ _____ get more financial help from your company.
  B I understand that and I agree. We can offer you a further $60,000.

6 A We want you to provide IT training in English, French, and German.
  B I'm sorry, but that's _____ _____. Our trainers only speak English.

TASK

9 Work in pairs. You work in the same company. Student A, you are the manager. Student B, you are a salesperson. B's contract ends next month and you are going to agree a new one. Student A, go to page 128. Student B, go to page 134.

10 Carry out the discussion. Follow the stages below.

Stage 1	A, find out what B wants.
Stage 2	B, find out what A wants.
Stage 3	A, make offers to B.
Stage 4	B, respond to A's offers and make your own requests.
Stage 5	Reach a final agreement.

Review

Grammar Zero, 1st, and 2nd Conditional

Form

Zero Conditional	*if* + Present Simple, Present Simple	If you press this switch, the computer comes on.
		If you hit it with a hammer, it doesn't make it work.
1st Conditional	*if* + Present Simple, *will* + verb	If I change my job, I'll move house.
		If I don't get the job, I won't move house.
2nd Conditional	*if* + Past Simple, *would* (or *could* / *might*) + verb	If they made me a director, I would be delighted.
		If I were you, I wouldn't apply for that job.

We usually put the *if* clause first in the sentence, but we can put it second.
Example I would be delighted if they made me a director.

Use

We use *if* to talk about conditions and outcomes.

Zero Conditional

We use the Zero Conditional to talk about events that generally occur based on a typical condition. We can talk about rules.
Example If the temperature goes below 0° [condition], water freezes [outcome].

We can also talk about typical situations.
Example When I have to give a presentation [condition], I always practise beforehand [outcome].

In these cases, the outcome is always, or almost always, the same. We can use *if* or *when* for the condition clause.

1st Conditional

We use the 1st Conditional to talk about future outcomes based on likely or possible conditions.
Example If I don't have enough time to finish the job, I'll ask someone to help.

In this case, it is likely or possible that I won't have enough time.

2nd Conditional

We use the 2nd Conditional to talk about future outcomes based on unlikely or imaginary conditions.
Example If he didn't get the job, he'd be very disappointed.

In this case, it is likely that he will get the job.

PRACTICE

1 Match 1–5 with a–e to make conditional sentences.

1 If everyone worked from home, ___
2 If both parents work full-time, ___
3 If we were living in the 17th century, ___
4 If you learn another language, ___
5 If you don't study, ___

a we'd probably be working in agriculture.
b you won't increase your qualifications.
c we wouldn't need to use our cars so much.
d it will increase your job opportunities.
e someone else has to look after the children.

2 Complete the sentences with the correct form of the verbs in brackets.

1 What would you do if computers _____ (not exist)?
2 When you _____ (put) the information on a USB stick, it's easier to take with you.
3 If you _____ (can) only have one piece of digital technology, what would it be?
4 If you take your phone on holiday, you _____ (check) your emails and you _____ (not relax).
5 If you _____ (go) to Hong Kong rather than New York, you would find that computer equipment is cheaper.
6 If you _____ (not read) the instructions, how will you know what to do?
7 If I can't do something immediately, I just _____ (give up).

3 Complete the text with the correct form of the verbs in brackets.

Is change an opportunity or a threat?

None of us know the future. If we did, we _____¹ (probably find) life rather boring. Think about it: if you _____² (know) the events of the day before they happened, would you be happy? But we can predict some things. For example, if we _____³ (work) hard and do a good job, we usually get paid. If we work for a good company for a number of years, we _____⁴ (probably get) a pay rise and promotion. Maybe, if we worked really hard, we _____⁵ (make) it right to the top of the company. But change, and its consequences, isn't always easy to predict. If your company _____⁶ (offer) you a job in another country, would you see it as an opportunity or a threat? Perhaps you would think, 'If I _____⁷ (not take) this chance, I'll regret it for the rest of my life'. Or maybe you would think, 'I would lose all my friends and family if I _____⁸ (move) abroad'. If you don't take the opportunities, then there's a good chance that life _____⁹ (become) boring and predictable. One thing is certain: change will always happen. And if you _____¹⁰ (stop) pedalling the bicycle, you fall off.

Vocabulary Money and finance

1 Complete the sentences with these words. Change the form of the verb where necessary.

deposit   enter   pay   set up   transfer   withdraw

1 Can I _____ by credit card?
2 I _____ €600 in my account yesterday, but it will be three days before the money is in my account.
3 She's _____ a standing order to pay her rent.
4 Please check the amount and _____ your PIN.
5 He _____ $200 from an ATM yesterday.
6 I'd like to _____ €400 to my son's account on the last day of each month.

2 🔊 **7.6** Listen to the conversation between a customer and a telephone banking advisor. Answer the questions.
1. What is Ms McDonnell's sort code and account number?
2. How much does she want to transfer?
3. Why can't she transfer the money?
4. What is the balance of her account?
5. What money was she expecting to receive?
6. How much did she withdraw from an ATM?
7. What is her standing order for?

3 Choose the correct words to complete the text on mobile banking.

SouthlandBank

Instant Banking

With Southland Bank's new Instant Banking app, you can access your bank account on your mobile phone. The app allows you to:
- *check / deposit / set up*[1] your balance
- *enter / transfer / withdraw*[2] money to other accounts
- *deposit / open / set up*[3] standing orders and direct debits
- keep track of your bills and other *inflation / insurance / outgoings*[4]

If you need to *deposit / close / withdraw*[5] money from an ATM, the app has a map function that allows you to find your nearest ATM. It also has a StockEx function with live updates from major stock exchanges, so you can check the current value of your *savings / shares / inflation*[6]. The Instant Banking app is secure and is protected by our Internet Banking Guarantee, so your *insurance / outgoings / savings*[7] will be safe. To access your account, you'll need to enter a *direct debit / PIN / sort code*[8] and password.

How you can get an Instant Banking account

If you're not already a customer of Southland Bank, you'll need to *close / open / borrow*[9] a current account with us. We offer a competitive 1.8% *outgoing / interest / savings*[10]. To open an account, please visit your nearest Southland Bank branch.

Work skills Emails 2: job applications

Complete the email with these phrases.

| attached to | Post Ref | experience | in response |
| available for | a Front Desk Manager | qualification | you will see |

Subject: Edinburgh position
Attachment: 📄 CV

Dear Ms Dann

I am writing _____[1] to your advertisement for _____[2] in your new 5* Edinburgh hotel (_____[3]: HR/Ed071).

As _____[4] from my CV, which is _____[5] this email, I have a _____[6] in hotel management. I have also worked as a trainee front desk manager for the past two years, so I believe I have the necessary customer service skills and _____[7] for the post.

I am _____[8] interview most days.

I look forward to hearing from you.

Yours sincerely,

Paul Finlay

Functions Discussing and reaching agreement

We use these phrases to put forward a proposal.
Examples We can offer you a discount of (% / $, etc.).
What we can offer you is …
What I propose is …

We use these phrases to ask about requirements.
Examples What are your main concerns?
What's your priority here / the most important thing for you?

We use these phrases to negotiate.
Examples In return, would you consider a further discount?
We cannot offer this unless …

We use these phrases to agree to a proposal / request.
Examples It's a deal!
That would be fine for us.
We can agree to that.

We use these phrases to reject a proposal / request.
Examples I'm afraid that wouldn't be possible.
I'm sorry, but that's not possible.

PRACTICE

1 Rewrite the sentences using the words in brackets.
1 We cannot give you a discount on golf equipment if you aren't a member of the sports club. (unless)
2 We have a special price of $20 per ticket. (offer)
3 Can you help with my presentation? If you say 'yes', I'll help you with your website. (return)
4 What is the number one thing for your company? (priority)
5 Sorry, but we cannot offer you a 15% discount. (afraid)
6 Our suggestion is a price of $20 for the first 1,000 books, and then $18 after that. (propose)
7 What are you most worried about? (concerns)

2 ◆)) 7.7 Listen to five conversations. Do the people agree to (A) or reject (R) the proposal / request?
1 ___   2 ___   3 ___   4 ___   5 ___

3 ◆)) 7.7 Put the words in the right order. Listen again and check.
1 (*possible / I'm / but / that's / sorry / not*) _____ . All our flights are fully booked today.
2 (*for / yes / would / that / fine / me / be*) _____ . I'm looking forward to working with you.
3 The price is £3,000. (*with / happy / are / that / you*) _____?
4 So we work the same number of hours, but we don't work on Friday afternoons? OK. (*that / we / to / agree / can*) _____ .
5 (*be / afraid / wouldn't / possible / I'm / that*) _____ because these uniforms are already at our lowest possible price.

Review Unit 7

8 Processes

Grammar Passives: Present Simple, Present Continuous, Present Perfect Simple, Past Simple, *will*

INTRODUCTION   1   How much do you know about chocolate? Do the quiz with a partner.

1. Who were the first people to make chocolate?
   the Swiss ☐   the Brazilians ☐   the Mayans ☐
2. When was chocolate first made?
   more than 2,000 years ago ☐   1,000 years ago ☐   500 years ago ☐
3. Chocolate is made from the seeds of which tree?
   cacao ☐   cocoa ☐   coconut ☐
4. In which of these countries is the bean grown?
   Côte d'Ivoire (Ivory Coast) ☐   Thailand ☐   Ghana ☐
5. Which of these ingredients is not used to make chocolate?
   flour ☐   milk ☐   sugar ☐

2   ◆)) 8.1   Listen to a chocolate maker talk about the chocolate industry and answer the questions.
1. Where was chocolate first produced?
2. How did Europeans learn about chocolate?
3. Was chocolate originally drunk or eaten?
4. Which is the largest market for chocolate these days?
5. What is the current situation in the Asia markets?
6. What is the likely trend for consumption of chocolate in Asia?
7. What is the situation regarding child labour?

Watch the video for more practice.

3   Is chocolate popular in your country? What sort of chocolate products are available? How much chocolate do you think is consumed?

90   Unit 8   Grammar   ■☐☐☐☐

Focus

Read the sentences. Find examples of the Present Simple, Present Continuous, Present Perfect Simple, Past Simple and *will* future.

But as Asian economies grow, it is likely that more chocolate products **will be consumed**.
Less than 1% of the trillion dollars **has been used** to improve the working conditions.
Thousands of children **are being forced** to work in West Africa.
Chocolate **was** first **produced** in Central America and Mexico.
This is hard work and they **are paid** very little.

Read the examples and answer questions 1–3.

Where **was** chocolate first **produced**?
It **wasn't made** into the chocolate that we know now.
Nearly half of all the chocolate consumed … is eaten **by** Europeans.

1 How do we form questions and negatives in the Passive?
2 Do we use the Passive to focus on the agent or the object?
3 Do we put *by* before the agent or the object?

Find other examples of the Passive in the script on page 149.

> For more details and practice, go to the Review section on pages 98 and 99.

PRACTICE

4 Complete the text about a Mexican chocolate manufacturer with the correct form of the verbs in brackets. Decide whether the verb is Active or Passive.

A chocolate-making business

The Cancun Chocolate Factory _____¹ (set up) in 2006. We _____² (produce) chocolate the traditional way. All our beans _____³ (source) from sustainable farms and plantations. All the chocolate _____⁴ (make) by hand. Since 2006, we _____⁵ (expand) throughout Mexico. We _____⁶ (open) our first Chocolate Café last year. The café _____⁷ (sell) chocolate products, coffee and chocolate drinks, and chocolate desserts. Our café _____⁸ (appear) on network TV last year, and we _____⁹ (describe) as 'the best chocolate in Mexico'.

This week, we _____¹⁰ (launch) a new range of exciting products. Next year, we _____¹¹ (offer) tours of the factory. You _____¹² (take) on a one-hour tour and tasting experience. Why not try our chocolate? We know you _____¹³ (love) it.

You _____¹⁴ (find) more information on our website, which _____¹⁵ (currently update).

5 Work in pairs. Ask questions for the sentences in the text in **4**.

Example When was the Cancun Chocolate Factory set up?

6 Change these sentences into the Passive using *by* for the agent.

1 The Spanish brought chocolate to Europe in the 16th century.
2 Europeans added sugar to the chocolate as they found the original taste too bitter.
3 J.S. Fry made the first chocolate bars in Britain.
4 Up to the 19th century, rich people, rather than the general public, drank chocolate.
5 The Swiss, Italians, and British started chocolate-making businesses from the early 1800s.
6 Company founders often used their family name for the brand, for example Hershey, Cadbury, and Lindt.
7 African countries produce around 70% of the world's cocoa.
8 African consumers eat only 3% of the total amount of chocolate consumed.

7 Work in pairs. Take turns to describe a process in your company (e.g. the recruitment process). Use the Passive in your description where appropriate.

TASK 8 Work in pairs. Learn about how chocolate is made. Student A, look at the instructions and information below. Student B, go to page 133.

Student A

1 Match the six sentences a–f to the stages 1, 3, 5, 8, 9, and 11 of the 'Making chocolate' diagram below. Then complete the chart by asking Student B questions about the process. At the same time, answer Student B's questions.

 a The cooling process helps to give the chocolate a shiny appearance.
 b Foil and a paper sleeve are used to wrap the chocolate.
 c To make the chocolate smooth, the paste is mixed and beaten.
 d The beans are harvested by hand.
 e The paste is dried until all the liquid is removed and turns into crumbs.
 f The beans are roasted to develop the chocolate flavour.

Making chocolate

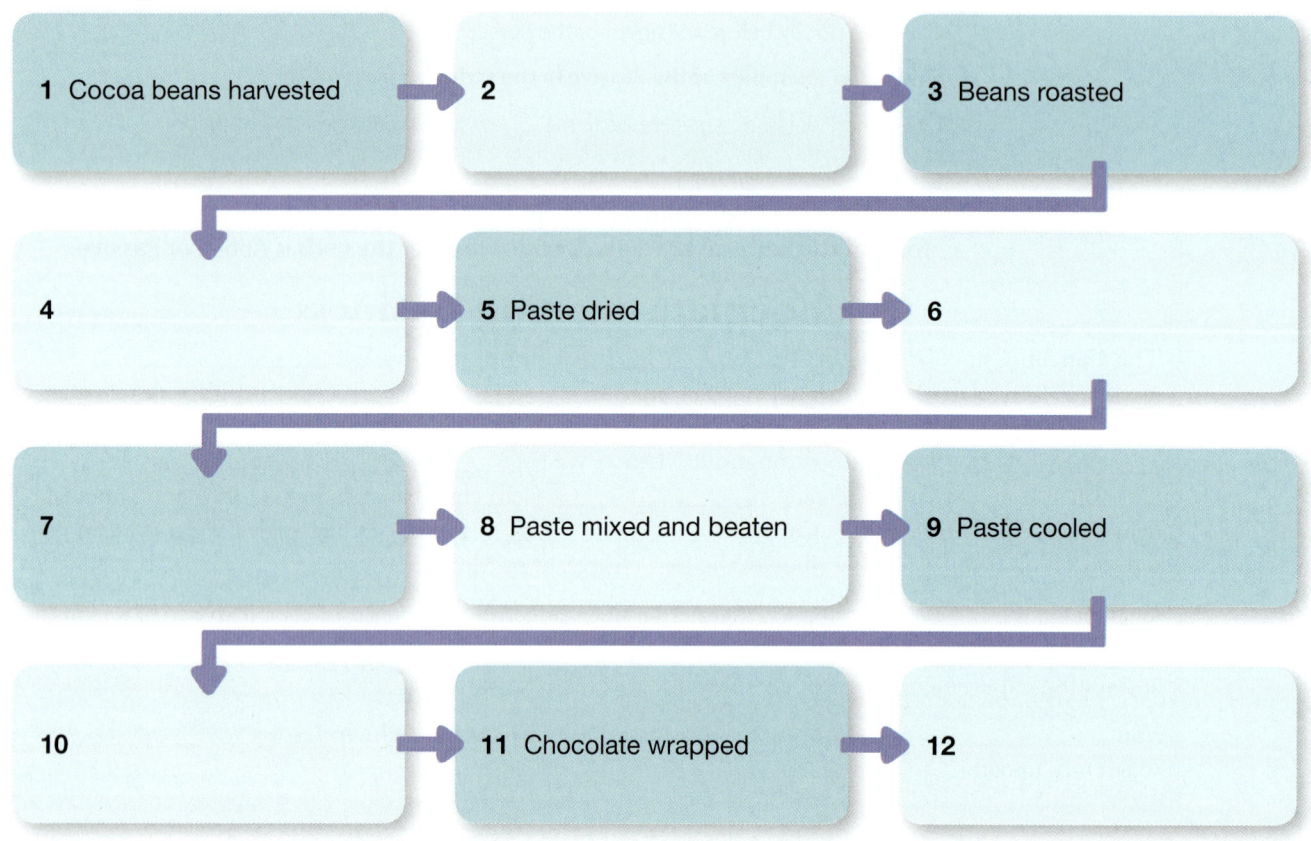

1 Cocoa beans harvested	→	2	→	3 Beans roasted
4	→	5 Paste dried	→	6
7	→	8 Paste mixed and beaten	→	9 Paste cooled
10	→	11 Chocolate wrapped	→	12

2 Take turns to ask and answer questions to complete these sentences about chocolate production.

1 Chocolate can be made from _____ types of cacao bean. The most common of these is forastero. (How many …?)
2 Cacao is grown in tropical countries where the climate is hot and moist.
3 About _____ are used to make 100 grams of chocolate. (How much …?)
4 Production of cocoa beans has grown from around 1.5 million tons in 1974 to over 4 million tons in 2012.
5 Cocoa beans can be picked _____ in most countries. (When …?)
6 One concern about cocoa production is that children in the Ivory Coast are being used to harvest and pack the beans.

Vocabulary Product journey

1 **Work in pairs and discuss these questions.**
   1 What do you think a mobile phone is made of? How much of it is recyclable?
   2 How could our old mobile phones help people in developing countries?

2 **Read the 'Product journey' for a smartphone and put these headings with the appropriate stages.**

Distribution   Production   Retail   Testing
Packaging   Design   Materials

1 _____
When a new smartphone is being developed, decisions are made about the various aspects of the design: the shape, size, and materials used to make the phone. Most smartphones are about 8 mm deep and rectangular in shape. Smartphones weigh between 110 and 120 grams.

2 _____
Phones are made of about 40% plastic, 40% metal, with glass and other materials making up the other 20%. The metals used to make a phone include copper, gold, and lead. The raw material has to be extracted and processed. For example, copper is mined, ground, heated, and treated with chemicals before it is ready to be used.

3 _____
All the parts of the phone are made by various suppliers and have to be transported to the main assembly plant. Here the parts are assembled including the touch-screen display, microphone, speaker, circuit board, camera, battery, and casing.

4 _____
All the features and functions of the phone are checked and tested in the QA (Quality Assurance) Department. For smartphones, the important functions are the voice quality, the clarity of the display, how tough the phone is, how reliable it is, how long the batteries last, and its overall functionality.

5 _____
All new smartphones are packed in a box with the accessories and instruction manual. The packaging is designed to reduce the amount of waste produced and to protect the contents during transportation. The main materials are cardboard and plastic.

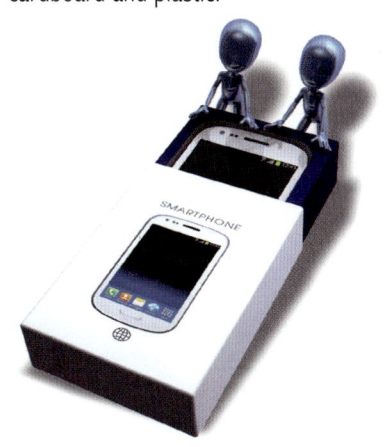

6 _____
After the phones have been assembled and packed, they are either air freighted or transported by sea to the various markets. On arrival, they are transported by container lorry to warehouses and then on to the retail outlets.

7 _____
Retail outlets advertise the phones in the shop windows, provide customers with product demonstrations and advice, both before and after purchase. They also provide customer service including repair, refunds, and replacements.

Vocabulary Unit 8   93

3 Read the 'Product journey' again and answer the questions.
1. What are three of the design characteristics of a smartphone?
2. What is a smartphone made of?
3. Where do the phone parts come from?
4. Which aspect of the phone's display is tested?
5. What is important about the design of the packaging?
6. Which three ways are used to transport the finished product?
7. Name three services that shops provide to customers.

4 Complete the lists with appropriate nouns and verbs from the 'Product journey'.

	Noun	Verb
1	development	_____
2	_____	distribute
3	process	_____
4	extraction	_____
5	assembly	_____
6	testing	_____
7	_____	produce
8	packaging	_____
9	_____	transport
10	advert	_____
11	_____	demonstrate
12	_____	replace

5 Work in pairs. Think of a product and describe its product journey. Use as many words from **4** as you can.

6 What is the best thing to do with the items below: reuse them, recycle them, or throw them away? Give a reason where possible.

Example   The best thing to do with glass bottles is reuse them because it saves energy.

glass bottles   mobile phones
crisp packets   books
cars   coffee cups (two types)
newspapers   batteries
packaging   bathwater

7 ◉) 8.2 Listen to an ecology expert talking about the advantages (+) and disadvantages (−) of things being recyclable or reusable. Complete the table with notes.

	recyclable	reusable
+	saves raw materials	
−		

8 Work in groups and discuss these questions.
1. In what ways can we reduce our use of some of the things in **6** and **7**?
2. What recycling facilities are there where you live?

Work skills Time management

1 **Work in pairs and discuss these questions.**
   1 Are you happy with the way you manage your time? Could you be more efficient?
   2 Do you have any techniques for managing your time effectively?

2 **Look at this list of time-management devices and techniques. Do you use any of them?**
   a 'to do' lists
   b the calendar function on your computer or mobile phone
   c paper diary or calendar
   d post-it notes
   e timed deadlines for particular tasks
   f 'do not disturb' periods (e.g. with phone switched off and door shut)
   g time audits (when you make a detailed note of everything you do throughout one day)

3 ◆)) 8.3 **Listen to three people describing the techniques they use to manage their time. Which of the techniques in 2 are they talking about?**
   1 ___   2 ___   3 ___

4 **Look at the list of 'dos and don'ts' for time management. Use the ideas you have discussed to add more. Cross out ones you don't think are useful.**

DO ...	DON'T ...
• plan your day	• try to push yourself to the limit
• prioritize important tasks	• waste time on unnecessary activities
• delegate to others where possible	• blame others for your workload
• be realistic about what you can and can't do	• miss breaks and rest periods
• tell your manager if your workload is too much	• be frightened to ask for help
• try techniques such as 'time audits'	• agree to do everything people ask you to do
• _____	• _____
• _____	• _____

5 **Work in groups. Think about a typical day in your working life. Make a list of all the things you do. Try to be as specific as possible.**

   Example answer emails from clients, prepare reports, speak to colleagues on the phone, browse the internet, make coffee, etc.

6 **Put the activities from your list in 5 into the chart below. Decide if the time you spend on each activity is *too much*, *not enough*, or *just about right*.**

Activity	Too much	Not enough	Just about right
1 _____	☐	☐	☐
2 _____	☐	☐	☐
3 _____	☐	☐	☐
4 _____	☐	☐	☐
5 _____	☐	☐	☐
6 _____	☐	☐	☐
7 _____	☐	☐	☐

7 **Discuss with the rest of your group what action you can take to improve your efficiency and time management. Are any of the devices and techniques in 2 and 4 useful?**

Functions Checking understanding and clarifying

INTRODUCTION

1 Work in groups. Look at the adverts for three team-building events and discuss these questions.

1. Which team-building event looks the most fun?
2. Which event would work best for you / your company? Why?
3. Can you think of any other team-building events? Have you ever done one?

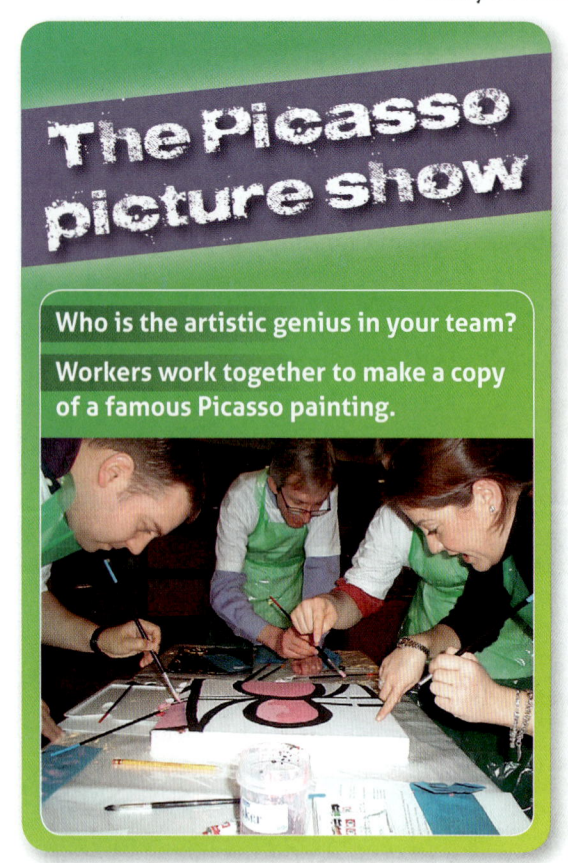

The Picasso picture show

Who is the artistic genius in your team?
Workers work together to make a copy of a famous Picasso painting.

Get in gear

It's time to get your hands dirty. Your team is going to make a real bike using the real parts – and you have just one day to do it!

HAPPY SUNDAES

Find out who is the Gordon Ramsey or Jamie Oliver on your team. Your team's task is to make a brand new ice cream flavour, using our exotic and unusual ingredients.

2 ◆)) 8.4 Listen to three people doing the team-building events in **1**. Which event are they doing?

1 _____ 2 _____ 3 _____

3 ◆)) 8.4 Work in pairs. Complete the sentences with your ideas. Listen again and check.

1. In conversation 1, Steve is not happy because Rhona _____.
2. In conversation 2, Makoto hasn't seen the picture because _____.
3. In conversation 3, Kath complains because Dieter _____.

4 ◆)) 8.4 Listen again and complete the sentences with one word in each gap.

1. a I see what you _____ .
   b Do you see how it _____ ?
   c Can you _____ me that again?
2. a Sorry, I don't _____ you.
   b Can you _____ what you mean by 'assemble the picture'?
   c Yes, I'm _____ you.
3. a Would you like me to go _____ that again?
   b OK, that _____ sense.
   c Is everything _____ ?

5 How do you think the people feel after the team-building events? Do you think they work better together afterwards?

96 Unit 8 Functions

Focus

Complete the table with the phrases from 4.

Checking someone understands you	Saying you understand
Do you follow me? Are you with me?	I follow you.

Saying you don't understand	Asking for clarification
I don't understand how to …	Can you just clarify what I need to do?

▶ For more details and practice, go to the Review section on page 101.

PRACTICE

6 ◉ 8.5 Work in pairs. Look at the picture below. Guess the missing words in the summary of the team-building exercise. Then listen to Katarina and Alfonso discussing the exercise and check.

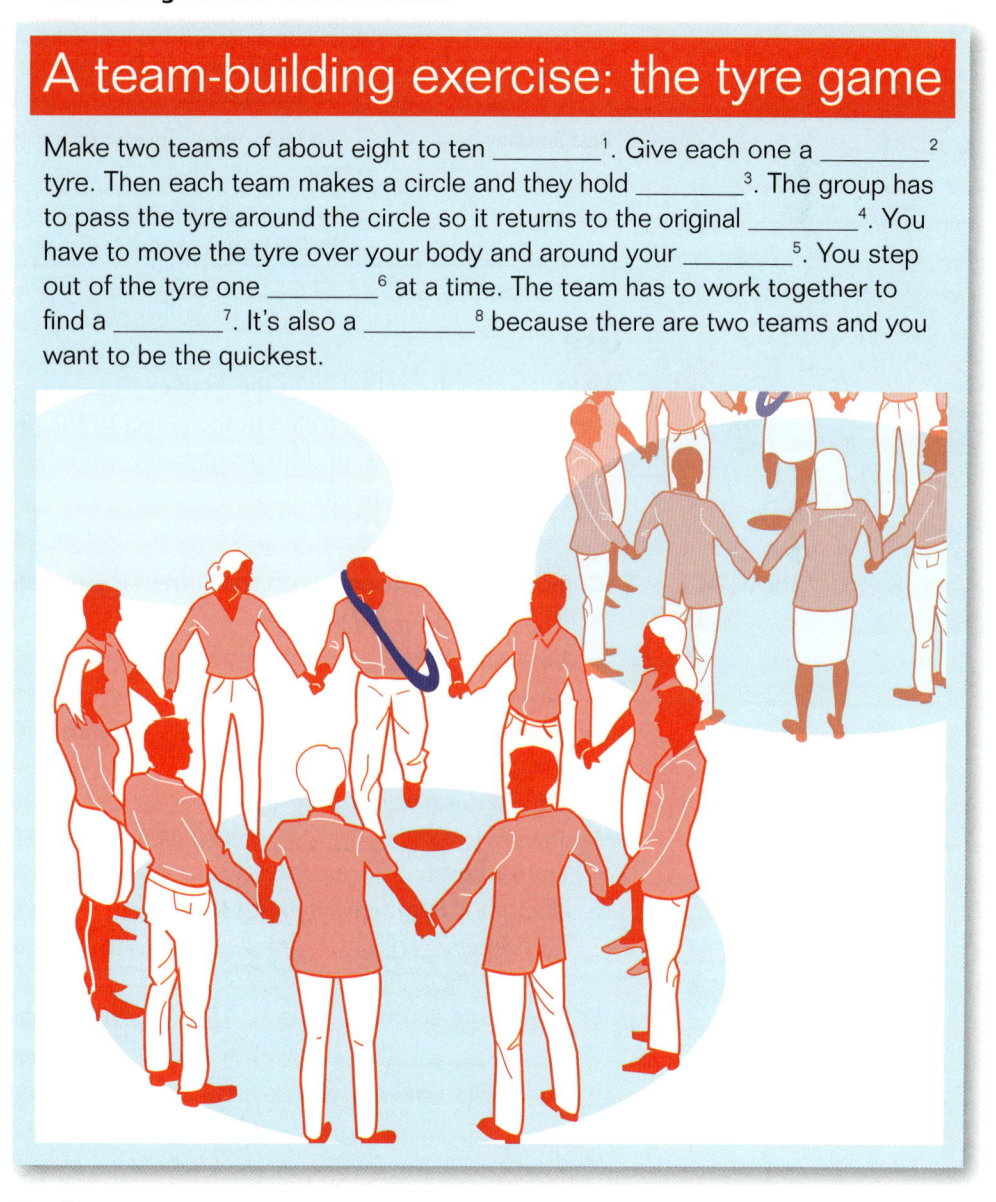

A team-building exercise: the tyre game

Make two teams of about eight to ten _____ [1]. Give each one a _____ [2] tyre. Then each team makes a circle and they hold _____ [3]. The group has to pass the tyre around the circle so it returns to the original _____ [4]. You have to move the tyre over your body and around your _____ [5]. You step out of the tyre one _____ [6] at a time. The team has to work together to find a _____ [7]. It's also a _____ [8] because there are two teams and you want to be the quickest.

7 ◉ 8.5 Listen again and tick ✓ the phrases you hear in the table in the Focus section.

TASK

8 Work in pairs. You are going to explain how a new expenses system works. Go to page 137.

Review

Grammar Passives: Present Simple, Present Continuous, Present Perfect Simple, Past Simple, will

Form

We form the Passive with *be* and the past participle.
If we want to say who or what did the action (the agent) we use *by*.
We can use the Passive with all tenses.

Present Simple	English is spoken on all factory tours.	Is tasting included in the price?
Present Continuous	Production is being increased to meet demand.	Is more chocolate being produced this year?
Present Perfect Simple	We have been asked to take a different route.	Have they been shown the packaging room?
Past Simple	The factory was opened last year.	Where were you based before then?
will future	No tours will be held over the Christmas period.	Will we be given any free samples?

Use

We use the Passive rather than the Active:
- when we are more interested in the object or the process than in the agent
- when we don't know, or don't want to say, who the agent is
- for more formal contexts

PRACTICE

1 Complete the sentences with the correct Passive form of the verbs in brackets.

1. The Natural Pizza Company _____ (open) by Lucy Franks last year.
2. Since then, over 10,000 pizzas _____ (serve).
3. Previously, Lucy _____ (employ) by one of the big pizza companies.
4. Only natural organic ingredients _____ (use) in her pizzas.
5. Pizzas _____ (cook) using traditional methods in a wood-smoked oven.
6. Their new Summer Surprise pizza _____ (launch) yesterday.
7. Customers _____ (invite) to come to the restaurant tonight for a free tasting.
8. A cooking demonstration _____ (hold) next week.
9. It _____ (give) by Lucy Franks herself.
10. A mystery celebrity chef _____ (invite) to come as well.

2 Write the questions for each of the sentences in **1**.

1 When _was the Natural Pizza Company opened_ ?
2 How many _____?
3 Where _____?
4 What sort of ingredients _____?
5 How _____?
6 What _____?
7 Why _____?
8 What _____?
9 Who _____?
10 Who _____?

3 Which of the sentences in **1** can also be used in the Active?

Example   Lucy Franks opened the Natural Pizza Company last year.

4 Complete the article with the verbs in brackets. You need to decide: a) Passive or Active? b) which tense?

What do you know about pizza?

What _are you eating_ ¹ (eat) for dinner tonight? There's a good chance it's pizza, especially if you _____ ² (come) from the USA. Pizza _____ ³ (become) more and more popular throughout the world. Next year, more than 5 billion pizzas _____ ⁴ (eat) worldwide – and Americans _____ ⁵ (eat) 3 billion of them. In fact in the USA 350 slices of pizza _____ ⁶ (eat) every second.

The famous Margarita Pizza _____ ⁷ (invent) by an Italian restaurant owner in 1889 and he _____ ⁸ (name) it after the Queen of Italy at the time. The first pizza in the USA _____ ⁹ (serve) in Lombardi's restaurant in New York City in 1905. Since then, more than 75,000 pizza restaurants _____ ¹⁰ (establish) in the USA.

Today, the Tricolore Pizza _____ ¹¹ (colour) like the Italian flag: red tomatoes, white mozzarella cheese, and green basil. But over the years, pizza makers _____ ¹² (try) every type of topping: from octopus and squid to peanut butter and jelly. What's your favourite?

At the moment, you can be fairly sure that a pizza _____ ¹³ (eat) somewhere in every country in the world.

Vocabulary Product journey

1 Complete the sentences about the 'Product journey' with these words.

tested   retail   packed   design   production   materials   distributed

a Products are _____ by air freight, ship, or container lorry.   ___
b The _____ of a smartphone includes the shape, size, and materials.   ___
c Shops and online stores are two types of _____ outlet.   ___
d All phones are _____ to make sure they are reliable and work properly.   ___
e The _____ process involves assembling all the parts of the phone to make the final product.   ___
f The finished phones are _____ in cardboard boxes which are wrapped in plastic.   ___
g The _____ used to make a phone are metal, plastic, and glass.   ___

2 Number the sentences in **1** in the order they occur in the product journey.

3 Complete the tables with the appropriate verbs and nouns.

	Verb	Noun
1	develop	
2		process
3	distribute	
4		production
5	extract	
6		assembly

	Verb	Noun
7		testing
8	pack	
9		advert
10	demonstrate	
11	replace	
12		transportation

4 Complete the sentences using the appropriate words from **3**.
1 Samsung _____ some of the best-selling smartphones.
2 The _____ of raw materials is an expensive process.
3 The sales assistant gave a very good _____ of the new tablet.
4 My new smartphone isn't working. I'm going to ask for a _____ .
5 The company needs to reduce its _____ costs. Air freighting is too expensive.
6 Some of the parts for the Galaxy X5 have not arrived at the _____ plant.

Work skills Time management

1 Match the time-management techniques 1–5 with definitions a–e.
1 delegation ___
2 'do not disturb' ___
3 time audit ___
4 'to do' list ___
5 digital phone alerts ___

a You tell people that they mustn't interrupt you for a fixed period. You turn your phone to voicemail and possibly close your door.
b You make a note of exactly what you spend your time on in a 24-hour period (not just work), and decide if it's what you want to do and if it's a good use of your time.
c You write a list of tasks for the day. You can put them in an order of priority if you want. You cross them off the list as you do them.
d You set reminders on your computer or mobile phone so that you do things at particular times. The reminder will ring or buzz at regular intervals until you have done it.
e You get someone else to do it. But remember, you still have to check they've done it!

2 Make phrases using these nouns and verbs 1–7. Some nouns can go with more than one verb.

meetings	colleagues	customers	paperwork	exercise	trade fairs
research	emails	texts	documents	accounts	clients
coffee	photocopies	friends	conferences		

1 check _____
2 attend _____
3 meet _____
4 chat to _____
5 do _____
6 make _____
7 send _____

3 Which of the activities in **2** do you do in a typical day? Which do you do too much / not enough / just about right?

Functions Checking understanding and clarifying

We use these phrases to check that someone understands instructions, etc.
Examples Are you with me? / Do you follow me?
Do you see how it works?
Is everything clear? / Would you like me to go through that again?

We use these phrases to say we understand instructions, etc.
Examples I follow you. / Yes, I'm with you.
I see what you mean. / OK, that makes sense.

We use these phrases to say we don't understand instructions, etc.
Examples I don't understand how to …
Sorry, I don't follow you.

We use these phrases to ask for clarification.
Examples Can you explain what you mean by …?
Can you show me that again? / Can you just clarify what I need to do?

PRACTICE

1 Complete the conversations with appropriate phrases.

1. A Our company will pay taxes under tax code 115.
   B Er … Sorry. _____ 'tax code 115'?
2. A The office will be closed for national and local holidays.
   B _____ days the local holidays are?
3. A I'm sorry, I didn't understand everything you just said.
   B _____? I'm happy to repeat it.
4. A Everyone needs to choose a nine-letter password, mixing numbers, symbols, and capital and lower-case letters. _____?
   B Yes, I do. In fact, my password is already like that.
5. A To order equipment for the office, you need to use this program.
   B _____ use that program. Can you help me?
6. A To operate the machine, press here, hold down this button, and turn the wheel to the left. OK?
   B Er, no. _____? Just once more.

2 8.6 Listen to three conversations. In which conversation (1–3) do they talk about the following?

a a boat ___   b a blog ___   c a visa ___

3 8.6 Complete the missing words in the extracts. Listen again and check.

1. A To get hits, you need to use tags.
   B Sorry, I d_____ f_____ you.
2. A Look, click here … and add the tag. Do you see how i_____ w_____?
   B Yes, that's fine.
3. A You need to arrange a Russian visa. This is the form you need to complete. I_____ e_____ clear?
   B Er, no, I have a problem.
4. A In that case, get a business double entry visa. That gives you permission to leave and re-enter the country.
   B OK, t_____ m_____ sense.
5. A When the wind is strong, pull this rope. That helps control the boat.
   B I don't understand h_____ t_____ use all these ropes.
6. A Would you like me to g_____ t_____ the instructions again?
   B Yes, please. This is the first time I've been sailing in my life.

9 The business of sport

Grammar Relative clauses

INTRODUCTION

1 How many international sporting events can you think of? How are these events paid for? Who makes money from them?

2 Read about the 2012 Olympics in London. How are the Olympics and business related? Here are some ideas to help you.

infrastructure   local employment   television rights
advertising   equipment   sponsorship

Take the money and run

The modern Olympic Games, which have been held since 1896, are the biggest single sporting event in the world. They are organized by the International Olympic Committee (IOC).

Nearly 10,500 athletes took part in the London 2012 Olympics. There were 4,688 women and 5,802 men from 204 nations who competed in 26 sports.

$19 billion was spent on the construction of the venues and security during the Games.

200,000 people were employed during the Games. 70,000 of these were volunteers who were selected from more than 240,000 applicants.

Around four billion people watched the Games online or on television.

900,000 sports items such as balls, paddles, and bicycles were used.

Over 50 companies were involved either as sponsors or providers.

3 ◯) 9.1 Listen to a journalist asking about how the Olympics are financed. Are these statements true or false? Correct the false statements.

1 The IOC's policy regarding sponsorship changed in 1970.
2 The main sponsors for the London Olympics paid $100 million to use the Olympic symbol.
3 Apple Inc. provided the computer services for the 2012 Games.
4 There are four different types of sponsor altogether.
5 About half the money from sponsorship goes towards the athletes and the Games.
6 The television coverage of the London Olympics was more than twice the coverage in Beijing.

Focus

Read the examples.
a The Olympic Programme, **which Samaranch designed to encourage sponsorship**, had dramatic results.
b Avery Brundage, **who was the President of the IOC from 1952 to 1972**, actually refused to allow corporate sponsorship.
c The nation **which is hosting the games** chooses these sponsors.
d The person **who really changed the attitude of the IOC** was Juan Antonio Samaranch.
e The athletes **that compete in the Olympics** receive some of the money.
f The company **that supplied all the timing equipment for the games** was Omega.
g The sponsors **(that) the IOC chooses** are given different marketing rights.

Which of the relative clauses in bold above are
1 *defining*: they give information we need to identify the person or thing we are talking about?
2 *non-defining*: they give extra information about the person or thing we are talking about?

Answer the questions.
1 Underline the correct relative pronoun in this rule:
In relative clauses we use *who / which* for people and *who / which* for things.
2 In which type of clause can we use *that* instead of *who* or *which*?
3 In which type of clause do we use commas?
4 In which example sentence can we omit the relative pronoun? Is the pronoun the subject or the object of the clause?

▶ For more details and practice, go to the Review section on pages 110 and 111.

PRACTICE

4 Complete the sentences with *who*, *which*, or *that*. Then decide if the relative clauses are defining (D) or non-defining (ND).

1 In the first London Olympics, _____ were held in 1948, only 59 countries took part. ___
2 The athletes _____ won the most gold medals were the swimmers Michael Phelps and Melissa Franklin. They both won four gold medals. ___
3 Sebastian Coe, _____ used to be an Olympic athlete, was the chairman of the London Organizing Committee for the Olympic Games. ___
4 The equipment _____ the athletes used was supplied by companies like Adidas. ___
5 The race _____ generated the highest viewing figures was the Men's 100 metres final. ___
6 Usain Bolt, _____ comes from a small town in Jamaica, is the most successful sprinter in Olympic history. ___
7 The Opening Ceremony, _____ the film director Danny Boyle created, was an amazing spectacle. ___
8 The country _____ was chosen to host the 2016 Olympics was Brazil. ___

5 Combine the two sentences using *who* or *which* to make non-defining relative clauses. Remember to use commas.

1 Avery Brundage was the fifth president of the IOC. He was an Olympic athlete.
2 Women's boxing was included in the Olympics for the first time in 2012. It featured 36 competitors.
3 The Orbit is a 115-metre-high tower in the middle of the Olympic Park. It was designed by Anish Kapoor and the engineer Cecil Balmond.
4 The Olympic tennis matches were held at Wimbledon. They were very popular.
5 Mo Farah is the Olympic 10,000 metres and 5,000 metres champion. He was born in Somalia.

6 Read the article about Pelé, one of the world's great sportsmen. Add these relative clauses to complete the article. Write the letters in the gaps.

a which includes football boots and shirts
b which earns him up to $20 million a year
c that celebrate the 1,283 goals Pelé scored during his football career
d who is better known as Pelé
e who comes from Brazil
f which helps children recover from serious diseases
g he scored
h that records the goal

Edison Arantes do Nascimento, _____¹, is considered to be the best football player of all time. Pelé, _____², started playing for the São Paulo football team Santos when he was 15. He started playing for the national team when he was 16 and won his first World Cup at 17. In total he played 1,106 first-team matches. He was voted Olympic Committee Athlete of the Century in 1999. Pelé was famous for his skill and goal-scoring ability. One of the most famous goals _____³ was at the Maracanā stadium in 1961. A plaque _____⁴ can still be seen at the stadium with the inscription 'the most beautiful goal in the history of the Maracanā'.

When he retired in 1977, Pelé became a worldwide ambassador for football and has started various commercial ventures. One of the most profitable ventures, _____⁵, has been his endorsement of major brands. He has worked with Coca-Cola, Petrobras, Nokia, Samsung, and MasterCard, for whom he has appeared on more than two million credit cards.

Pelé supports the Little Prince Research Institute, a charity _____⁶. The Institute is partly funded by the sale of medals _____⁷. Pelé has also launched his own brand of sportswear, Pelé Sports, _____⁸. Pelé has also published several autobiographies, starred in films, and composed musical pieces, including the entire soundtrack for the film *Pelé* in 1977.

7 Think about some friends or people in your family. Write two pieces of information about each of them, like the examples in the table. Then tell your partner about the people using relative clauses.

Relationship	Company / Job	Residence	Life story	Hobby
Friend	Fujitsu		lived for year in Egypt	
Brother		Aberdeen		loves watching football

Example   My friend, who works for Fujitsu, lived for a year in Egypt.

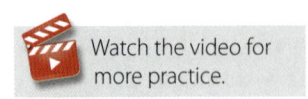

TASK

Watch the video for more practice.

8 Work in pairs. Make your own sports quiz. Student A, use the sentences below. Student B, use the sentences on page 134.

Student A
Complete the sentences using the appropriate relative clauses. When you are ready, quiz your partner. Your answers are on page 128.

1 Which Jamaican athlete / won the 100 metres gold medal in 2012 / is famous for doing the 'Lightning Bolt'?
2 Which sport / originated in ancient Greece / is 42 kilometres long?
3 Which organization / has a symbol of five rings / started in 1896?
4 Which computer company / is based in Taiwan / provided the computer services for the 2012 Olympics?
5 Which film director / directed *Trainspotting* and *127 Hours* / was artistic director for the Opening Ceremony in London?

104   Unit 9 Grammar

Vocabulary Describing personal qualities at work

1 Match the pictures to the industry sectors 1–5.

1 finance   ___
2 IT   ___
3 manufacturing   ___
4 retail   ___
5 sales and marketing ___

2 Do you know anyone who works in these sectors? What skills do they need? What personal qualities do they need?

3 Read the job adverts. Which of the industry sectors in **1** do the companies operate in?

1 Do you like working in an exciting modern industry? We are looking for web designers to join our **talented** team. We need **creative** thinkers, but you also need to be **practical**. Of course, you'll also be **hard-working** – the hours are long, but the rewards are high! Have you got what it takes?

2 With a chain of stores throughout the country, we can offer an exciting career for **ambitious** people. We are looking for trainee managers, so we need people with **good leadership skills** who are also **team players**. Find out more at …

3 Do you want to be part of our busy call centre team? We are recruiting now for sales staff with **good communication skills** and the ability to be **independent** and **self-motivated**. Excellent telephone skills are essential in this job. Call us now for more information.

4 Match these definitions with the words and phrases in blue in the adverts.

1 able to work alone   _independent_
2 good at working with other people in a group   _____
3 good at talking to people and explaining things   _____
4 having a natural ability to do something well   _____
5 putting a lot of effort into a job   _____
6 willing and able to work hard without being told what to do   _____
7 determined to be successful, rich, powerful, etc.   _____
8 able to think of new ideas or produce something new   _____
9 able to lead a team successfully   _____
10 sensible and realistic   _____

Vocabulary Unit 9 105

5 ◉ **9.2** Listen to five people talking about their colleagues. Choose two words or phrases from **3** to describe each person.

1 Salma: _____ , _____
2 Javier: _____ , _____
3 Olga: _____ , _____
4 Tomas: _____ , _____
5 Jae Min: _____ , _____

6 Work in pairs. Sort these adjectives into six pairs with opposite meanings. Use a dictionary if necessary.

| reliable | sensible | hard-working | lazy | enthusiastic | reckless |
| experienced | laid-back | unreliable | uptight | inexperienced | unenthusiastic |

7 Work in pairs. Match the descriptions to six of the adjectives in **6**.

1 Barbara is really relaxed. She never seems to get stressed! _____
2 Martin always turns up late and doesn't do much work. _____
3 You can depend on Tippawan. She always gets her work done. _____
4 Vasily takes too many risks. He needs to calm down a bit. _____
5 Irwan has been doing this job for 15 years so he really knows what he's doing. _____
6 Jenny has a really positive attitude to work. She's always very keen and approaches each new task with a smile. _____

8 Which of these qualities apply to you or people you know? Give examples of things you (or people you know) do.

Qualities	Example for you	Example for someone you know	Your score (0 to 5)
practical	I always plan realistic schedules for our projects.	My friend Paul likes to work out the cost of something before he agrees to it.	
ambitious			
reliable			
hard-working			
independent			
experienced			
enthusiastic			
be a good team player			
have good communication skills			
have good leadership skills			

9 Give yourself a score for each of the characteristics (0–5). Explain to a partner why you gave the score.

10 Work in pairs. Say which of the qualities are most important in your current job or in a job you would like to have.

11 Write a job advertisement for a job in your company (or a company you would like to work for).

Work skills Job interviews

1 **Work in pairs and discuss these questions.**
   1 How do you prepare for job interviews?
   2 What are the typical questions asked at interviews? Make a list.

2 **Look at some of the common questions asked at interviews.**
   1 Do you agree with the tips?
   2 Can you think of any more common questions?

Question	Tip	Reply
a What do you think are your key skills / strengths?	Make sure you choose something specific that is relevant to the job.	___
b What do you think are your main weaknesses?	Choose something that was a weakness but you've improved. Describe how you've done this.	___
c Why did you leave your last job?	Whatever the reason, don't criticize your previous employer!	___
d Why do you want this job?	Match your skills to the company, and say how much you like what the company is doing.	___
e Can you tell us about a difficult situation you've had at work and how you dealt with it?	Choose a situation that had a positive outcome.	___
f Can you tell us about an achievement of which you are proud?	Make sure you choose work-related examples that helped the company.	___
g What do you know about our organization?	Find out about the company before interview; give your opinion of their website (but be positive!).	___
h Do you have any questions for us?	Prepare questions that show you're interested in the company.	___

3 **9.3 Listen to eight extracts from interviews for a sales team leader post. Match what the people say to the questions in 2. Write the number in the table.**

4 **9.3 Listen again. Did the interviewee follow the advice given in every case?**

5 **Work in pairs.**
   1 Think about your own job or another job that you know well. Describe it to your partner. Think about the key skills, experience, and qualifications.
   2 Your partner is going to interview you for 'your' job, so think about the way you will answer the questions in **2**.
   3 Role-play the interviews.

Functions Changing plans

INTRODUCTION

1 Read the email and answer the questions.
1. What is the purpose of the meeting?
2. Who is going to the meeting?
3. What was the original plan?
4. What has changed?

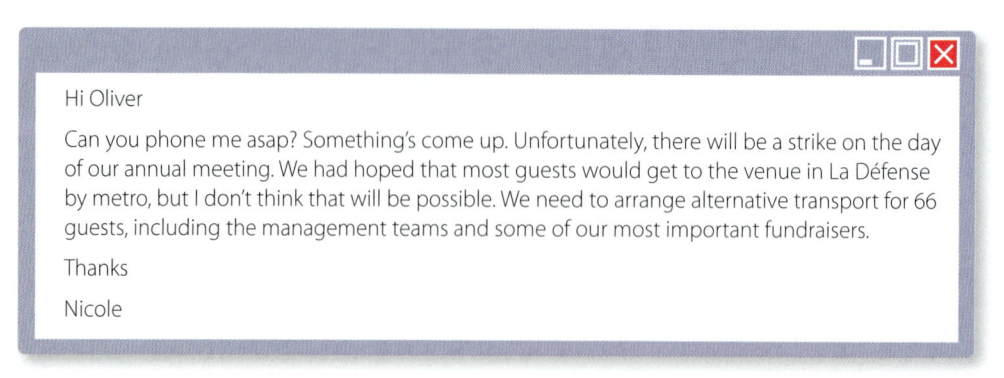

Hi Oliver

Can you phone me asap? Something's come up. Unfortunately, there will be a strike on the day of our annual meeting. We had hoped that most guests would get to the venue in La Défense by metro, but I don't think that will be possible. We need to arrange alternative transport for 66 guests, including the management teams and some of our most important fundraisers.

Thanks

Nicole

---

2 9.4 Look at the map of Paris. Then listen to Nicole and Oliver. Make a note of:
1. the number of people who will arrive at each place
2. how these people will get to the meeting

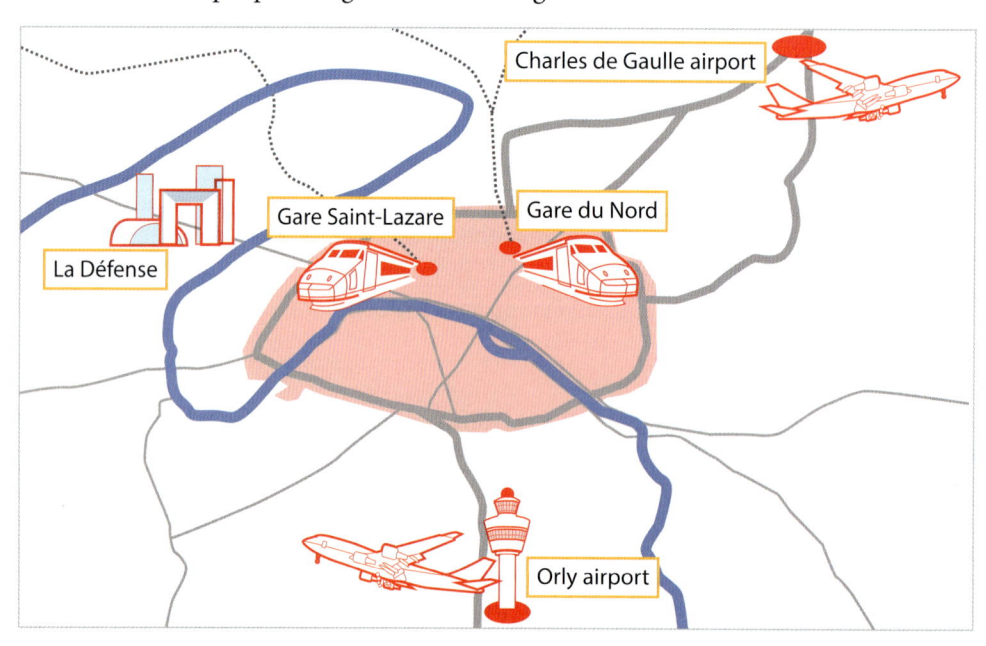

3 9.4 Listen again. Choose the correct options.

1. **Nicole** I was wondering *that / whether* you could send some information about the buses to everyone? Timetables, routes …
   Oliver Well, *I'd / I'll* like to, but the problem is that the buses may go on strike too.

2. **Nicole** Would you mind *booking / to book* some coaches for our guests?
   Oliver No, I'm happy *for / to* do that.

3. **Oliver** *Could / Do* you tell me how many people are coming?
   Nicole *Certain / Certainly*.

4. **Nicole** Do you think you *could / must* book one coach for both groups of people?
   Oliver No, we won't be able to *do / make* that because the airports are quite far apart.

5. **Nicole** *Are / Do* you mind booking a taxi for us as well?
   Oliver That's *no / not* problem.

108 Unit 9 Functions

Focus

Look again at the email in 1. Find phrases we use
1 to say an unexpected problem has recently appeared.
2 to show we are sorry to say something.
3 to talk about previous plans that won't happen.

Complete the table with the phrases from 3.

Making requests	Agreeing
Could you tell me how many people are coming?	Don't worry, it's fine.

	Politely refusing
	I don't think that will be possible.

▶▶ For more details and practice, go to the Review section on page 113.

PRACTICE

4 ◉) 9.5 **Complete the conversation with these phrases. Listen and check.**

could you send   do you think   I'm happy   I was also wondering
that will be possible   unfortunately   we had hoped   would you mind

Nicole   _____¹, the company has some budget problems so we need to save money. _____² flying to the meeting in Paris on a budget airline?

Rick   No, _____³ to do that.

Nicole   Before we discovered the budget problems, _____⁴ to book you a hotel too, but that will be expensive. So _____⁵ you could fly back the same day?

Rick   Don't worry, it's fine. I think it's important to save money too.

Nicole   _____⁶ whether your team could travel on public transport instead of by taxis.

Rick   I don't think _____⁷ because there's a strike on the day of the annual meeting.

Nicole   That's right. I forgot. _____⁸ an email to everyone about that?

Rick   Certainly. Leave it with me.

5 **Work in pairs. Respond to these requests from your boss. Refuse at least one request.**

1   Could you tell me the marketing manager's email address?
2   Would you mind staying late tonight for a videoconference with Japan?
3   I was wondering whether you could write a blog entry on the company website next week.
4   Do you mind working on all the national holidays this year? We need someone in the office 365 days a year.
5   Do you think you could send me your schedule for the next six months?
6   I was wondering whether you could organize a birthday lunch on Friday for Jodi, my PA.

TASK

6 **Work in pairs. Role-play two situations which involve changing plans. Student A, go to page 129. Student B, go to page 135.**

Review

Grammar Relative clauses

Form

We use a defining relative clause to identify a person or a thing. We do not use commas to separate it from the rest of the sentence as the information is essential to the meaning of the sentence and cannot be left out.
Example   The revenue which the games generate is given to the IOC.

We use a non-defining relative clause to add extra information about a person or thing. We use commas to separate it from the rest of the sentence as the information is not essential and the sentence still has meaning if it is left out.
Example   Pelé, who comes from Brazil, was voted Athlete of the Century in 1999.

Relative pronouns

We use *who* for people, and *which* for things. In defining relative clauses, we can also use *that*.
Examples   The woman who / that lives next door works at my company.
     Marie Lehoux, who is French, works at my company.
     The painting which / that he bought last year is very valuable.
     The *Mona Lisa*, which was painted by Leonardo, is priceless.

When the relative pronoun is the object in a defining relative clause, we can omit it.
Example   The report (that) they wrote contained a lot of mistakes.

Use

Relative clauses identify and give extra information about the nouns or clauses which precede them. They are particularly common in (formal) written English and in formal speech, such as presentations or lectures.

PRACTICE

1   Look at the sentences. Are they defining (*D*) or non-defining (*ND*) relative clauses? Add commas where necessary.
    1   The 2012 World Cup which was held in South Africa was won by Spain. ___
    2   The man that I met just now was very amusing. ___
    3   The IT Conference which will take place in Berlin starts on 7th July. ___
    4   Usain Bolt who broke the 100 metres world record at the Beijing Olympics also won gold in the 200 metres. ___
    5   The meeting which I attended yesterday was very productive. ___
    6   Have you still got the DVD that I lent you last month? ___

2   Look again at the relative clauses in **1**. In which clauses can the relative pronoun be left out?

3   Add these defining relative clauses to complete the sentences.

    that set up our IT system   Angela is talking to   that I bought in the sales
    I sent you   I'm presenting the paper to who fixed my shower

    1   The plumber _____ has sent me a large bill.
    2   The shoes _____ don't fit very well.
    3   Have you read the email _____?
    4   The company _____ is based in Prague.
    5   The people _____ are all scientists.
    6   The woman _____ is Matt's wife.

4 **Combine the sentences using non-defining relative clauses and commas. Sometimes more than one answer is possible.**
1 The *Titanic* sank in 1912. It was built in Belfast.
2 Marius is an electrical engineer. He works for NASA.
3 Our company was founded in 1982. It now has factories all across the world.
4 Cairo has a population of about 9 million people. It is one of the largest cities in the world.
5 My manager is Russian. She speaks four languages fluently.
6 Thomas Edison invented the light bulb and the phonograph. He held 1,093 US patents in his name.

5 **Choose the correct pronoun to complete the text: *who*, *which*, *that*, Ø (= no pronoun). Sometimes more than one answer is possible.**

The publicity game

Fame can be measured in dollars and cents. The amount _____¹ companies will pay a sportsperson to endorse their company is astonishing. According to a report by Forbes magazine, it is often far more than the money _____² they earn from their sport. We can see this if we look at Tiger Woods and Roger Federer, _____³ both have very valuable sponsorship deals. Woods, _____⁴ earned $4.4 million in prizes in 2012, received $55 million in sponsorship deals. Similarly, Federer won $7.7 million but received $45 million in advertising. Do the players _____⁵ are the best at their sport receive the most advertising? Not always. Christiano Ronaldo, _____⁶ was the highest-paid footballer in the world in 2012, was paid $20.5 million for playing football and received $22 million for endorsements. However, David Beckham earned more than him: he received $9 million in pay, but $37 million in advertising revenue. This difference is due to the value of fame and celebrity. Companies _____⁷ sponsor sportspeople are paying for their fame. This is mainly related to their skill and success but, as in the case of Beckham, not completely.

Some celebrities use their fame for charitable purposes. The Pelé Little Prince Research Institute, _____⁸ the footballer Pelé set up in 2005, carries out research into diseases that affect children and adolescents. Their aim is to investigate complex diseases such as cancer. The charity has a team of scientists _____⁹ has already had some successes. The Roger Federer Foundation, _____¹⁰ supports projects in Africa and Switzerland, concentrates on the improvement of early learning and education. Mia Hamm, _____¹¹ was the captain of the women's US football team, has set up a charity to support families with bone marrow disease. The list goes on. The publicity _____¹² these sportspeople create helps the charities to raise a lot of money, so celebrity endorsement can sometimes be used for the good.

Vocabulary Describing personal qualities at work

1 **Choose the correct adjectives to complete the sentences.**
1 I'm an *experienced / practical* hotel manager. I've been a manager at this hotel for 15 years.
2 Arturo always shows a lot of excitement and interest about the projects he works on. He's very *reckless / enthusiastic*.
3 Are you able to work alone? We need someone who is *laid back / independent* and can make their own decisions.
4 Siobhan is a *talented / reliable* designer. She has a natural ability to create unusual designs.
5 I don't think I can depend on Marcia to meet you at the airport. She's a bit *unenthusiastic / unreliable*.
6 Jorge is a *practical / creative* member of the team. He's always sensible and realistic about what we can do.
7 I wish I was more relaxed and calm. I often feel *reckless / uptight* and worried.
8 We're looking for a *hard-working / sensible* office manager – someone who is willing to work long hours and put a lot of effort into the job.

2 Complete the two job adverts with the words and phrases above each one.

experienced   self-motivated   good leadership skills
creative   team player

hard-working   good communication skills   ambitious
laid-back   independent

Assistant Project Manager: Web Design

We are looking for _____ ¹ and talented web designers who can create innovative websites for a range of different clients. The candidate will be _____ ² in all aspects of web design. This position requires you to be independent and _____ ³: you must plan your own work schedule in order to meet strict deadlines. You must also be a _____ ⁴ who is able to work with other members of the web design team. The ideal candidate will have _____ ⁵ and will be able to motivate team members and delegate tasks appropriately.

Area Sales Representative: Western Europe

Great opportunity, with good promotion prospects, for an _____ ⁶ and enthusiastic graduate to join our sales team in Western Europe. The position involves working long hours and some weekend work, so the candidate will be _____ ⁷ and reliable. We are looking for people with _____ ⁸, ideally with experience in giving presentations to clients. The post requires you to plan your own sales visits, so you must be organized and _____ ⁹ although we provide training and support. But it's not all hard work! We are a young, _____ ¹⁰ team, so the atmosphere in the office is fun and relaxing. Apply now! We look forward to welcoming you to our team.

Work skills Job interviews

1 Complete the interview questions with these words.

~~strengths~~   questions   your last job   an achievement
our organization   situation   weaknesses   this job

1 What do you think are your key _strengths_?
2 Can you tell us about _____ of which you are very proud?
3 Do you have any _____ for us?
4 What do you know about _____?
5 Why do you want _____?
6 Why did you leave _____?
7 What do you think are your main _____?
8 Can you tell us about a difficult _____ you've had at work, and what you did about it?

2 Match these answers to the questions in **1**.

a I am easy to get on with and I think people like working with me. I'm also very organized. ___
b I think that sometimes I need to prioritize more. I sometimes spend too long on a project because I want to get it right. ___
c My husband had to take a job in another city so we had to relocate. ___
d I discovered that a close colleague of mine was making false expenses claims. I had no choice but to tell my line manager. ___
e Yes, in April, I was given a prize for 'Fundraiser of the Month'. ___
f I think it would be really interesting and would give me more responsibility than I have at the moment. ___
g I know that you are the leading medical research organization in this country. ___
h Yes, can I ask how many other people are in the team? ___

Functions Changing plans

We use these phrases to talk about changes to our situation.
Examples Something's come up.
Unfortunately, …
We had hoped that …, but …

We use these phrases to make requests when we change plans.
Examples Would / Do you mind (+ -ing) …?
Could you / Do you think you could …?
I was wondering if / whether …

We usually use just *can* or *could* for basic requests, but we use the phrases above to make more formal or difficult requests. These are more polite because it is easier for the other person to refuse the request.

We use these phrases to agree to requests when plans change.
Examples Certainly. / I'm happy to do that.
Don't worry, it's fine.

We use these phrases to politely refuse requests when plans change.
Examples I don't think that will be possible.
I'd like to, but …
We won't be able to do that because …

PRACTICE

1 Rewrite the sentences using the words in brackets.
1. Do you want to have a meeting tomorrow? (wondering)
2. Can you work at the weekend? (mind)
3. I need to know your ID number. (could)
4. I want to do some research, but I don't have enough time. (like)
5. There's a new problem. (come)
6. It's OK for me to chair the meeting. (happy)

2 ◆)) 9.6 Listen to four conversations. Do the people agree (A) to the request or refuse (R) it?

1 ___   2 ___   3 ___   4 ___

3 ◆)) 9.6 Complete the conversations with one word in each gap. Listen again and check.

1 **A** We need someone to translate our website pages into Russian. Could you _____¹ Ivan to do that, please?
   B I don't think that _____² be possible. Ivan's on a six-month contract in Brussels at the moment.
   A OK, well … Can you arrange a translation agency to do it, please?
   B _____³ like to, but the problem is that I don't know any translation agencies.

2 **A** I had _____⁴ to run the training course for our new employees, but now I have to go to London on business. Would you mind _____⁵ the course for me?
   B No, don't worry, that's _____⁶.

3 **A** _____⁷, the conference in Miami has been cancelled due to the hurricane. Do you _____⁸ you could cancel our flights?
   B We won't be _____⁹ to do that because we've already printed our boarding passes.

4 **A** Something's _____¹⁰ up. Er …We're going to do the product launch in Chennai, not in Delhi. Would you _____¹¹ contacting the press to tell them? Here's the new address.
   B _____¹². Leave it with me.

10 Great partnerships

Grammar 3rd Conditional; *should / shouldn't have*

INTRODUCTION

1 Work in pairs. Match the people's names to make famous partnerships. What brand or activity do you associate with the partnerships?

Example   Charles Rolls and Henry Royce – Rolls-Royce luxury cars

William Harley	Coco Chanel	Charles Rolls
Ben Cohen	Steve Jobs	Bill Hewlett
Wilbur Wright	Neil Armstrong	Arthur Davidson
Pierre Wertheimer	Henry Royce	John Lennon
Jerry Greenfield	David Packard	Orville Wright
Paul McCartney	Steve Wozniak	Buzz Aldrin

2 Read the texts and answer the questions below.

The two Steves (& Ronald)

The two Steves first met in 1971, and in 1976 started attending the Homebrew Computer Club. At a club meeting, Wozniak demonstrated his new microcomputer. It was very basic with no keyboard, mouse, or casing, but Jobs saw its commercial potential. With a third partner they founded Apple Computers and Jobs got an order for 50 Apple 1s from The Byte Shop. That was Apple's first sale. The third partner was Ronald Wayne, who owned 10% of the company. He sold his shares for $2,300. If he had waited just a year, they would have increased hugely in value. And if he had kept them, he would have become a billionaire.

NUMBER FIVE

In the 1920s, Coco Chanel, a French fashion designer, developed a new perfume. It was very popular with her customers and so she decided to manufacture it on a large scale. Unfortunately, she did not have enough capital and needed a partner. At Longchamp Racecourse near Paris she met Pierre Wertheimer, a wealthy businessman, who owned one of the most successful cosmetics businesses in the world. They formed a new company called Les Parfums Chanel and produced the perfume Coco had created. This was one of the world's most famous scents, Chanel No. 5. However, Wertheimer's family owned 70%, and Chanel was offered only 10% of the business. Chanel shouldn't have accepted the deal and she spent many years trying to increase her shareholding. She never succeeded.

1 Which club did the two Steves attend?
2 What did Wozniak make?
3 Who was Apple's first customer?
4 Where did the Chanel partners meet?
5 What did Coco Chanel make?
6 What did Coco Chanel try to change?

3 ♪) **10.1** **Listen to a discussion about two more partnerships and answer the questions.**
1 What business did Ben and Jerry think about opening?
2 Why were Ben and Jerry successful?
3 How do they use some of the profits?
4 Where did John Lennon and Paul McCartney meet?
5 Where did Lennon first hear George Harrison play guitar?
6 What mistake did Decca Records make?
7 Why did the Beatles change their drummer?

4 ♪) **10.2** **Listen and complete the sentences.**
1 If they _____ a bagel business, they might not have been so successful.
2 So if Paul hadn't gone to the event, he _____ John.
3 So if George _____ that bus, John would never have heard him play.
4 Decca _____ signed them when it had the chance.
5 If Pete Best had been a better drummer, he _____ a superstar.

Focus

Look at the sentences in 4 and choose the correct words to complete the rules.
We use the 3rd Conditional to talk about the *real / imaginary* past.
We use the *Past Simple / Past Perfect* in the *if* clause.
We use *would / will* + *has / have* in the main clause.

We can also use modal verbs such as *might* and *could*.
If they had started a bagel business, they **might** not have been so successful.
If Pete Best had been a better drummer, he **could** have become a superstar.

should / shouldn't have
Read the examples and choose the correct words to complete the rules.
Decca **should have** signed them when they had the chance.
Chanel **shouldn't have** accepted the deal.

We use *should have* to talk about the *best / wrong* thing to do.
We use *shouldn't have* to talk about the *best / wrong* thing to do.

▶ For more details and practice, go to the Review section on pages 122 and 123.

PRACTICE **5** **Work in pairs. Match 1–8 with a–h to make conditional sentences.**
1 If Steve Wozniak hadn't met Steve Jobs at the Homebrew Computer Club, ___
2 If Ronald Wayne hadn't sold his shares in Apple, ___
3 If Coco Chanel hadn't met Pierre Wertheimer, ___
4 If Pierre Wertheimer had agreed to give Coco Chanel 50% of the company, ___
5 If Ben and Jerry hadn't been friends at school, ___
6 If Ben had been able to taste normally, ___
7 If Paul McCartney hadn't gone to the church festival, ___
8 If Decca records had offered the Beatles a contract, ___

a Coco would have become a very rich woman.
b he would have created a different type of ice cream.
c they might not have met the producer George Martin.
d he would not have met John Lennon.
e they might not have started the Apple company.
f Chanel No. 5 might never have been produced.
g they might not have gone into business together.
h he would have made millions of dollars.

6 ◉ **10.3** Listen and complete the sentences. Practise saying the short forms.
1 You _____ offered her a bigger share.
2 She _____ accepted his offer.
3 They _____ offered them a contract.
4 If _____ to different schools, _____ started companies with other people.
5 If he _____ demonstrated his computer, he _____ met Steve Jobs.

Watch the video for more practice.

7 Complete the comments about the characters in the four stories.
1 Pete Best _____ (practise) drumming more often.
2 Pierre Wertheimer _____ (offer) Coco Chanel only 10% of the company.
3 Decca Records _____ (realize) that guitar music was becoming popular.
4 Ronald Wayne _____ (sell) his shares in Apple.
5 Some people think that Ben and Jerry _____ (sell) their company to Unilever.
6 Pete Best probably thought George Martin _____ (criticize) his drumming.

8 Read the text and complete the sentences below.

Hudson River heroes

On 15 January 2009, an Airbus A320 took off from LaGuardia Airport in New York. The two pilots were Captain Sullenberger, who had 29 years' flying experience and was a safety expert, and co-pilot Jeff Skiles, who had just finished training to fly the Airbus A320.

Co-pilot Skiles was at the controls when, only three minutes into the flight, a flock of geese flew right into the aircraft stopping both engines.

Captain Sullenberger took the controls, while Skiles began going through the three-page emergency procedures checklist in an attempt to restart the engines. Sullenberger and Skiles decided that they couldn't reach an airfield because they were flying too low. Instead, they turned south towards the Hudson River.

Showing great skill, Sullenberger landed the plane not only intact but also close enough to the ferry terminal so that rescue boats could arrive quickly.

All 155 passengers escaped and the last person to leave was Captain Sullenberger. The entire flight crew of Flight 1549 were awarded the Guild of Air Pilots and Air Navigators Master's Medal in 2009.

1 If Captain Sullenberger hadn't _____.
2 If co-pilot Jeff Skiles hadn't done _____.
3 If a flock of geese hadn't flown _____.
4 If they had been able to restart the engines _____.
5 If the plane had been flying higher _____.
6 If the captain hadn't landed so near the rescue boats _____.

TASK 9 Work in pairs. You are going to tell your partner about a narrow escape. Student A, go to page 129. Student B, go to page 134.

Vocabulary Changing careers; -ing vs infinitive

1 **Work in pairs and discuss these questions.**
   1 What is your career? Have you ever thought of other careers? What attracts you to these careers?
   2 What do you think are the advantages and disadvantages of changing careers? Make a list.

2 ◆)) **10.4 Listen to three people who have changed careers. Complete the table with six of these words.**

lawyer   editor   accountant   caterer   events manager
marketing manager   teacher   website developer   landscape gardener

	1st career	2nd career
1 Mariam		
2 Liam		
3 Beatrice		

3 ◆)) **10.4 Work in pairs. Choose the correct words to complete the sentences. Listen again and check.**
   1 a She suggested *doing / to do* some charity work.
     b I enjoy *being / to be* out in the open air.
     c I managed *getting / to get* some work experience.
   2 a It's quite hard *meeting / to meet* people.
     b It is easy *spending / to spend* time with my family now.
   3 a I'm pretty good at *organizing / to organize* things.
     b I was afraid of *not having / not to have* any money.
     c I decided *starting / to start* my own catering company.

4 **Complete the table using the sentences from 3.**

-ing	Examples
after prepositions The thought **of changing** career was scary.	
after some verbs I really **missed going** into the office.	
infinitive	**Examples**
after adjectives It's not **easy to change** career.	
after some verbs I **offered to stay** at home.	

5 **Work in groups of three. Look at the script on page 153. Choose one person each and find more examples to add to the table in 4.**

6 Work in pairs. Complete the sentences with the correct form of these verbs.

apply   break into   use   give   go   make   manage   play   cut   learn

1. I enjoy _____ golf. It's really relaxing.
2. She's decided _____ for a new job.
3. Our company specializes in _____ anti-virus software.
4. They tried _____ the American market but failed.
5. We've managed _____ our costs by 6%.
6. This software is really easy _____. I'll show you.
7. She's involved in _____ the new IT project.
8. He's not very good at _____ presentations.
9. It's hard _____ Russian. It's a difficult language.
10. He's suggested _____ to Italy for our next holiday.

7 Work in pairs. Ask and answer the questions.

1. What are you good / bad at?
2. What do you enjoy doing at the weekend?
3. What are you interested in doing in your career over the next five years?
4. What is easy or difficult to do in your job?
5. What have you decided to do recently?
6. Where would you suggest visiting in your town?
7. Is there anything you're afraid of doing?
8. What do you plan to do this evening / this weekend / this year?

8 Complete the article with the correct form of the verbs in brackets.

HIGH*flyer*

Changing careers

Changing career is a big step. Here's some advice on how to prepare for the change.

Plan ahead

If you decide _____[1] (change) career, it's important to plan ahead. You need _____[2] (have) a clear strategy. Think about where you want to be five years from now, and then work out how you can get there. This means _____[3] (identify) what skills and qualifications you need.

Develop your network

If you want _____[4] (do) a different job, then talk to people who do that job. Go to conferences and try _____[5] (meet) as many people as you can. Don't be afraid of _____[6] (ask) for advice.

Save money

Changing career will probably mean _____[7] (earn) a lower salary at the beginning, so it's important to have some savings. To gain experience, you could offer _____[8] (work) on a voluntary basis for a short period. If you have a family and a mortgage, it may be difficult _____[9] (work) for less money – you may need to do your old job and gain experience in your new career at the same time.

Market yourself as a package of skills

Always remember you already have skills and experience from your previous job. You may be good at _____[10] (manage) people or public speaking. This gives you an advantage in the job market.

Mix with supportive people

It's hard _____[11] (make) a fresh start. You are nervous about _____[12] (have) no money. You may be afraid of _____[13] (appear) foolish. For this reason, it's important to have friends who will support you. Other people who are interested in _____[14] (do) your new career can help you at this time.

9 Work in groups. Choose a career that you know well. Write down five or more suggestions for someone who would like to do that career. Try to use some of the structures and vocabulary in **4**.

10 Change groups. Tell the people in your new group your suggestions from **9**.

Work skills Teleconferencing and videoconferencing

1 **Work in pairs and discuss these questions.**
   1 Have you ever been involved in a teleconference or a videoconference?
   2 What are their advantages compared to a face-to-face meeting? What problems can happen?

2 **Work in pairs. Read the guidelines below for teleconference leaders and participants.**
   1 Did the leaders and participants in the teleconferences and videoconferences you discussed in **1** follow these guidelines?
   2 Which of the guidelines are more important for teleconferences than videoconferences? Can you add any guidelines?

Leading a successful teleconference or videoconference

- Have a clear agenda and timings. Send these to participants in good time before the meeting.
- Establish clear rules for participants to follow (for example, ask participants to say their name before they speak so everyone knows who is speaking).
- Announce each person who joins and introduce people who don't know each other.
- Allow some 'small talk' at the start: it is an opportunity to check people understand the rules and that the sound is OK.
- Say the person's name before you ask them to talk. It prevents people speaking at the same time.

Participating in a successful teleconference or videoconference

- Make sure you know who is in the conference.
- Say who you are each time you speak.
- Speak clearly and outline what you are going to say before you say it.
- Stay focused: do not do other tasks while you are in the conference.

3 **10.5 Listen to two conference calls and answer the questions.**
   1 Which one is a teleconference and which is a videoconference?
   2 What is the topic of each meeting?

4 **10.5 Listen again and answer the questions.**
   1 Which guidelines in **2** are demonstrated in each conference call?
   2 What problems do they have and how do they solve them?

5 **Work in pairs. Complete the phrases in the table. Look at the script on page 153 to check your answers.**

Meeting	Troubleshooting	Turn-giving	Turn-taking
1	Hanif, are you _____ 1?	Please go _____ 3.	_____ 5 is Renata speaking.
	You both sound a little quiet. Could you turn up the _____ 2 a little?	Magda, would you like _____ 4 something about …?	Sergio, _____ 6.
2	The picture's _____ 7 up. I'm not sure we can all see it.	Tom, did you want to _____ 9 on that?	_____ 11 is Junko.
	Hold on, before you go on, we need to _____ 8 the technical problem.	Tom, did you want to say _____ 10?	Could I just _____ 12 something?

6 **Work in groups of three or four. Go to page 138.**

Functions Catching up

INTRODUCTION

1 Work in pairs. When you meet people again after a long time, it's an opportunity to catch up with them. Tick ✓ the topics you would talk about when catching up with an old colleague or business contact.

☐ your company ☐ mutual friends / acquaintances
☐ family ☐ your salary
☐ your home town ☐ the economy
☐ sport or hobbies ☐ industry gossip

2 ◉) 10.6 Valerie Bridge meets her colleague Jordi Foix at the Mobile World Congress in Barcelona. Listen. Which topics in 1 do they discuss?

3 ◉) 10.6 Work in pairs. Complete the information about Valerie and Jordi. Listen again and check.

1 Where Valerie works: _____
2 Where Jordi works: _____
3 What their company does: _____
4 Why they are at the congress: _____

4 ◉) 10.7 Listen to Valerie meeting different people at the congress. In which conversation (1–5) does she meet the following?

a an ex-colleague ___
b a competitor ___
c a journalist ___
d someone she studied with ___
e someone who works with her now ___

5 ◉) 10.7 Listen again and complete the sentences.

1 I _____ actually. I'm now a project leader.
2 I _____ California. I live in the San Diego area now.
3 _____, the programmers in India accepted the deal.
4 I _____ again last year. Now I'm at Apple.
5 We _____ creating eight different versions of the game.

Focus

Complete the table with these headings.

Asking for news *Giving news about yourself*
Meeting someone again *Saying goodbye*

1	2
Long time, no see. I haven't seen you in ages. How's everything going?	Are you still working at Slipstream Apps? What have you been doing since I last saw you? What happened with our India project in the end? How are things at Microsoft?
3	**4**
I changed jobs last year. I got a promotion … In the end, the programmers … We ended up creating …	Sorry, I have to go now … I'll see you later. It was lovely to meet you again.

▶ For more details and practice, go to the Review section on page 125.

PRACTICE

6 Complete the conversation between Ruth and Zubeda with phrases from the Focus section.

Ruth   Zubeda! How are you? _____¹.
Zubeda Hi, Ruth. I think it must be two years. _____²?
Ruth   Very well thanks. _____³. I'm now Head of Marketing for the whole US.
Zubeda Wow, that's great news.
Ruth   How about you? _____⁴ the Dubai project in the end?
Zubeda _____⁵, it was a real success. We only had problems at the beginning. The rest was OK.
Ruth   _____⁶ that construction company?
Zubeda No, I _____⁷ about three months ago. I now work for a management consultancy in Jordan.
Ruth   That sounds great. Sorry, Zubeda, _____⁸ because I have a meeting. Let's meet up this evening. Are you staying in this hotel?
Zubeda Yes, I am – Room 112. So _____⁹.
Ruth   Yes, OK. Maybe about 6 p.m. in the bar? It _____¹⁰.
Zubeda You too. Bye for now. Good luck with the presentation.

7 Put the words in the right order to make questions.

1 going / how's / everything?
2 you / course / still / English / are / that / doing?
3 doing / have / saw / you / you / what / last / since / been / I?
4 are / things / work / how / at?
5 with / in / what / your / end / last / project / happened / the?

8 Work in pairs. It is next year. You meet your partner again at a conference. Ask and answer the questions in **7**.

TASK

9 Work in pairs. You worked together two years ago. One day, you are on a business trip and you meet in the airport. Role-play your conversation. Student A, go to page 130. Student B, go to page 135.

Review

Grammar 3rd Conditional

Form

We form the 3rd conditional with *if* + Past Perfect, and *would* + past participle.

Use

We use the 3rd Conditional when we imagine a situation that didn't actually happen and talk about the likely consequences.

Might and *could* can be used instead of *would* to show that we are not certain about the result.

Examples If she **had asked** someone, she **would have known**. (*She didn't ask, so she didn't know.*)
If he **hadn't invited** me, I **wouldn't have gone**. (*He did invite me, so I went.*)
If the exam **had been** easier, I **might have passed**. (*The exam was difficult, so I didn't pass.*)

should have / shouldn't have

Form

We use the subject + *should have / shouldn't have* + past participle.

Use

We use *should have* and *shouldn't have* to criticize a past action.

Examples I **should have remembered** that you don't eat meat. (*but I forgot*)
We **shouldn't have gone** to that restaurant: the food is terrible. (*but we did go*)

PRACTICE

1 Join the two sentences to make a 3rd Conditional sentence about how the past could have been different.

Example I didn't study hard at school. I didn't get good exam results.
If I had studied harder at school, I would have got better exam results.

1. I bought an expensive car. I wasn't able to afford a holiday.
2. They didn't realize red and yellow were bad luck colours. They bought red and yellow flowers.
3. I left my mobile at home. I didn't call you.
4. He got a bonus. He worked very hard last year.
5. We didn't listen to the instructions. We went to the wrong room.
6. I didn't give the waiter a tip. I didn't know service wasn't included.
7. I lost my temper with my boss. I lost my job.
8. We didn't make a better offer. We didn't win the contract.
9. My flight was delayed. I stayed at the airport hotel.
10. He didn't go on the course. He didn't know how to use the new software.

2 **Make sentences using *should have* or *shouldn't have* from the notes in the email.**

   Example   We should have planned our trip in advance.

   The trip to our friends in Egypt started off as a disaster. We got so many things wrong.
   1 didn't plan in advance
   2 didn't check the weather
   3 took too many clothes
   4 booked tickets to wrong airport
   5 didn't tell our hosts when we were arriving
   6 forgot to take a phone / laptop
   7 didn't pack any suncream
   8 didn't take any presents for our hosts

3 **Change the sentences in 2 into 3rd Conditional sentences. Use these ideas to help.**

   *be so disorganized   know about the hurricane   suitcases be so heavy   arrive on time
   someone meet us   contact our families   get sunburnt   feel embarrassed*

   Example   If we had planned our trip in advance, we wouldn't have been so disorganized.

4 **Write about Jack's 'lucky break' using the prompts and the 3rd Conditional.**

   Example   If I'd remembered to set my alarm, I wouldn't have overslept.

   Forgot to set alarm¹… Overslept²… Missed bus³… Late for work⁴…
   Boss fired me⁵… Went to café to think things over⁶… Bought a paper⁷…
   Saw advert for diving instructor⁸ … Called the company⁹… Got an interview.

Vocabulary Changing careers; *-ing* vs infinitive

1 **Choose the correct forms to complete the sentences.**
   1 I'm afraid of *flying / to fly*.
   2 She enjoys *learning / to learn* languages.
   3 My job involves *managing / to manage* a team of 20 people.
   4 He's managed *getting / to get* a job with a law firm in Boston.
   5 Our new notebook is light and easy *carrying / to carry*.
   6 I've decided *buying / to buy* a new car.
   7 She's planning *having / to have* a party for her birthday.
   8 Their company specializes in *designing / to design* microchips.
   9 He offered *helping / to help* me with my proposal.
   10 I'll miss *seeing / to see* my friends after I move.

2 **Complete the text with the correct form of the verbs in brackets.**

The sweet taste of success

Tina and Phil Freer have always enjoyed _____¹ (experiment) with flavours. A few years ago, they decided _____² (start) up their own company, selling unusual jams and spreads. 'It started off with our friends. We used to make them jams as presents. We were keen on _____³ (mix) up unusual flavours and they all thought they were delicious,' Tina says. They wanted _____⁴ (start) selling their jams and they managed _____⁵ (get) a stall at the Borough Market in London. They were good at _____⁶ (create) unusual flavours, such as raspberry and vanilla, watermelon marmalade, and fig and honey. The stall went well and they were soon contacted by a supermarket chain. 'They were interested in _____⁷ (sell) our jams in their stores. Their first order was for 2,000 jars! At that time, we were still making the jams in our apartment, so it wasn't easy _____⁸ (do),' Tina says. 'It was also difficult _____⁹ (get) enough money to pay for all the ingredients and the jars. Supermarkets don't pay in advance.' Luckily, they managed _____¹⁰ (borrow) money from friends and family, and now their jams are being sold across the UK.

3 Answer the questions about the text in **2**.
1 Who did Phil and Tina make their jams for at first?
2 Where did they start selling their jams?
3 What were they good at doing?
4 Who was interested in selling their jams?
5 Why was it hard to supply the supermarket's order?
6 Who lent them money?

4 Write answers to these questions. Write full sentences.
1 What are you good at doing?
   _____

2 What are you interested in doing in the future?
   _____

3 Where do you want to go for your next holiday?
   _____

4 What does your job involve?
   _____

5 What does Apple specialize in making?
   _____

6 What are you afraid of doing?
   _____

7 What is difficult about the job of a doctor or politician?
   _____

8 What do you plan to do tonight?
   _____

Work skills Teleconferencing and videoconferencing

1 Match sentences 1–9 with functions a–c.
1 This is Ainara.
2 I can't hear you. Could you turn up the volume a little?
3 Please go ahead, Leo.
4 The picture's breaking up.
5 Maiko, would you like to say something about the proposal?
6 Javier, did you want to say something?
7 This is Andreas speaking.
8 Eva, here.
9 Hold on, before you go on, we need to sort out a technical problem.

a saying who is speaking: ___, ___, ___
b saying there is a technical problem: ___, ___, ___
c asking someone to speak: ___, ___, ___

2 ◀)) 10.8 Listen to the conference call and answer the questions.
1 Is the conference call a videoconference or a teleconference?
2 What is the technical problem?
3 How many people are at the meeting?
4 What is the first agenda point about?
5 Why does Rose interrupt Marina?
6 What is Marina going to talk to them about?

Functions Catching up

We use these phrases when we meet someone we haven't seen for a long time.
Examples How's everything going?
I haven't seen you in ages. / Long time, no see.

We use these phrases to ask someone for their news.
Examples Are you still working at / How are things at (company)?
How did that project go? / What happened with (project) in the end?
What have you been doing since I last saw you?

We use these phrases to give news about ourselves.
Examples I changed jobs (last year / six months ago, etc.).
I got a promotion.
I moved to (place).
In the end, …
We ended up (+ -ing) …

We use these phrases to say goodbye after catching up.
Examples I'll see you later.
It was lovely to meet you again.
Sorry, I have to go now.

PRACTICE

1 Match 1–6 with responses a–f.

1 Long time, no see. ___
2 Are you still working at Morgan Stanley? ___
3 What happened with your new product launch in the end? ___
4 What have you been doing since I last saw you? ___
5 How are things at the shop? ___
6 It was lovely to meet you again. ___

a It was a disaster. Nobody came!
b You too. Bye for now.
c I know. It must be two years since we last met.
d Very good, thanks. Our business is growing all the time.
e Yes, I am. I've been there five years now.
f This and that. Life is pretty much the same.

2 Complete the missing words in the conversations.

1 **Suraj** Louise! L_____ time, no see.
Louise Suraj! Hi! How's everything g_____?
Suraj Good thanks. I have some news for you, actually. I got a p_____ at work.
Louise Really? So what are you doing now?
Suraj I'm an engineer for Shell. I work on oil platforms.
Louise Congratulations.

2 **Nina** How are t_____ at Thames Water, Becky?
Becky I don't work for them any more. I c_____ jobs last year.
Nina Who do you work for now?
Becky Sydney Water. I m_____ to Australia about eight months ago.

3 **Pietro** So, what h_____ with your catering business in the end?
Tracy We were very successful. We e_____ up selling the company to a multinational.
Pietro That's good news. Oh. Sorry, Tracy. I have to go now.
Tracy OK. I'll see you l_____, Pietro.

Task and activity notes

1 Grammar p.8

Questions	Interview 1	Interview 2
What do you do?		
Can you explain what that means?		
What are the main areas of your job?		
And how is business at the moment?		
Can you tell me a bit about your current project?		
How many people are working on the project?		
How's the project going?		
What's a typical week for you?		
Do you enjoy your job?		

2 Grammar p.20

Student A

1 Ask Student B questions about John Rocha and complete the table.
2 Give Student B details about Jimmy Choo using the information in the table.

	Jimmy Choo	John Rocha
Occupation	Fashion designer – shoes	
Born	Malaysia (Chinese parentage), 1957	
Grow up	Malaysia	
Training	London (London College of Fashion)	
Home	London, since 1980	
Residence in other countries	Malaysia only	
Started own business	1996 – set up Jimmy Choo Ltd, but sold share in 2001	
Main achievements	Successful shoe design business; winner of World's Outstanding Chinese Designer 2011	
Recent activity	Set up shoemaking institute in Malaysia	
Interesting facts	Made his first shoe when he was 11	

2 Functions p.25

Student A
You are the chairperson of the meeting.

- Begin the meeting. You also choose when to move to a new agenda item.
- Find one person to do each job on the agenda. You can do one job yourself.
- You want all the jobs done in the next few days.
- At the end, check you have discussed everything.

2 Vocabulary p.22

1. You are a group of entrepreneurs. You are going to present your idea for a new company to a group of investors. Prepare a five-minute presentation. Think of the following things.
   - The name of your company
   - What is your business model (e.g. what product or service are you selling)?
   - What location will you choose for your business?
   - Who are your potential customers?
   - How much start-up money do you need? What will you spend this on? How much income do you hope to make in your first year? What are your predicted profits for the first five years?

2. Take turns as groups to present your company. The rest of the class can question the group about their business plan. At the end of the presentations, each group can vote to invest in one company (not their own!). The group with the most votes receives the investment.

4 Functions p.49

Student A

You researched the Liverpool area. Read the information. Then plan the tour together. Use the table below. You need about a day to travel between the different areas of the country. If you travel, you cannot do anything else that day.

- You want people to see a Liverpool football match (price around £44).
- You think a fun activity is to do a tour of the Beatles' homes and neighbourhoods – the harbour of Liverpool is a World Heritage Site (cost £15.95).
- Your idea for accommodation is a bed and breakfast (a small hotel in people's houses). This is £45 per night.

	Visit and activity	Accommodation
Plan day 1		
Plan day 2		
Plan day 3		
Plan day 4		
Total cost		

Tasks and activities 127

5 Grammar p.56

Student A

Read the rules and then discuss them with your partner. Decide which rules you think are best. You can modify the rules if you wish.

1 People are allowed to drive from the age of 16.
2 Smoking is not permitted in private or public areas, only in special smoking zones.
3 Everyone has to carry an identity card with them at all times.
4 All public transport is free.
5 You don't need a permit to own a gun.

6 Functions p.73

Student A

1 Read the information then ask Student B for help. Listen to B's suggestions and choose one.

> Your smartphone is not working. It is impossible to download apps and it cannot save photos. This problem only started yesterday. Ask B for help. Note that your smartphone is three months old.

2 Student B asks for help with a laptop. Listen to B's problem and suggest solutions. Use this information to help you.

Possible causes of problem	Possible solutions
- The laptop is broken. - The laptop has a hardware problem. - The laptop has a virus.	- Take the laptop to a repair shop (cost about $100). - Buy a new anti-virus program and look for the problem (cost about $40). - Delete everything on your computer and re-install all the software (the Operating System).

7 Functions p.85

Student A

You like B's work and you want him/her to stay at the company. Have a discussion with B and reach agreement on a new contract.

What you want	What you can offer
- Another salesperson, Maria, is going on maternity leave. You need B to do some of her work. - You want B to help train the less experienced salespeople. - You want B to stay on the same salary this year.	- five weeks' holiday a year - one day to work from home every month - a new company car - possibly a 10% pay rise next year

9 Grammar p.104

Student A

Answers

1 Usain Bolt
2 the marathon
3 The International Olympic Committee
4 Acer
5 Danny Boyle

9 Functions p.109

Student A

1. You work for a charity that provides sports equipment for children around the world. You have arranged a videoconference with your local managers tomorrow. Unfortunately, the International Director is ill and cannot do the conference. Speak to B, who is the Asia manager of your charity.
   - Give B the news. Ask B to rearrange the conference for tomorrow.
   - Ask B to contact the country managers in India and Sri Lanka today to confirm a new date.
   - If B refuses your requests, find a solution (new date for the conference).

2. You are the boss of a watch company. You have arranged a big meeting on 1st June with your clients to show them your new watches. Your sales director calls you with some bad news.
   - Listen to B's news.
   - August is not acceptable. All your customers are on holiday.
   - You want to speak to the head designer. Ask B to arrange a meeting tomorrow.
   - Suggest a new date for the meeting (you are free in July).

10 Grammar p.116

Student A

Look at the picture and make up your version of what happened.

Imagine what happened and describe how someone helped you escape. Make at least one sentence starting with 'If X hadn't, …' and 'X should / shouldn't have …'.

10 Functions p.121

Student A

Read the information. Then ask and answer questions to catch up with Student B.

- You start the conversation. Express surprise to see B.
- Respond to B. You last saw B two years ago.
- You remember B worked for Sony. Ask about now.
- Last year, you got a project with the German government. It's a success. You now have a better job in the same company (Regional Manager).
- You remember that B lived in Paris. Ask about B's life there.
- Listen to B's response and end the conversation.

2 Grammar p.20

Student B

1. Give Student A details about John Rocha using the information in the table.
2. Ask Student A questions about Jimmy Choo and complete the table.

	Jimmy Choo	**John Rocha**
Occupation		Fashion designer – clothing (hand-crafted and beaded)
Born		Hong Kong – Chinese and Portuguese parents, 1953
Grow up		Hong Kong
Training		London, Croydon School of Art
Home		Dublin, Ireland, since 1970s
Residence in other countries		China (Hong Kong), Italy (Milan), and the UK
Started own business		1977 in Ireland
Main achievements		Successful fashion designer; won Designer of the Year Award 1993
Recent activity		Running his design business (Three Moon Design) in Dublin
Interesting facts		Also designed glassware and interiors of hotels in Dublin and Birmingham

2 Functions p.25

Student B
You are in charge of the sports department.
- You can do any job in sports.
- You are on holiday for the next month.
- You love video and film – you want to work on this.

Student A is the chairperson and begins the meeting.

3 Work skills p.35

Student A

1 You have to travel to a meeting in Moscow next week. Write an email to your colleague in Moscow.
   - Confirm your travel arrangements: Monday 7 June, 8.30 a.m., flight AF1470, Paris (Charles de Gaulle Airport) to Moscow (Domodedovo Airport).
   - Check that someone will meet you at the airport. You arrive 1.30 p.m.
   - Send the agenda for the meeting. Ask your colleague to book a room for the meeting.

2 Exchange emails with your partner. Write the reply.

4 Functions p.49

Student B
You researched Wales and south-west England. Read the information. Then plan the tour together. Use the table below. You need about a day to travel between the different areas of the country. If you travel, you cannot do anything else that day.

- You want people to visit Stonehenge, a World Heritage Site (price around £8).
- Your idea for a fun activity is to go to Snowdonia and go hiking in the mountains (free).
- Your idea for accommodation is to go camping. This costs £20 a night (visitors bring their own tent).

	Visit and activity	Accommodation
Plan day 1		
Plan day 2		
Plan day 3		
Plan day 4		
Total cost		

5 Grammar p.56

Student B

Read the rules and then discuss them with your partner. Decide which rules you think are best. You can modify the rules if you wish.

1. People are allowed to drive from the age of 20.
2. Smoking is permitted in private areas and open spaces.
3. No one has to carry an identity card with them.
4. Transport is run by private companies. The company decides how much to charge.
5. The private ownership of guns is prohibited. Guns are only for use by the military.

6 Grammar p.68

Student B

Read the text and complete the diagram. Then tell Student B about the Sundrop Farms story.

Sundrop Farms

Many areas in the world don't have enough fresh water, and most farms use large amounts of water to grow vegetables and fruit.

Sundrop Farms developed a system that uses sea water and the sun's energy to produce fresh water and energy. This provides water for the plants in the greenhouses and energy to heat up or cool down the air in the greenhouses. The end result is fresh produce – fruit and vegetables.

After Sundrop Farms had developed this new system, they began operating their first commercial farm in South Australia in 2010. And farmers who had previously found it very difficult to grow fresh produce in the world's drier regions can now do so without using electricity or fresh water.

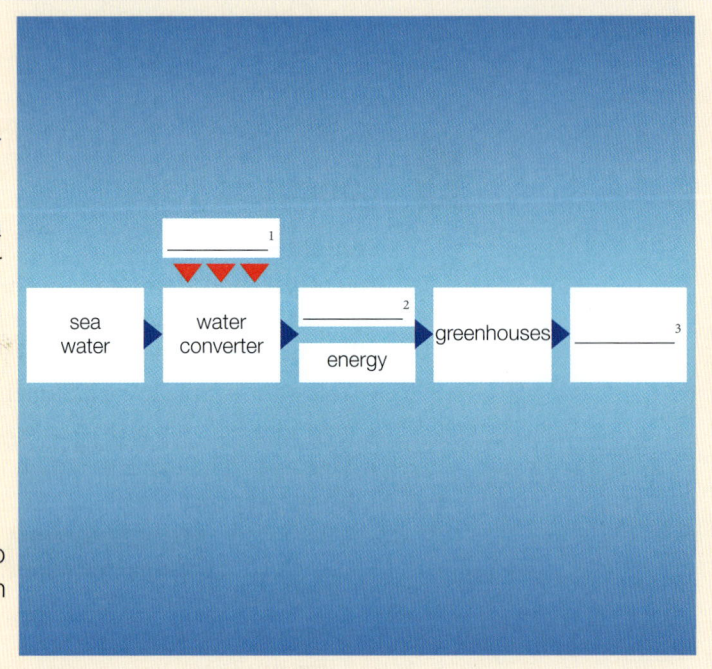

Diagram: sea water → water converter → [2 _____ energy] → greenhouses → _____ 3

(1 _____ above water converter)

6 Functions p.73

Student B

1. Student A asks for help with a smartphone. Listen to A's problem and suggest solutions. Use this information to help you.

Possible causes of problem	Possible solutions
• The smartphone is broken. • The smartphone is very old. • There is a problem with the smartphone's memory.	• Restore factory settings (you lose all information, but the phone is the same as when you bought it). • Return the phone to the shop and ask them to repair it. • Look online for help (maybe someone had the same problem in the past).

2. Read the information then ask Student A for help. Listen to A's suggestions and choose one.

> Your laptop is doing strange things. It makes a lot of loud noises when you are doing nothing. It is also very slow. Ask A for help. Note that your laptop is about a year old. You once dropped it in the street, but you think it is OK. You use a free anti-virus program that you got on the internet.

8 Grammar p.92

Student B

1 Match the six sentences a–f to the stages 2, 4, 6, 7, 10, and 12 of the 'Making chocolate' diagram below. Then complete the chart by asking Student B questions about the process. At the same time, answer Student B's questions.

a The crumbs are rolled to make them smooth.
b Sugar, vanilla, and other flavouring are added to the mix.
c Finally, the finished product is distributed around the world.
d The beans are crushed to form a dark brown paste.
e The beans are mixed with dirt and twigs so they are washed.
f Before the chocolate becomes hard it is made into different shapes.

Making chocolate

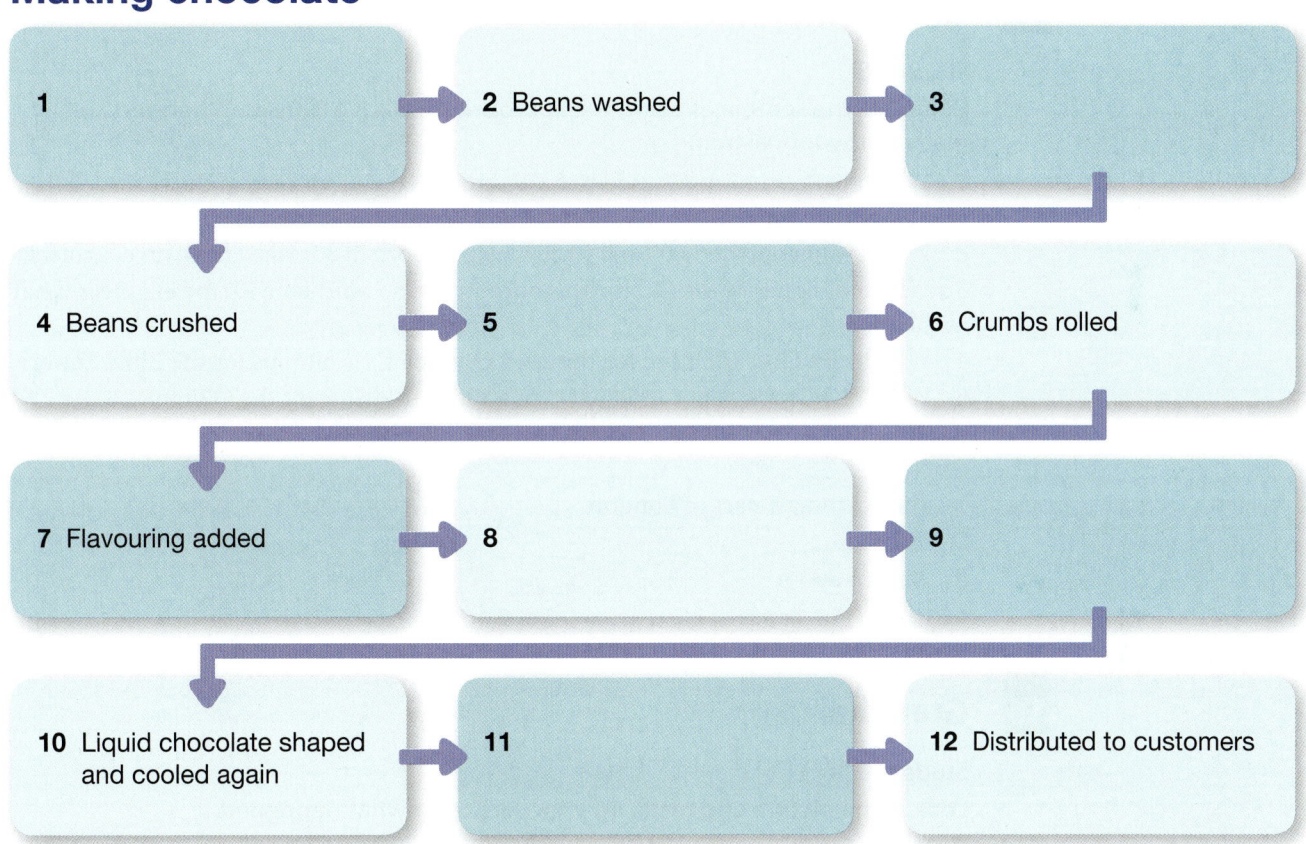

1	→	2 Beans washed	→	3
4 Beans crushed	→	5	→	6 Crumbs rolled
7 Flavouring added	→	8	→	9
10 Liquid chocolate shaped and cooled again	→	11	→	12 Distributed to customers

2 Take turns to ask and answer questions to complete these sentences about chocolate production.

1 Chocolate can be made from three types of cacao bean. The most common of these is forastero.
2 Cacao is grown in _____ where the climate is hot and moist. (Where …?)
3 About 30 to 60 beans are used to make 100 grams of chocolate.
4 Production of cocoa beans has grown from around 1.5 million tons in 1974 to over _____ million tons in 2012. (How many …?)
5 Cocoa beans can be picked at any time of year in most countries.
6 One concern about cocoa production is that _____ in the Ivory Coast are being used to harvest and pack the beans. (Who …?)

7 Functions p.85

Student B

You really want to stay at your company, but there are some things you are not happy about. Have a discussion with A to agree a new and better contract.

What you want	What you can offer
• You want a 5% pay rise as soon as possible. • You currently have four weeks' holiday a year. You would like six weeks. • You want to work from home whenever you can.	• You can take on some more work because one of your clients has gone out of business. • You can help work with newer employees (you like training people). • You think there are two new potential customers that you can bring to the company.

9 Grammar p.104

Student B

Complete the sentences using the appropriate relative clauses. When you are ready quiz your partner.

1 Which part of London / used to be an industrial site / provided the space for the London Olympics?
2 Which winner of the 5,000 and 10,000 metres / born in Somalia / has twin daughters?
3 Which designer of the Orbit / was born in India / worked with the engineer Cecil Balmond?
4 Which city / lost their bid for the 2012 Olympics / is famous for the Eiffel Tower?
5 Which IOC president / used to be an athlete / didn't want the Olympics to be influenced by business?

Answers
1 The north-east part of London
2 Mo Farah
3 Anish Kapoor
4 Paris
5 Avery Brundage

10 Grammar p.116

Student B

Look at the picture and make up your version of what happened.

Imagine what happened and describe how someone helped you escape. Make at least one sentence starting with 'If X hadn't, …' and 'X should / shouldn't have …'.

3 Work skills p.35

Student B

1 You have a meeting in Tokyo next week. Write an email to your friend who lives in the same city.
   - Your friend has already agreed to meet you in Tokyo after your meeting: Tuesday evening 6.30 p.m. Confirm that Tuesday is OK, but you want to meet later. Suggest a time and ask for confirmation.
   - Ask your friend to text you where to meet for dinner.
   - Send a photo of the hotel where you are staying.
2 Exchange emails with your partner. Write the reply.

9 Functions p.109

Student B

1 You are the Asia Manager for a charity that provides sports equipment for children around the world. A is the head of the charity. There is a videoconference with all the local managers tomorrow. Listen to A's news and react. Use this information.
   - You cannot have the videoconference tomorrow: it's a national holiday in India.
   - You cannot contact the Sri Lanka manager today (she is flying to Australia).
   - Suggest a new day for the conference (next week).
2 You are the sales director for a watch company. You have agreed to present the company's new watches to your main customers on 1st June. The designs will not be ready. Speak to Student A (your boss).
   - Give A the news. Ask A to rearrange the presentation of the watches for 1st August.
   - A cannot speak to the head designer because she is in hospital for an operation this week.
   - Find a new date for the meeting (July?).

10 Functions p.121

Student B

Read the information. Then ask and answer questions to catch up with Student A.

- A starts the conversation. Respond to A. Say it's been a long time since you last saw each other.
- You last worked for Sony 18 months ago. Now you work for Toyota.
- You know A wanted to do a project for the German government. Ask about this.
- Answer A's question. In the past, you lived in Paris. Now you live in Stuttgart.
- Respond to A and end the conversation.

2 Functions p.25

Student C

You are in charge of young fashion.

- You have one free day next week (Wednesday).
- You want the mannequins to represent young people and teenagers.
- At the end of the meeting, tell the others that a famous person (choose one) will visit the store next Thursday. Someone has to meet this person (you can't do it).

Student A is the chairperson and begins the meeting.

4 Functions p.49

Student C

You researched Northern Ireland. Read the information. Then plan the tour together. Use the table below. You need about a day to travel between the different areas of the country. If you travel, you cannot do anything else that day.

- You want people to visit Belfast and hear some traditional Irish music in the evening (price around £10).
- Your idea for a fun activity is to go to the Giant's Causeway (a World Heritage Site) and walk over the rocks (£9).
- Your idea for accommodation is to stay in four-star hotels (price £120 per night).

	Visit and activity	Accommodation
Plan day 1		
Plan day 2		
Plan day 3		
Plan day 4		
Total cost		

2 Functions p.25

Student D

You are in charge of adult fashion.

- The theme of the display is summer and it will look like a beach (this is finished).
- You have a very good relationship with the company's main suppliers.
- You are not sure what clothes to show.
- You are not free this week, but you can do any job next week.

Student A is the chairperson and begins the meeting.

4 Functions p.49

Student D

You researched Scotland. Read the information. Then plan the tour together. Use the table below. You need about a day to travel between the different areas of the country. If you travel, you cannot do anything else that day.

- You want people to visit Edinburgh and see its castle (a World Heritage Site) (£14.50) and historic city centre (free).
- Your idea for a fun activity is to go to Loch Ness and take a boat on the lake (£12.50).
- Your idea for accommodation is to stay in five-star hotels (price £175 per night).

	Visit and activity	Accommodation
Plan day 1		
Plan day 2		
Plan day 3		
Plan day 4		
Total cost		

8 Functions p.97

Take turns to be the employee and the manager. Use the prompts to make a conversation.

Employee: You don't understand the new system for expenses (money the company pays for food / accommodation when you travel for business).

Manager: Your company has recently introduced a new expenses system. People are confused about the 'multiplier'.

Employee	Manager
can / clarify / how / the / new / expenses system / works?	Employees get maximum $200 a day. you / with / me?
can / explain / what / mean / by 'maximum' $200?	$100 = accommodation. $50 = transport. $50 = food, breakfast + lunch. you / follow?
that / make / sense. What happens in very expensive places like Moscow or London?	In very expensive countries, there is a higher budget. It might be $200 x 1.25, 1.5 or 1.75. you / see / how / it / works?
sorry / I / not / understand /you.	Some countries have expenses plus extra money, 'a multiplier'. This depends on the country. like / me / go / over / again?
I / not / understand / how / to find / the / information about the multiplier.	It's on the company intranet. Look at this document. be / everything / clear?
yes / with / you. It's very complicated, especially for new employees.	I / see / you / mean. Everyone will understand it soon.

3 Functions p.37

Complete the diary for next week with:
- four work commitments (meeting, training course, etc.)
- one day when you are not at work (day off, doctor's appointment, etc.)
- two events that may or may not happen
- one lunch meeting

Time	Monday	Tuesday	Wednesday	Thursday	Friday
Morning					
Lunchtime					
Afternoon					

Arrange a time to meet together next week. Can you arrange a meeting or just pencil one in?

4 Work skills p.47

Choosing visual aids

a Use visual images rather than words. A picture speaks a thousand words.
b Have a variety of visual aids. It keeps your presentation interesting.
c Don't put too many words on the screen. Less is more.
d Don't just read out the text on the screen. It will send the audience to sleep.

Presenting visual aids

e Don't stand in front of the screen.
f Check that the audience can see the screen. If they can't, explain what's on it.
g Point out the parts of the visual you want the audience to notice.
h Give the audience enough time to look at the screen.
i Always remember: your visual aids should aid your presentation, not *control* it.

10 Work skills p.119

Decide if you are going to have a teleconference or videoconference. Choose one of the topics below. Before you start the conference, do the following.

1 Choose someone to chair the conference.
2 On your own, think of some ideas to bring to the discussion. Include a 'problem' (e.g. the sound is bad, etc.).

Topics
- Planning an itinerary for the new managing director of your company (who wants to visit all offices / departments in your company)
- Designing a web page giving 'cultural tips' to people visiting your country
- Planning a party to celebrate the 50th anniversary of your company

Scripts

1

1.1
J=James Martin, G=Geoff Walker
- J What do you do, Geoff?
- G I'm a social media manager.
- J Can you explain what that involves?
- G Yes, it basically means that I'm responsible for marketing our products using social media sites.
- J What are the main areas of your job?
- G There are two main areas. Firstly, I promote our latest products or offers by posting information on social networking sites like Facebook and Twitter. Secondly, I check the information that we get from prospective customers' interactions with each other and the various websites. For example, comments people make, which questions people are asking online, and the number of times a message is passed on or retweeted.
- J And how is business at the moment?
- G We're very busy. We have a lot of new products coming out later this year, so now we're planning the next phase of marketing.
- J Can you tell me a bit about your current project?
- G Yes, sure. We're developing the mobile device side of our marketing. In marketing these days, smartphone users are becoming more and more important. So we're sending messages to individual users on their smartphone or tablet to keep them up to date with any new promotion or sales event.
- J How many people are working on the project?
- G In the office, about ten people are working on the mobile project.
- J And how's the project going?
- G It's going very well. But there's a lot to do before our main sales season in October.
- J What's a typical week for you?
- G I have a typical five-day nine to five sort of week. But I do work quite a lot of weekends, going to conferences, trade fairs, and so on.
- J Do you work mainly in the office during the week?
- G Yes, I spend most of my time in the office in front of a computer. But I do have a lot of team meetings during the week as well. I need to keep everyone up to date, solve any ongoing problems, and make sure that we're on schedule, that sort of thing.
- J What sort of problems do you usually have?
- G We have lots of technical problems. For example, we have to make sure that everything works on both iPhones and Android phones, which is quite complicated. And there's a huge amount of information that we process – the number of hits, comments, retweets, and so on. We need all this information to help plan our future marketing campaigns.
- J It sounds like you're very busy. Do you enjoy your job?
- G It can get pretty stressful, but yes, generally, I enjoy it. I always enjoy a challenge.

1.2
I=Interviewer, C=Cat Shaeffer
- I Today we have Cat Shaeffer on the show to give us some tips about how to use social media safely. Welcome to the show, Cat!
- C Thanks, Tom, glad to be here!
- I So, Cat, everyone is on Facebook, Twitter, and other social media sites nowadays. What's your advice for our listeners on how to use these media?
- C Well, first of all, I'd say be careful what you upload onto a social networking site. A lot of people post any photo or video they think is funny onto the web, without thinking about who might see it or when. Just remember that whatever you put online will probably still be available years from now. Do you really want a possible future employer to see you with your friends at 18, dressed in a policeman's uniform?
- I I know what you mean! I've got some really embarrassing photos from when I was younger that I'd hate anyone to see now. So what other advice do you have?
- C Well, I'd say be careful about putting too much private information about yourself online. Identity theft is a common crime nowadays, so you need to be careful.
- I Could you explain a bit more about what you mean by 'identity theft'?
- C Sure. Identity theft is when someone pretends to be you by using your personal details, like your name, address, email address, etcetera. Criminals may use your details to log in to a website and then buy goods. In the worst case, they can access your bank account and steal money directly from your account.
- I I see. You really don't want that to happen.
- C Of course not. So that's why you need to make sure you don't post too much private information that a criminal might be able to use.
- I I see. So do you have one more tip for our listeners?
- C Yes, my last tip is be careful what you say online. People often forget that the internet is in the public domain. In terms of the law, it's not really any different to print media like a book or newspaper. You would be very careful about printing bad comments about someone, but people think that posting negative or untrue comments on the internet is OK. They're wrong! If you say untrue comments about a person online, they can sue you. So watch out!
- I Good to know! I'll be more careful what I post online in the future. Thanks, Cat.
- C You're welcome. And happy networking!

1.3
L=Lisa, P=Pete, D=Diane
- L Oh, excuse me. It's Pete Shen, isn't it?
- P Yes, that's right.
- L We met last year at the Virtual Reality conference.
- P Yes, in Atlanta. Er … I'm sorry, I don't remember your name.
- L Lisa. Lisa Jamieson.
- P Lisa. Of course. It's nice to see you again.
- L You too, Pete. So what are you doing at the conference?
- P Well, currently, I'm working on a technology website.
- L Uh-huh.
- P We want to find some new products to review on our blog.
- L Really? Interesting. Would you like to meet my colleague, Diane Smith?
- P Diane?
- L She's looking for people like you.
- P Great, yes, please introduce us.
- L Diane! Diane, I want you to meet Pete Shen.
- D Pleased to meet you, Pete.
- P And you.
- L Pete writes a blog about new technology.
- D Do you? That *is* interesting. Tell me about your blog, Pete.

1.4
P=Pete, D=Diane
- P Well, Diane, I'm a technology journalist. I write a blog for a magazine. I'm based here in San Diego and I write about new technology.
- D Are you familiar with recent developments in hardware?
- P Yes. Previously I worked as a programmer for a computer manufacturer. Then I changed jobs and became a journalist.
- D That's very interesting. I worked as a journalist too about five years ago. I worked on the radio.
- P Did you?
- D Yeah, but now I'm a marketing manager. I'm in charge of marketing a new laptop for our company.
- P Well, I deal with reviews of hardware, computers, laptops, and tablets.
- D Maybe we can work together. Look, here's my card. I work in LA.
- P Thanks. Sorry … I don't have one.
- D That's OK. Give me your email and I'll save it on my phone.

P Great! My email address is Pshen (all one word) at pshen dot com.
D Pshen.com. OK. So you have your own website too.
P That's right. I have a website and you can follow me on Twitter.
D Well, nice to meet you, Pete. I hope we can work together in the future.

1.5

1 A=Adriana, F=Felipe, C=Chizuko
A I want you to meet Chizuko Honda. Chizuko, this is Felipe Diaz.
F Pleased to meet you, Chizuko.
C Nice to meet you too, Felipe.
A Chizuko is in charge of our hotels in Osaka.
F Really? I didn't know that.

2 B=Brian, J=Julienne
B Excuse me. It's Julienne Blanc, isn't it? We met last year at the WA Forum.
J That's right. I'm so sorry, I don't remember your name.
B Brian. Brian Smith.
J Nice to meet you again, Brian.
B Are you working here in New York now?
J No, I'm not. I'm based in Washington. I work for an advertising company there.

3 C=Chloe, N=Nikolai
C Are you familiar with our software, Nikolai?
N No, I'm not. I'd like to know more about it. We're always interested in new software.
C In that case, let's talk again in the future. Here's my card.
N Thank you. Here's mine. My email has just changed actually. It's now nik@purplesoftware (all one word) dot com.
C I'll change that on the card.
N Thanks. I'll look forward to hearing from you after the conference.

2

2.1

J=James Martin, A=Aisha Hayek
J Aisha, hello.
A Hi.
J So, can you tell us something about Nada Debs?
A Sure. Nada is a successful designer from Beirut.
J OK. And how did her story start?
A Well, Nada's story is an interesting one. She was born in Lebanon, but she grew up in Kobe, Japan.
J Did she stay in Japan?
A No, she left Japan in 1982 and went to the USA where she studied at the Rhode Island School of Design.
J I'm guessing she didn't stay in the USA.
A That's right. She moved to London where she stayed till 1999.
J Where did she go next?
A She went back to her home country and she's been living in Beirut ever since.

J And what's been happening in terms of her business?
A Well, she founded her company, Nada Debs Furniture and Design, in 2000, and since then she has gradually been developing her unique style.
J And how would you describe her style?
A I guess you could say it's a style based on her experience. She has lived in four different countries with four very different cultures. So she combines the artistic traditions of the Middle East with the pure forms of Japan.
J And how is the business doing?
A Recently, her business has been expanding. She has opened stores worldwide, from New York to Dubai to Cairo. So she's doing amazingly well.

2.2

1 A What've you been doing?
   B I've been looking after a visitor.
2 A What's she done today?
   B She's done all her marketing reports.
3 A Has she been in the office yet?
   B No, she hasn't. She's been working from home.
4 A What's the weather been like?
   B It's been really sunny.

2.3

C=Carl, L=Liza, S=Sara, K=Koichi
C OK, I think we're nearly all here. We're just waiting for Pieter and Liza. Ah, here's Liza now.
L Sorry I'm late, Carl. The traffic was terrible.
C No problem. Do you know where Pieter is?
L Pieter can't make the meeting today. There's a family problem.
C Nothing serious, I hope?
L No, I don't think so.
C OK, good. In that case, let's start. The first item on the agenda is the product launch next month. Sara, can you start us off? How are the plans for the launch going?
S Things are going well. We're ahead of schedule.
C What about costs? We were a bit worried about that last time.
S Yes, we're still over budget. But we're working on it.
C Could you be a bit more specific? What have you done exactly?
S Well, we've put together an action plan, but it's proving quite hard to make savings.
C We really need to stay within budget if we can. Would you like me to help?
S Could you? That would be great.
C Sure, no problem. Do you want to schedule a meeting and we can discuss it?
S OK, I'll send you an invite.
C Good. Right, let's move on to the next point. Liza, I think that's you … the sales conference in April. Would you like to fill us in on what's happening with that?
L Sure. Well, as you all know …
…

C Great, well thanks very much for that, Liza. So you're going to draw up a list of people to invite to talk at the sales conference.
L Yes, I'll do that this week.
C Good. OK, I think we've covered everything. Twenty minutes. That's not bad! Does anyone have anything else they want to discuss? Koichi?
K We still haven't discussed arrangements for the launch party. I was hoping to run some ideas by you all regarding dates and venues.
C OK, do you think that could wait until the next meeting? Maybe you could send us all your suggestions and we could discuss it then? OK with you?
K Sure, I'll email round the suggestions this week.
C Great. Are there any other issues that people want to raise? … No. OK, well to sum up, we've agreed that Sara and I will meet to discuss the budget for the launch, Liza is going to put together a list of potential speakers for the sales conference, and Koichi is going to email us all a list of possible dates and venues for the product launch. Can everyone have a look at it and then we can discuss it at the next meeting?
L Same time, same place?
C The next meeting will be at the same time, but we'll have to hold it in Sara's office. They're using mine for an interview. OK, well thanks very much, everyone. Have a good day!

2.4

D=Donna, B=Britta, T=Takeshi, C=Colin
D How are we doing with the autumn collection window display? Britta?
B Well, we want to do a retro theme this year – Old London. We want old buildings and streets, and a penny-farthing.
T Sorry?
D Yes, Takeshi.
T What's a penny-farthing?
B It's an old bike, with one enormous wheel and one tiny wheel.
T Oh yes, I know.
B Does that sound OK to you?
T Yeah, it's a good idea.
D Have we ordered the bikes yet? We need one for every shop.
B I don't think so.
D Britta, I'd like you to handle that.
B OK. Leave it with me.
D Colin, tell us about the colours of the display.
C Typical autumn colours, Donna. Red, orange, and yellow.
B Yes, it always works.
D I have a question about the mannequins. Last year they all looked the same. We need to change them so they look like our customers.
B Absolutely.
T Yeah.
D Someone needs to order the new ones, probably in the next couple of days. Colin?
C I'd rather not because I have a lot of other work.

D Ah … Is anyone free to organize the mannequins?
B I'm not free, I'm afraid.
D Takeshi?
T Yes, I can do that. How many do we need?
D Great, thanks. We need three people: a man, a woman and a child, and a model of a dog too. The dog will be fun.
T Yes, no problem.

2.5
D=Donna, C=Colin, T=Takeshi, B=Britta
D We also need to choose the clothes for the display. Who's going to look after that? Colin?
C Yes, I can handle that.
D We need to arrange a meeting with our main clothing suppliers, perhaps next week.
C I won't be able to do that because I'll be in New York. What about at the beginning of June?
D That's fine. Now who's responsible for the lighting of the display?
T Britta is.
D Britta, last year the lighting was all wrong. The wall behind the display was black. The window looked like a mirror – people couldn't see the clothes.
B I remember. It wasn't good.
D This year the lighting has to be better. Can you deal with that?
B Yes, no problem.
D Good. So, have we covered everything?
T Er … no. There's just one more thing.
D Ah. What's that, Takeshi?
T We need a designer to build the display, but our usual designer, Julia Romero, is on maternity leave. We need to find a new one.
C Don't worry. I know a good designer. Sven Olsen.
D Brilliant, Colin. Can I leave this with you?
C Yeah, leave it with me.
D OK. Thanks everyone. It's been a very successful meeting.

2.6
C=Claudia, M=Mila
C Hey, Mila, how's it going?
M Oh, hi, Claudia. I'm OK, thanks.
C What's up? You don't sound so good.
M No, I'm fine. I'm just a bit worried, that's all.
C Why? What's the matter?
M Well, you know I had a meeting with a financial advisor to talk about my business plan?
C Yes, the plan for the fashion website you want to set up. You mentioned it to me last time I saw you.
M Well, I met her yesterday. She wasn't very positive.
C Why? What did she say?
M Well, she says I need to carry out more research into existing fashion websites. She thinks there's a lot of competition and my concept isn't new.
C But you've already looked into the competition, haven't you?
M Yes, I have. But she pointed out that my idea is easy to copy. Another big website could easily do it and they're already established.
C Don't let that put you off. I thought your idea was great.
M Yes, I think it's good. I'm still going to do it, but she made me think.
C So are you going to meet with her again?
M Yes, next week. I need to put together a marketing plan. She wants me to break it down into markets: you know, what age group we want to attract, in which countries, all that kind of thing.
C Well, that makes sense. So it sounds like you'll be busy.
M Yes, very. I also need to sort out a few problems with our web designer. He missed his last deadline. Anyway, enough about me. How are you? Are you meeting someone?
C Yes, I'm meeting Paolo, but you know him. He always turns up half an hour late! I'm just going to read the paper for a while.
M Well, I hope he turns up soon. Anyway, I'm afraid I've got to run. Good to see you. Do you fancy meeting for a drink next week sometime?
C Sure, sounds good. Text me when you're free.
M OK, will do. See you soon.
C See you and good luck!

2.7
N=Noel, J=Jay, V=Virginia
N Hello, thanks for coming. Let's get started – we have a lot to get through. First of all, apologies from Rita. She can't make the meeting today. She's at a conference in Frankfurt. So, first on the agenda we have Jay. Jay, can you fill us in on what's happening with the new advertising campaign? How's it going?
J Pretty good. We've agreed the adverts for the newspaper campaign. We've also started work on the adverts for the radio.
V Which radio stations will the ads be on?
J Radio 6 and Jazz FM. The market research showed that these are the stations that our target market listens to most.
N I see. So what have you done exactly? Can you be a bit more specific?
J Well, we've contacted some writers who work on radio ads. I had a meeting with them last week and we discussed some ideas. They're going to get back to me in a couple of weeks with some scripts.
N OK, that sounds hopeful. Did they seem good?
J Yes, they're good. We worked with them on our last radio campaign.
N Good. Jay, do you have anything else you want to add?
J No, that's about it for now.
N OK, in that case, let's move on. What's next on the agenda? …Virginia and the TV campaign. Virginia, how's the new TV campaign going?
V Well, the TV campaign is going well. We've begun …

2.8
1 A Have we paid the staff bonuses yet?
  B Not yet, but the money is available.
  A We need to pay them soon. Can I leave this with you, Barry?
  B No problem.
2 A Who's going to look after the lighting for the photo shoot tomorrow? Mia?
  B I'd rather not because I have a doctor's appointment in the afternoon.
  A Sorry, I forgot about that.
3 A So we're going to use Travis Move to deliver our products. OK?
  B Yes, I think they're a good company.
  A Then we need to have a meeting with the sales director of Travis. Gordon, I'd like you to handle that. Tomorrow?
  B No, I'm not free, I'm afraid.
  A OK. Let's find another day.
4 A We're going to choose the BMW as the new company car next year.
  B Yes, that's fine.
  A Who's responsible for organizing the cars?
  B That's me.
  A OK, Eva. Can you talk to the car showroom?
  B Fine. Leave it with me.

3

3.1
P=Presenter, PK=Professor Sarah Kean, DB=Dr Leo Blavatnik
P I have with me two experts – Professor Kean and Doctor Blavatnik – and we're going to discuss predictions made over a hundred years ago by the American engineer John Watkins.
Professor Kean, what did you think about John Watkins' predictions?
PK They were amazingly accurate. One of his predictions was 'wireless telephone circuits will cross the world'. This sounds very similar to the internet. And Watkins made the prediction before computers and just after the invention of the telephone.
DB That's right. He also predicted 'newspapers will publish colour photographs of an event one hour later'. We can do this now with digital cameras and news websites, but in 1900 this was an extraordinary thing to predict.
P Absolutely. What other things did he write about?
PK Well, he also predicted ready-cooked meals.
P And today we buy ready-cooked meals from supermarkets.
PK Yes, that's right. Watkins believed that we would buy the meals from bakeries, which is very close.
P Indeed. So, Dr Blavatnik, are there any predictions Watkins got wrong?
DB Well, he predicted 'all fast traffic within the city will be below ground or above ground level'. I think traffic here means any kind of fast transport rather than

Scripts 141

just cars. He probably meant trains and buses as well.
P So he was partly right.
DB Yes, he was. Subway systems in big cities mean that a lot of traffic in Watkins' sense is underground. However, it is unlikely that *all* traffic will be below ground or above ground level in the future.
PK I think you're right about cities that already exist, like New York and Tokyo. I think they will have some traffic running at ground level. But for new cities, cities that we build in the future, we will probably use subway systems or overground monorails, but it *is* likely that there'll be a car-free zone in the centre of big cities.
P Good. OK. Can we look at the next prediction? 'Powerful electric light will speed up the growth of vegetables.'
DB This is another amazing prediction; artificial light *is* used in greenhouses.
P And what about the future? Will we use electricity to grow vegetables in the next hundred years?
DB No, we definitely won't. It's a waste of electricity, basically. There are some cutting edge companies that can grow vegetables in very hot areas without fresh water and that only use natural light. It's a very efficient system and in the future it might be the main way we produce fresh vegetables.
PK Yes, that makes sense. We probably won't have enough electricity to heat or light greenhouses in the future. I'm sure that the global population will grow so fast in the next hundred years we'll only use natural resources like sunlight.
DB And we will definitely use fresh water more carefully. Water will be our most precious and important resource in the next hundred years. With the right technology, it is possible that there will be enough water for everyone.
PK Some areas may actually run out of water if climate change continues. As weather patterns change, some places may not get any rain for years.

3.2

D=Dmitri, Y=Yolanda, H=Haruka
D So, Yolanda, do you think you'll ever buy a house or apartment?
Y Well, I'm living with my parents right now and I'm trying to save enough money to rent my own apartment. Most people where I live rent; property is so expensive. So I probably won't buy a house. How about you, Dmitri?
D It's the same situation in my country. Houses are too expensive. For me a house costs ten times my salary for one year. So I don't think I'll be able to afford a house until I'm in my 40s. I'm 25 now, so that's a long time to wait. But who knows, it's possible.
Y And what do you think, Haruka?
H I'm married and my partner and I are saving to buy a house. So we might have enough money in about ten years'

time. But it depends on house prices. They may go up or down. No one really knows.
Y It's the same with the economy. Some people think it will get better, others are sure it will get worse. So it's really hard to plan anything long-term.
H How about family? Do you have any plans?
Y I want to have a family. But I probably won't have more than one child. These days it's very expensive to have children. Education, clothes, food, everything costs a lot of money. How about you, Dmitri?
D I love kids, but I don't think I'll have a family. And you, Haruka?
H We'll definitely have more than one child. But I'm working now and I'm still young, so I probably won't have a baby just yet. Also I'll probably quit work when I have a family, so I need to save up first.
D Will you go back to work?
H It's unlikely. People expect you to look after your family and for the husband to have a career.
Y How long do you think your husband will work for?
H Probably till he's 65.
D I'll probably work till I'm 70.
Y I'm sure you'll be rich and famous before then. As for me, it will depend on our financial situation, but I'd like to finish work before I'm 65. So it's unlikely I'll work till I'm 70.

3.3

1 Because of the growing popularity of 3-D television, I think TV will have a bigger impact upon sport in the future. The Wimbledon tennis championship is now shown in 3-D in some countries. I think 3-D technology will be used for all sports in future. It makes watching the games a lot more exciting. I also think there will be more sporting events in Asia and Africa. In these areas, sports viewing figures are growing rapidly. Due to this, I think we'll see a lot more sportspeople coming from these countries.

2 I think the number of people living alone will rise dramatically in the next few decades. This will be a major trend. In the 15 years between 1996 and 2011, the number of people living alone globally rose from 153 million to 277 million – an increase of around 80%. In the UK, 34% of households have one person living in them. In Sweden, the figure is even higher: 47% of Swedish households now only have one person living in them. As a consequence, one of the big problems will be social isolation. People may suffer from loneliness. This may also result in a rise in property prices.

3 For me, one of the most interesting future trends is the movement of people to other countries. In the future, an increasing number of retired people

from Europe or the USA will retire in developing nations, such as in Latin America, Africa, etcetera. This growing trend is the result of economic changes. As the value of their pensions falls, older people will find that they can live more cheaply in developing nations. For the developing nations, this will lead to many social changes. It will create new jobs and bring more money into the country. Hopefully, everyone will benefit.

4 I work in publishing and the big future trend for me is the change to digital publishing. There is an increasing demand for digital content. People want to access books through digital devices, such as a Kindle or a tablet. As a result, the way we publish books is changing. I think people will always want printed books, but we'll also need to provide e-books or other digital content. Digital publishing will cause major changes to the way we work. It's an exciting development and I'm looking forward to seeing what happens over the next few years.

3.4

D=Dave, E=Elke
D Thanks for meeting with me, Elke.
E No problem, Dave. Are you enjoying your trip to Switzerland?
D Yes, I am. This is a beautiful country.
E We're pleased you're here, Dave. There are a lot of things to discuss about the merger between our two companies.
D Yeah, it's complicated. There are a lot of mergers in the insurance industry, but this one is unusual.
E Yes, I think there are some differences in business culture between Switzerland and the USA.
D Yeah, and a lot of people are worried about the future and their careers.
E Oh, absolutely.
D So the new director has asked if I can talk to you about organizing a meeting for the management teams.
E A meeting? Yes, good idea. Do you want it in Texas?
D No, in Switzerland. The team could do a two- or three-day visit to your offices here.
E OK.
D To start the visit, we should have a dinner. That way, the managers in the US can get to meet the managers in Switzerland.
E Uh-huh.
D We need to get to know each other.
E I know a great restaurant here in the mountains. It would be perfect.
D Yeah? Great.
E When shall we have the meeting?
D Soon. Perhaps we can have the dinner on August 30th? Then we can have two days of meetings afterwards. I'll speak to the team in the US and can you speak to yours? We can talk again next week on Skype to confirm.
E That sounds good to me.
D OK, Elke. Let's make some calls!

3.5

R=Reto, E=Elke, D=Dave, T=Tony, C=Cheryl, A=Anna

1   R   Hello?
    E   Reto, it's Elke.
    R   Hi, Elke. What's up?
    E   We're trying to arrange a meeting with the US managers and the Swiss managers, here in Switzerland. Are you free on August 30th for a dinner?
    R   The 30th? Hmm … I'm busy then because I'm in Geneva all day. I can make the 31st though.
    E   OK, thanks. I can't confirm the date now because I need to speak to the rest of the team. I'll get back to you.
    R   No problem. I understand.
2   T   Hello.
    D   Tony, have you got a moment?
    T   Sure, Dave. What is it?
    D   We're arranging a meeting between our team and the Swiss team.
    T   That's a good idea.
    D   It'll be two days. And we want to have a dinner to start the meeting.
    T   A dinner. Fine. When were you thinking of?
    D   Is August 30th convenient for you?
    T   August 30th? Yeah, that should be fine. I just need to check with my PA. I'll get back to you tomorrow, OK?
    D   Great. Thanks, Tony.
3   C   Cheryl Goldblatt.
    D   Cheryl, it's Dave.
    C   Hi, Dave. I read your email about the meeting and the dinner.
    D   Great. Are you free?
    C   I'm afraid that August is no good for me because I'm away on vacation.
    D   I'm sorry, I forgot.
    C   Why don't we meet in September? Er … Is September 4th good for you?
    D   September 4th? Hmm. I need to check that with Elke in Zurich.
    C   September is best for me.
    D   I'll try and change the date. As soon as I know, I'll let you know. OK?
    C   OK.
4   A   Hello.
    E   Hello, Anna?
    A   Elke! Hi.
    E   I'm calling about the meeting.
    A   Yes, I read your email.
    E   Reto suggested August 31st for the dinner. Does that sound OK to you?
    A   I can't make August 31st. It's my daughter's wedding.
    E   How about the following week? Is September 3rd good for you?
    A   That suits me fine.
    E   Great. Let's pencil in September 3rd.
    A   OK, I'll wait for you to confirm that.
    E   Perfect. Thanks, Anna.

3.6

1   A   Are you free tomorrow lunchtime for a chat about our new projects?
    B   That should be fine.
2   A   Why don't we have the sales conference on 21st May?
    B   I need to check that with my team. As soon as I know, I'll let you know.
3   A   Let's all go out for a meal to celebrate the new contract. Does next Friday sound good to you?
    B   I'm not sure. Let's pencil in Friday for now.
4   A   Harry, we need to arrange a meeting with our new clients. Er … Is Thursday 19th convenient for you?
    B   The 19th? Sorry, I'm busy then.
5   A   Now, the visit to the warehouse. I can make Tuesday 3rd. Jim?
    B   I'm afraid that the 3rd is no good for me.
6   A   I'm trying to arrange flights to London for the sales team. Is nine o'clock on Friday night good for you?
    B   Nine o'clock on Friday … That suits me fine.

4

4.1

The National Gallery in London, the Musée du Louvre in Paris, and the Metropolitan Museum of Art in New York are the three most popular art museums in the world. They exhibit some of the most famous and popular paintings as well as many rare and beautiful sculptures and objects.

They all have long names, so I'm going to call them the National, the Louvre, and the Met.

The National is the oldest museum. It opened in 1753 and is just a little older than the Louvre which opened in 1793. The Met is the most recent of the three. Even so, it has been an art museum since 1870.

The Met is the largest of the three. It's 190,000 square metres, more than twice the size of the second largest museum, the Louvre, which is only 60,000 square metres. The Met has a very wide-ranging collection including North American, Asian, and European art. It also has a huge collection of 13,000 works of modern art. However, the Met has a relatively small collection of European paintings, only 1,700 works, compared to the Louvre which has an amazing 7,500 works including some of the most famous paintings in the world. The most famous painting of all is the *Mona Lisa* by Leonardo da Vinci. The National has 2,300 paintings on display including another very famous work, Van Gogh's *Sunflowers*.

It's paintings like the *Mona Lisa* that attract a lot more people to the Louvre than either the Met or the National. A staggering 8.8 million people visited the museum last year, that's 2.8 million more than the Met, and 3.6 million more than the National. The Louvre has better transport connections and is close to some of Paris' favourite tourist attractions, which helps to keep a flow of tourists and visitors coming through its doors. The Louvre is not free: the standard adult charge is €11, but it's less expensive than the Met which charges $25. The National is the only free museum, though it does charge for special exhibitions. This means that the Louvre has a very substantial turnover and this allows it to invest in more works of art and to maintain and improve the museum.

The National recently held an exhibition of Leonardo da Vinci's works. The exhibition was very popular and more than 330,000 people came. But this wasn't as many as the Met's fashion exhibition by Alexander McQueen. Surprisingly, this was more popular than the National or the Louvre's Rembrandt show, which was the least popular of the three. It attracted just 225,000 visitors. A sign of the times, perhaps?

4.2

1   The National is the oldest museum.
2   It opened in 1753 and is just a little older than the Louvre.
3   The Louvre is less expensive than the Met, which charges $25.
4   The most famous painting of all is the *Mona Lisa* by Leonardo da Vinci.
5   The Louvre has better transport connections.
6   But this wasn't as many as the Met's fashion exhibition by Alexander McQueen.
7   Surprisingly, this was more popular than the Louvre's Rembrandt show.
8   The Louvre's Rembrandt show was the least popular of the three.

4.3

interesting
dirty
educational
relaxing
exciting
dangerous
beautiful
independent
expensive
international
enjoyable
professional

4.4

1   This graph shows our visitor numbers in the past five years. The horizontal axis shows the year and the vertical axis indicates visitor numbers. As you can see from the way the line rises, visitor numbers have risen in recent years. I'd now like to look at this in more detail …
2   On the next screen you can see two pie charts. These pie charts represent the main nationalities of our visitors five years ago compared to today. Look carefully at the two charts … Sorry … You can't see? My apologies, I'll move to the left. Is that better? … If you look at the blue segment, you can see the percentage of visitors from Europe. It clearly shows how this figure has fallen dramatically. The purple segment represents visitors from Asia, the yellow segment is Latin America, the green is the Middle East, and the red is visitors from North America. I'll just give you a moment to compare the two charts …
3   Can you all see the screen? Good. Can you read everything OK? No? The

writing is quite small I'm afraid – there was a lot to include. I'd better just take you through it. At the bottom of the screen, you can see a table. This describes our pricing structure. As you can see, we charge $25 dollars for an adult, $15 dollars for a student, and $10 for a child or senior citizen. We also offer a family-pass for two adults and two children for $40 …

4.5

M=Mona, B=Bradley, C=Clive, S=Sumiko

M We're ready to start, Bradley.
B Thanks, Mona. Right, today we're putting together our new Kenya Safari. Clive, would you like to start? How long should the tour be?
C From a financial point of view, it needs to be two weeks. People won't pay a lot of money for a seven-day tour.
M Yes, that's a good point, Clive. I agree.
B Good, a fortnight. Now, what do you think about the dates for the tour? Mona?
M I think we should run the tour all year. There are always people who want to go on holiday to Kenya.
B Sumiko?
S I'm afraid I completely disagree. We can't do the tour from April to June because it rains a lot then.
B Uh-huh.
S Personally, I think January and February are the best months. The weather is perfect then.
M I take your point, but we need to do at least four tours every year.
C Er … In my opinion, we should do one tour in January, one in February, one in October, and one in November. They're all nice times to visit Kenya. That's four tours a year.
B Yes. I see what you mean. Right, so four tours every year: one in January, February, …
C October and November.
B OK. That's clear. Now the cost. What's your opinion of that, Mona?
M $6,000 US per person. We could do a great tour at that price.
S $6,000? I'm sorry, but I don't agree. Last year, our Botswana tour was $6,000. We cancelled it because no one signed up for it.
M Yes, but remember, we generally only make a 10% profit.
C Our most successful tours are usually $4,500.
B Can we do Kenya for $4,500?
C I'll check the figures.
B Great. Thanks, Clive. I'll pencil in $4,500 for now. OK?

4.6

B=Bradley, S=Sumiko, C=Clive, M=Mona

B OK, let's look at the route for the Kenya Safari. One USP of our trip is that it includes visits to World Heritage Sites. We can start in Mombasa and also visit the island of Lamu. Lamu is one World Heritage Site. What are your views?

S I'm not sure about that. Lamu is a beautiful place for diving, but that's not really a safari holiday.
C Hmm, I can see where you're coming from, Sumiko. Let's think about this. You also need to fly from Mombasa to Nairobi. That's expensive.
M Let's not include Lamu and Mombasa. Let's just include Nairobi.
B I agree with that. So we start in Nairobi. What then?
C We go directly to Mount Kenya.
B And Mount Kenya is a World Heritage Site?
C That's right.
B OK.
C I think we should arrange a bus from Nairobi to Mount Kenya.
M I'm not sure about that. This is an adventure holiday. Our customers don't want a bus. They want to travel by jeep.
B I agree with that provided that the jeeps are new ones. Carry on, Clive.
C OK, well … Next our tourists go to the Lake Nakuru National Park. The park will be the second World Heritage Site. They spend two days there and then they go to the Great Rift Valley.
S Definitely. There are zebras, hippos, and flamingos in the Great Rift Valley. It's beautiful.
C Then the tourists go to the Masai Mara Game Reserve. They sleep in tents and they might see lions, giraffes, and crocodiles.
S May I make a suggestion? You can travel in a hot-air balloon over the Masai Mara.
B You're right. Thanks for raising this, Sumiko. The hot-air balloon is a trip of a lifetime, but it's expensive. In my view, the balloon ride should be an extra thing. People pay more money if they want to do it.
M I completely agree, Bradley.
S After the Masai Mara Game Reserve?
C They return to Nairobi for a day or two in the city.
B Excellent. It sounds like a very nice trip.

4.7

C=Clive, S=Sumiko, M=Mona

C Bradley is thinking of organizing a new package of trips for people over 55. What do you think about that, Sumiko?
S From a marketing point of view, it's a good idea. There are particular websites where we can advertise the trips.
M I see where Bradley is coming from, but I don't think it's a good idea. Our customers enjoy travelling with people of all ages: young and old.
C Yes, I completely agree. Our customer feedback tells us that they like the mix of people.
S I don't know. Personally, I think we should do some research on the idea. Maybe there's a new market of older travellers out there for us.
C Yes, that's a good point. I agree. Are you able to do the research?
S Sure, leave it with me.

4.8

1 A Would you like me to help you?
    B Thanks! That would be great!
2 A Do you fancy watching a movie?
    B No … sorry. I'm going to bed. I was up at six this morning …
3 A Have you heard? Mark's moving to Japan.
    B Really? But he's just bought a house in London!
4 A Do you mind if I speak to you a minute?
    B I'm a bit busy right now. Another time.
5 A I'm sorry, Juan. I'm not going to be able to meet you for dinner tonight.
    B Oh, really. That's a shame. I was looking forward to it.
6 A Have you heard? The company is opening a new office in Rome. They're looking for people to move there.
    B Are they? I'd love to work in Italy. Can you send me the details?

4.9

1 A I think we should give everyone a 10% pay rise this year. What do you think, Olga?
    B A 10% pay rise? I'm sorry, but I don't agree. That's too much money.
2 A Personally, I think we need to stop advertising in newspapers and move all our advertising onto the internet. What's your view, Tony?
    B I see what you mean. Online advertising is the best way of reaching new customers.
3 A Some people are saying we should close our factory in Germany. What's your opinion of that, Gloria?
    B I'm afraid I completely disagree. The German factory produces very high-quality products. We shouldn't close it.
4 A From a financial point of view, the company can save money if we replace our cleaners with an outside cleaning company. Satoko?
    B In my view, that's not a good idea. There are security problems with an outside cleaning company. I prefer the cleaning staff to work directly for us.
5 A We are doing a lot of business in the Middle East and we need a manager who is just working in that region. Er … What do you think, Wulfram?
    B Yes, that's a good point. I agree. I know a perfect manager for the Middle East: Nasrin in the Jordan office. She would be perfect.
6 A I think we should speak to a management consultant. The company needs some new ideas. Andrew?
    B Yes, I can see where you're coming from. Which are the best management consultants to contact?

5

5.1

1. A Can you tell me about the sort of clothes you need to wear for your job, Ken? Are there any particular clothes you have to wear?
   B Well, when we're at sea we usually have to wear special waterproof gear. It's often very cold and wet, and windy, so we need to keep as warm and dry as possible. We also have to wear gloves to protect our hands from ropes and sharp objects. When we're not actually working, we don't have to wear our waterproofs. We normally just wear jeans and a T-shirt.

2. A So, Mike, what special sorts of clothes do you have to wear for your sport?
   B It's a dangerous game so we need to wear protective clothing. We must wear helmets to protect our heads. We also have lots of padding on our shoulders and knees.
   A It's a very physical sport.
   B That's right. It's very competitive. The rest of the uniform has to be tight so the other team can't get hold of you so easily.

3. A I imagine your job can be very dangerous. Is clothing important, Jorge?
   B Yes, safety is the most important thing. When we change the tyres and refuel the car during pit stops, we have to work really quickly, and because there's always the risk of fire we must wear protective clothing.
   A Do you need to wear gloves?
   B Yes, gloves are really important in case any petrol spills when we refill the cars.

4. A Is your sport very different from American football, Ben?
   B It is. A lot of the rules are different. And the clothes too. In our sport, we're not allowed to wear a plastic helmet, for example, but we are allowed to wear some padding.
   A Are you allowed to wear gloves?
   B No, we can't wear gloves. They make it easier to handle the ball, but it's against the rules.

5. A Keira, I guess temperature is the most dangerous aspect of your job?
   B Indeed. In the winter, the temperature drops to minus 40. So we mustn't leave the building without warm clothing and protection for our faces and hands. We need to check the equipment outside every day, so good gloves and boots are really important.

6. A Your uniform is one of the most important parts of your job. Is that right, Yuko?
   B That's' right. We must look smart, but we also have to prepare and serve meals. So our uniform needs to look good but also be practical. When we're outside the aircraft, we have to wear the complete uniform including hats and gloves.
   A Can you take your hats off?
   B Yes, during the flight, we can take our hats and gloves off. We can also change into flat shoes if we want.

5.2

1. This warm colour is lucky in China, so people wear it on New Year's Day. Some people believe it's unlucky to write a person's name in this colour. In the UK, letter boxes and buses are painted this colour. Flowers that are this colour are usually pollinated by birds or the wind because it's invisible to bees. The colour has two very different meanings in sport. In football, if the referee shows a player a card this colour, the player is disqualified from the game and is sent off the pitch. On the other hand, in a boxing match, judges are more likely to give a player high points if the boxer is wearing clothes this colour.

2. This is the national colour of Ireland, and people wear it on St Patrick's Day. It also represents eco-friendly products and companies. It's considered to be the most relaxing colour for a room, and can improve your mood if you're feeling miserable, or dissatisfied with your life. It's one of the rarest and most unusual colours for diamonds. It's the colour of Islam.

3. This cool colour is the most popular colour. In the US, most mailboxes are painted this shade. A study found that if bars and restaurants use this colour lighting at night, it makes their customers more lively and they spend more money. It's the colour of the sky. If you are feeling this colour, it means you are feeling sad and unhappy.

4. This is possibly the happiest colour. It's often worn by people who are optimistic, if slightly irresponsible. In China, emperors in the Ming and Qing dynasties wore clothes that were this colour. It's impossible not to see this colour from a distance, so it's used for school buses and taxi cabs in the USA. It's also the most common colour for pencils in America.

5. This is the colour of the hidden, the unknown, and the mysterious. The ancient Egyptians believed that cats this colour had special powers. The colour also represents sophistication and power, for example, tuxedos, limousines, and judge's robes. We also use the colour with certain words to give a negative meaning, for example, 'list', and 'Monday'. When we use the colour with the word 'market', it means the illegal trade of goods or money.

5.3

1. R=Receptionist, P=Paolo
   R Good morning, Fashion World. How can I help you?
   P Good morning. Can you put me through to Simone Parker in the Public Relations Department, please?
   R Who's calling, please?
   P My name's Paolo Marconi.
   R Thank you. Please hold the line, … I'm sorry, Mr Marconi. I'm afraid she's on another call. Can I take a message?
   P Yes, could you tell her I called? It's about our meeting next Tuesday. I'd like to reschedule it to another date.
   R OK, I'll pass on your message. Does Simone have your number?
   P Yes, but let me give you my mobile number, just in case.
   R OK, let me just get a pen … OK, go ahead.
   P OK. So the number's oh seven six oh one three nine six two.
   R OK, let me just repeat that back to you. Oh seven six oh one three nine six two.
   P Yes, that's right.
   R Fine, I'll pass that all on to Simone.
   P Many thanks. Bye.

2. P=Paolo, S=Simone
   P Hello.
   S Hi, Paolo! It's Simone. I'm just returning your call. Sorry I missed you earlier.
   P Hi, Simone! No problem. Thanks for getting back to me. How are things? Still busy?
   S Really busy! You know how it is. And you?
   P The same unfortunately. That's why I was calling. I'm afraid some work has come up, so I won't be able to make the meeting next Tuesday. I was wondering if you'd mind if we rescheduled it to a later date? Maybe the following week?
   S Sure, no problem. How about–?
   P I'm sorry, I didn't catch that. Did you say Wednesday?
   S No, Thurs–.
   P Sorry. Your phone's cutting out, Simone. I didn't catch that either.
   S Sorry, Paolo. I'm on a train. It keeps going through tunnels. Can I give you a call later? I'll be back at the office in an hour.
   P Sure, no problem. Talk to you later.
   S Thanks. Bye.
   P Bye.

5.4

J=Jessica, I=Ian
J Hi, everyone. Last week, lots of people emailed me about my article on Hong Kong. One was Ian Hill. He's going on a trip to Hong Kong for five weeks. Ian, are you there?
I Yes, I am. Hi, Jessica.
J Hi, Ian. So how can I help you?
I Well, I have some questions about Hong Kong.
J OK. Fire away.
I First of all, how do I get around?
J I would just use the underground for everything. In Hong Kong, public

Scripts 145

transport is fast, modern, clean, and cheap.
I I'd rather not go on the underground because I don't like being underground in tunnels.
J Don't worry. Lots of people use the buses. Taxis are also very cheap in Hong Kong and you don't need to tip the drivers.
I Great. Thanks for the advice. Now, what about a fun excursion?
J Do you know that you can hire a helicopter and do a 15-minute trip over Hong Kong? It costs about $850.
I That's an interesting idea, but it's quite expensive.
J True, but if you go with an important customer, they'll really remember it.
I Yeah. I like the sound of that.
J Any more questions?
I What about language?
J In big companies, everyone speaks English. However, the main language of Hong Kong is Cantonese. Why don't you do a short course before you go? Then you can learn some basic phrases, like 'I'm lost'!
I Yes, that sounds like a good idea. I'll look for a language school. What about free-time activities?
J There are some amazing shops in the IMC mall by the harbour.
I I'm not keen on shopping, actually. I really want to find a quiet place to relax, to escape the city.
J One thing you could do is visit Victoria Park. It's a lovely green space in the centre of the city.
I Good idea. I like the sound of that. Thanks for your suggestions, Jessica.
J Any time, Ian. OK, that's all on our podcast today.

5.5

1 A One thing you should be careful about is travelling on the underground – there are lots of pickpockets!
   B Oh, right. Thanks for the tip.
2 A How about going to the Olympic Swimming Pool? It also has a gym.
   B That sounds like a good idea.
3 A Let's see. I'm not keen on spicy food.
   B Then you'd better not have the red curry – it's incredibly hot!
4 A If you like history, you should definitely go to the City Museum. There's a fascinating Roman exhibition there at the moment.
   B That's a good idea.
5 A Have you considered getting a coach? You can get there in about five hours.
   B I think I'd rather get the train than the coach. I don't like buses.
6 A Personally, I'd avoid the area round the park because it's very touristy.
   B Oh, I don't like the sound of that.

5.6

R=Receptionist, B=Barbara, V=Victor
R Good afternoon, Blue Star Electronics. How may I help you?
B Good afternoon. My name's Barbara Jones. Can you put me through to Manuel Herrera in the Sales Department, please?
R Certainly, Ms Jones. Hold the line, please. I'll just put you through …
V Hello, Victor Martinez speaking.
B Oh, hello. I'm sorry. The receptionist has put me through to the wrong number. I was calling Manuel Herrera.
V That's OK. Manuel's out of the office at the moment so his call has come through to me. I'm his assistant, Victor.
B Oh, hi, Victor. My name's Barbara Jones. Do you know when Manuel will be back at his desk?
V He's going to be in a meeting all afternoon, I'm afraid. Can I take a message?
B Sure. Could you tell him Barbara called and ask him to call me back later today or tomorrow? I'll be free until about 6.30 today. It's about the sales trip next week. I just wanted to check a couple of things with him.
V OK, I'll tell him. Does he have your number?
B I'm not sure he has my mobile number. I'm out of the office today, so he can reach me on that. Can I give it to you?
V Sure. Please go ahead.
B OK, so it's 07 … 8972.
V I'm sorry, Barbara. I didn't catch that. Your phone's cutting out. Could you say it again?
B Sure, it's 0731 8972. Did you get it that time?
V Yes, I think so. Let me just check. 0731 8972. Right?
B Yes, that's right …
V OK, good. The line's quite bad again. Anyway, I'll pass on your message and ask Manuel to call you.
B OK, thanks Victor. Nice talking to you.
V You too. Bye.
B Bye.

6

6.1

The long walk
When she was 16, Lila got up at 3 a.m. every day to collect water from a river 5 kilometres' walk away, just like Lila's mother and the other women in the village had done when Lila was younger. While they were walking to the river, many women and girls risked hurting themselves carrying heavy buckets or being bitten by snakes. One day, Lila was walking home when she fell over. She hurt her leg and could only walk slowly back to school. Lessons had already started by the time she got back to the village. When the teacher asked her why she was late, she explained that she had fallen over because she was so tired. She had already missed several classes the week before, so she was behind with her homework and her teacher was not happy.

Later that year, Lila heard about an organization that helped villages like Lila's to build fresh water wells. After she had found out more about the organization and talked to her mother, she applied for help to make a new well in the village.
The following year volunteers arrived and built a new well. By the end of the year, Lila and her family were drinking clean, safe water from a well just a short walk from her home.

6.2

improvement
development
management
agreement
encouragement
payment
investment
production
solution
reduction
definition
exploration
explanation
satisfaction
performance
appearance
disappearance
resistance
assistance
guidance
removal
refusal
denial
survival

6.3

1 Good morning, everyone, and thank you for coming. My name is Josh Ratner. I work here at MIT in the Engineering Department. My research concerns developing new technologies for use in water purification, that is, removing harmful bacteria from drinking water. Today, I'm going to talk to you about a very simple idea, but one which could save millions of lives. It could even change your life. I've divided my talk into three sections: the problem of water purification, the research we've carried out to find a solution, and what we need to do to put this into practice.
2 Let's begin with identifying the problem. Water sanitation is probably the greatest challenge facing the world today … So, we've looked at the problem of water purification and the terrible consequences it has for millions of people. Now let's move on to the second section. This is the science bit! Our researchers have discovered that … We've looked at the problem and the solution, my next point deals with how we put this into practice. For our plan to work we need to involve local people and to change the way they access and use water. It's about education and training. Let me explain …
3 So to sum up: we know the problem, we think we have the solution, the important thing now is to educate and

to train everyone involved, from the people in government to the families in poor villages. I'd like to leave you with one last point to think about: what can *you* do to help in this programme? Would you like to get involved? If you would, then please feel free to email me. My email address is on the handout … That brings me to the end of my talk. Thank you for listening. Does anyone have any questions?

6.4
T=Tariq, I=Ivana
1 T Can you help me please, Ivana?
 I Sure, Tariq. What's the problem?
 T The internet isn't working.
 I Yes, sorry, the internet's down at the moment.
 T How long has it been like that?
 I Only about half an hour. There's a problem with our servers.
 T Right. That must be the problem. If the servers aren't working, it's impossible to connect to the internet.
 I Don't worry. They should fix it soon.
2 I Is everything OK, Tariq?
 T Er … I have just one problem. I want to play a video in my presentation, but the speakers aren't working properly.
 I Really?
 T Yeah, there's a fault with the sound. Listen, you can't hear anything.
 I Oh, yes.
 T Have you noticed it before?
 I No, I haven't. It could be the speakers. Have you tried using the other ones?
 T No, I haven't.
 I What we need to do is change this cable and connect the new speakers.
 T OK.
 I There. Check it.
 T Great, that's fixed it!
3 T Oh!
 I What's wrong, Tariq?
 T My computer's crashed and my presentation is starting in ten minutes.
 I What happened?
 T There was a message about the antivirus and then the screen went black.
 I Oh, right, don't worry.
 T What do you think caused it?
 I It looks like a problem with an automatic update. I had the same problem on my PC. Why don't we try restarting your computer?
 T Yes, that might fix the problem. Fingers crossed!
4 I So, is everything OK now? Are you ready for your presentation?
 T Er … Something's wrong with the mouse. It keeps stopping. I need it to change the slides for my presentation. I'm not sure what the problem is. It may be the battery.
 I It can't be the battery because I put a new one in this morning.
 T So what we need to do is change the mouse.
 I I don't have a new one.
 T Oh.
 I One solution is to use the touch pad on your laptop.
 T But I want to walk around while I give the presentation.
 I Have you tried using the remote control? There's one here. You can use it to move forward and backwards through the slides.
 T A remote control? Perfect! I didn't see it. Thanks, Ivana. Now I'm ready.
 I And it looks like your audience is arriving. Just in time!

6.5
1 A I'm worried about my jeep. It keeps making a strange noise when I drive over 70 kilometres per hour.
 B Have you noticed it before?
 A No, I haven't.
 B What you need to do is take it to the garage as soon as possible.
2 A Something's wrong with the coffee machine. It isn't giving any money back.
 B How long has it been like that?
 A It started yesterday.
 B Why don't we put a notice on it saying 'Exact money only – no change given'?
 A Yes, that's a good idea.
3 A Oh, no!
 B What's wrong?
 A I want to buy some plane tickets but there's a problem with the website. I can't pay with my credit card.
 B Have you tried using a different one?
 A Yes, I have. It won't accept any of my cards.
 B Maybe there's a problem with the site. Perhaps their payment processing isn't working at the moment. Wait half an hour and then try again.
4 A I heard a noise. What happened?
 B My mobile was recharging and it suddenly exploded!
 A Oh, yeah. I see the smoke. What do you think caused it?
 B I'm not sure. Can you look at it?
 A Hmmm … it looks like a problem with the charger. Let's take it back to the shop.

7

7.1
R=Reporter, M=Matt, G=Grace
R Matt and Grace. How are you?
M&G Fine, thanks.
R Good. So, Matt, can we start with you?
M Sure.
R Do you think you're a good employee?
M I hope so.
R Well, let's try a few questions to check how good you are.
M Fine.
R OK. First, is this statement true for you? 'If my boss asks me to work at the weekend, I always say "Yes".'
M Mmm. Tricky question. My boss doesn't usually ask me. But if he does, I do say 'Yes'. If it's a tight deadline, for example. And if I do any extra work, I always get a day off later on.
R How about you, Grace?
G Weekends are really important for me, so I usually say 'No'.
R OK. Let's stay with you, Grace, for the next one. 'If it's one of my team's birthdays, I buy them a birthday card.'
G Oh, definitely. I think it's really important to look after your team and remembering someone's birthday is a nice way to show you care.
M Oh, dear. I feel terrible.
R I'm guessing you don't do birthday cards, Matt.
M I think it's a really good idea, but I'm really bad at remembering things like that. I know it's bad, but …
R OK, moving swiftly on. 'If I'm behind schedule, I don't panic.' Grace?
G Not me, I'm afraid. Keeping to schedules is a real problem for me. And I do tend to get quite stressed when I'm behind.
R I'm guessing you're pretty organized, Matt.
M Not bad. I don't usually panic because we have regular update meetings, so we know if we're falling behind and can do something about it.
R Sounds good. How about this one? 'If another employee has performance issues, I try to help them.' Grace?
G I have catch-up meetings with individuals on my team so I have a chance to talk about anything that they're struggling with. I usually ask them what they think first and get them to solve their own problems, but I do my best to help.
M Me, too. We work in a tough business and everyone is under pressure, so I make sure everyone gets the support they need.
R Great. You're both doing very well. Just two more questions to go. 'If someone does a great job, I tell them.'
G Absolutely.
M Yes, I do. And if I've got someone really good, I like to push them a bit harder.
R OK. And finally, 'If there's a tough decision to make, I don't avoid responsibility.' That sounds like you, Matt.
M That's true. I don't spend much time worrying. If it's got to be done, I don't hesitate.
G Mmm. I don't avoid responsibility either. But if there's a problem, I usually talk to the whole team first. Then I make a decision.
R Very good. Well, thank you both. Would you like to know who the winner is?

Scripts 147

7.2

1 R=Reporter, M=Matt
R So, Matt, what are the chances that you'll be promoted in the next year?
M Pretty good, I think.
R And what will you do if you are promoted.
M If I get promotion, I'll work really hard. The next level of my job is really tough. There's no room to make mistakes.
R And what about the opportunity to work abroad? Is that likely?
M It isn't very likely, to be honest. But if my company wanted me to work abroad, I'd say 'Yes'. I'd love to work in one of our overseas branches and learn more about the business.
R Do you have a family?
M No, so it's an easy decision. If I had a family, it would be much more complicated. Kids' school, and so on.
R Do you think you'll stay with your present job?
M Yes, I think so. If I don't change my job, I'll probably do some training while I have the chance. The technology in this business is developing so quickly I need to keep up.

2 R=Reporter, G=Grace
R Can you tell us a bit about your present job?
G I'm the Assistant Design Manager. I've been in the same job for five years, so I'm ready for a change.
R Do you think you'll change jobs or companies?
G No, I don't think so. But I've worked ever since I left college, so I'd like to take some time off.
R Have you thought about taking a gap year?
G I have. I really like the idea of doing something completely different. But if I take a gap year, I'll really need to save some money first. Not having a salary for a year isn't easy.
R I know you said it was unlikely, but if you changed jobs, what would you do?
G If I changed jobs? I'm not sure. I really like designing, so I'd probably do the same sort of job somewhere else.
R With another company?
G I think I'm pretty lucky with the company I'm with now. If I got a job with another company, it would have to be good.

7.3

A Hello, Southland Bank. How can I help you?
B Hello, I'd like to set up a standing order to pay my rent each month.
A Certainly, sir. Can I take your account details?
B Of course. The sort code of my account is 31-07-78. My account number is 61757275.
A Thank you. Let me just bring up your details. OK, Mr Johnson. So you'd like to set up a standing order. Can you tell me the amount you want to pay and when you want the money to leave your account each month?
B Yes, I'd like to transfer £800 on the first day of each month.
A OK, so that's £800 to leave your account on the first day of every month. And which account would you like to transfer the money to?
B To my landlord. Let me give you his account details. His name is …
A OK, Mr Johnson, your standing order is set up. The first payment will be on the first of next month. Is there anything else I can help you with today?
B Yes, can I check the balance on my account?
A OK, let me just look at your balance. You currently have £2,407 in your account.
B £2,407! I thought I had more than that. Can you check something? When did I last withdraw money from my account?
A Let me see. You withdrew £80 on 18th May from an ATM in Cambridge. That was the last withdrawal. I can see that you also had a bill for £854 for your credit card. That money was debited from your account on 17th May.
B I see. That explains it. I'd forgotten about my credit card bill.
A Yes, do you pay your credit card bill by direct debit?
B Yes, that's right. The credit card company debits my account automatically on the 17th of each month. I've just paid for a holiday by credit card and I'd forgotten that my bill was due.
A OK, well that explains it.
B I deposited £500 in my account yesterday. Is that money in my account yet?
A No, not yet. I can see a deposit was made yesterday, but it will take three more days before the money is credited to your account. Is there anything else I can help you with today?
B No, that's it, thanks. Thanks very much for your help.
A You're welcome. Have a nice day.

7.4

M=Martina, G=Georgios
1 M OK, Georgios, let's get down to business.
G Good idea. So, shall we start by discussing the first aid training package? What's the most important thing for you?
M Well, we already have some people with first aid training.
G Uh-huh.
M But we need some first aid courses for beginners. We also need refresher courses, where people return every year to improve their skills. So we'd like you to provide both beginner and refresher courses for our staff.
G We can agree to that. What I propose is a package of a beginner course plus refresher courses for more experienced people.
M That would be fine for us.
2 G So these are the courses that we offer. You can see all the dates and the prices here.
M Yes, I see.
G Tell me, Martina. What's your priority here?
M It's essential that our factories follow the law. We want to have all the necessary health and safety training, equipment, and notices.
G Really? What are your main concerns?
M The factories. We had two small accidents last month. We do not want accidents at work. We need our factories to be safe.
G I see. We can help there. In addition to our courses, we can provide a complete safety check of workplaces and factories. How does that sound to you?
M That would be great, Georgios. Can you also arrange a government inspection of the factory?
G I'm sorry, but that's not possible. We don't work directly with the government.
M OK, I'll organize that.
3 G Now, let's look at dates.
M We need courses for about a hundred employees. Can you complete the training in the next two months?
G Two months? I'm afraid that wouldn't be possible. We would need about three months, I think.
M OK. Three months. In terms of location, I think we can run the courses at our factories.
G Yes, you have all the facilities available.
M In return, would you consider a further discount?
G Absolutely, we can look at a full discount of 15%.
M Well, that's great news.
G Are you happy with everything?
M I am. It's a deal!

7.5

1 A I have to go to the bank tomorrow. Can you do my morning shift and I'll do your afternoon one?
B OK. In return, can we change our shifts this weekend so you work on Saturday and I work on Sunday?
2 A We can deliver 500 chairs to your furniture shop by the end of next month.
B It's a deal!
3 A We would like you to start construction of the research centre on 1st May and to finish the work by September next year.
B I'm afraid that such a short timetable wouldn't be possible. We'll need 24 months to complete the work.
4 A What we propose is a temporary contract of three months, followed by a possible permanent contract.
B That would be fine for us.

5 A We cannot do this project unless we get more financial help from your company.
   B I understand that and I agree. We can offer you a further $60,000.
6 A We want you to provide IT training in English, French, and German.
   B I'm sorry, but that's not possible. Our trainers only speak English.

7.6

A Hello, Southland Bank. How can I help you?
B Hello, I'd like to transfer some money from my account.
A Certainly, madam. Can I take your account details? Can I have the sort code for your account?
B Yes, the sort code is 25-04-43.
A And the account number, please?
B My account number is 9723678.
A Thank you. Let me just bring up your details. OK, Ms McDonnell. So you'd like to make a transfer. Can you tell me the amount you want to transfer?
B Yes, I'd like to transfer £500.
A OK, let me just check your balance. Hold on a moment, please … I'm sorry, Ms McDonnell. I'm afraid your account is currently overdrawn.
B What? Overdrawn! By how much?
A You're currently overdrawn by £105.65.
B Really? Can you check if my salary has been deposited in my account yet?
A Let me see. The last deposit in your account was on 16th March. So last month. Were you expecting a payment?
B Yes, my salary is usually paid in on the 16th of each month.
A Well, today's the 16th. It doesn't seem to have been paid. Perhaps you should contact your employer.
B Yes, I will. So what money has left my account recently?
A Well, I can see that you withdrew £150 from an ATM on 13th April. Also you have a standing order. £800 was transferred from your account yesterday.
B Yes, that's my rent. So is there a charge for being overdrawn?
A I'm afraid there is. Let me just check your account details …

7.7

1 A We've arrived very early for our flight. Is it possible to fly on an earlier plane?
   B I'm sorry, but that's not possible. All our flights are fully booked today.
2 A Would you be happy to start work with our company next Monday? 11th May?
   B Yes, that would be fine for me. I'm looking forward to working with you.
3 A Can you complete the heating installation before October?
   B No problem. The price is £3,000. Are you happy with that?
   A Yes, I am.
4 A We want the workers to have a shorter lunch break, but then we'll close the factory at midday on Friday.
   B So we work the same number of hours, but we don't work on Friday afternoons? OK. We can agree to that.
5 A If we order 400 uniforms from you, can you arrange a 5% discount?
   B I'm afraid that wouldn't be possible because these uniforms are already at our lowest possible price.

8

8.1

I=Interviewer, C=Chocolate maker
I Where was chocolate first produced?
C Chocolate was first produced in Central America and Mexico. The cacao tree was cultivated by the Olmecs, an early civilization which existed over 3,000 years ago. Then the Mayans, another civilization in Central America, found a way to use the cacao beans to make chocolate. But it wasn't made into the chocolate that we know now. For Mayans it was a drink rather than a food.
I Mm. How about Europe?
C Europeans knew nothing about chocolate until the 16th century when it was introduced by the Spanish: by the Spanish general, Hernán Cortés. At that time, chocolate was quite a bitter tasting, frothy kind of drink. Chocolate was exported to Europe for the first time at the end of the 16th century from Mexico to Spain. It was only at this point that sugar was added and chocolate became more like the hot chocolate drink we know today. The trend spread across Europe and chocolate became popular with royalty and the rich. It was still very expensive and it took another 200 years before it became generally affordable. It's also interesting to note that chocolate only became a solid food at the end of the 17th century when Doret, a French maker, made the first solid bar of chocolate.
I How about these days? How popular is chocolate?
C In terms of the present consumer trends, chocolate is currently an $83-billion-a-year business. Nearly half of all the chocolate consumed globally is eaten by Europeans. The average European consumer eats around 11 kilograms of chocolate a year. Chocolate is generally not as popular in the Asian markets. For example, in India only 165 grams of chocolate is consumed per person per year. Chinese consumers eat even less, only 99 grams.
I Do you think this trend will change?
C Yes. As Asian economies grow, it is likely that more chocolate products will be consumed. Chocolate sales in China, Indonesia, and India are expected to rise significantly in the next few years. In total, by 2016, a 20% share of the global market will be generated by the main Asian markets.
I So the future looks bright?
C Yes, but I should make one final point. Since 1971, the chocolate industry has made nearly a trillion US dollars. So it has been hugely successful. However, not everyone has benefited from this success. Thousands of children are being forced to work in West Africa, harvesting and packing the cacao beans. This is hard work and they are paid very little, and miss going to school. Less than 1% of the trillion dollars has been used to improve the working conditions for these children. This is a problem that should be addressed so that the children can live better lives.

8.2

First of all, let's look at things that can be recycled, for example drinks cans. Cans are made of aluminium, which can be used to make more cans or other products. The used cans are collected and taken to a recycling plant. Here they are shredded, melted, and the aluminium reused to make other products. This reduces the need to make aluminium again using raw materials. It also saves money because extracting and processing the raw materials is expensive.

Critics of recycling say that the recycling is actually an expensive process. It involves the collection, transportation, as well as the processing of used cans. All of this costs money. Critics also point out that some materials can only be recycled a limited number of times, for example paper. Supporters of recycling argue that a paper mill uses 40% less energy to make paper from recycled paper than it does to make paper from wood.

OK. Let's look at reuse next. One example is glass bottles. These can simply be washed, the labels removed, and the bottles refilled.

The advantages of reusing are obvious. One of the biggest advantages is that raw materials are saved. The extraction and processing of the raw material, in this case sand, is no longer required. The only costs are collection, transportation, and preparation for reuse. The second advantage is the reduction in the amount of rubbish produced. This in turn means savings in rubbish collection and disposal.

On the other hand, critics argue that not all products are reusable in the same way as glass bottles. Most clothes, for example, are less desirable when they are second-hand and slowly wear out and have to be thrown away. The other common argument against reuse is that older products are less efficient than more recent models. For example, if we reuse an old refrigerator, it will use more electricity and have fewer features than a new fridge.

8.3

1 I have a series of colour-coded notes for all the things I know I need to do in a day. It's a kind of 'to do' list, but I put each item on one of those sticky notes.

I use different colours depending on how urgent or important the task is. Red or orange are very important – the red ones have to be done that day. Oranges are usually just as important, but someone else might be able to do those; in other words, I can delegate those tasks. Yellows are not so important. I could do those tomorrow if necessary. Greens are usually the less urgent things, and sometimes they're more fun – you know, email a friend, go out for a lunchtime walk, that sort of thing.

2 I believe in being available to my colleagues and staff. I have an open door all day, except for one hour, usually between 2 p.m. and 3 p.m. I close my door and everybody knows they have to leave me alone. I get so much work done in that hour that it means I can be more available the rest of the day. Of course, some of my staff think that I'm just having a sleep – but that's really not true!

3 I learnt this technique from a colleague of mine. He said that once a month on a random day you should set your alarm clock on your phone to 'ping' every hour, at eleven minutes past the hour. You have a piece of paper next to you and you write down whatever you're doing at that moment. It gives you a really good picture of what you really spend your time on, rather than what you think you spend it on. Why eleven minutes past? Well, it's important to avoid doing it at the hour mark or half-hour because that's often when you tend to be changing activity.

8.4
R=Rhona, S=Steve, J=Jimmy

1 R OK, let's put the mixture in the machine.
   S Wait a minute. Why are you making all the decisions, Rhona?
   R I've made ice cream before. Have you, Steve?
   S Er … No, I haven't.
   J I'm happy for you to make the decisions, Rhona.
   R Thanks, Jimmy.
   S So what do we do?
   R OK. Jimmy, you assemble the machine. First, put in the grey bowl. Then you put the white plastic thing inside. That turns the ice cream round and round.
   J I don't understand how to put this in.
   R Turn it to the right.
   J Ah, I see what you mean. Like this.
   R That's it. Now start the machine. Do you see how it works?
   J Yeah, I follow you.
   R It turns the mixture for about 20 minutes. In the end, the ice cream looks like this picture.
   J OK, I see.
   S I don't. *How* does the machine work? Can you show me that again?
   R Sure, Steve. It's like this.

2 **I=Imogen, V=Veronica, M=Makoto**
   I OK, now, Veronica, we mix the paint with the oil like this. Do you see how it works?
   V Yes, I do.
   I Good, let's start.
   M Sorry I'm late, Imogen.
   I That's OK, Makoto.
   M So what are we doing?
   I Well, they showed us a picture by Picasso. We're all painting part of the picture. At the end, we're going to assemble the picture.
   M Sorry. I don't follow you. Can you explain what you mean by 'assemble the picture'?
   I Each group paints one section of the picture. At the end, we put the nine sections together. The nine sections make one big picture. Do you follow me?
   M Yes, I'm with you. But where's the picture that we are copying?
   I They showed it to us at the beginning, just for two minutes.
   M OK, I see.

3 **D=Dieter, K=Kath, H=Hans**
   D We should all work on different parts of the bike. What do you think? Kath? Hans?
   K Sure.
   H I agree.
   D Kath, I'll do the gears and you do the seat. The seat is made by connecting part A to part B and part C. OK?
   K No, I'm not OK, Dieter. You're talking too fast! It's too much information!
   D I'm sorry, Kath. Would you like me to go through that again?
   K Can you just clarify what I need to do?
   D Yes. This is part A. It connects to this – part B. Then you connect the seat. That's part C.
   K A with B and then C. OK, that makes sense.
   D Is everything clear?
   K Yes. That's fine now!
   D OK, team. Let's get to work!

8.5
K=Katerina, A=Alfonso

K So, how can I help you, Alfonso?
A Well, my team is going to have a training day. I need a fun team-building exercise to start the day: one that we can do in the office.
K Uh-huh. Can you explain what you mean by your 'team'? Do these people work together every day or do they work in different offices?
A No, it's a real team. Everyone works together.
K OK, well, why don't you try the tyre game?
A The tyre game?
K Yeah, you need two teams of about eight to ten people. Each team needs a bicycle tyre. Do you follow me?
A Yes.
K OK. Each team makes a circle and they hold hands.
A Yes, I'm with you.
K The group has to pass the tyre around the circle so it returns to the original position. Do you see how it works?
A Er, but how can you pass the tyre if you're holding hands?
K You have to move the tyre over your body and around your legs. Like this. I'll mime it for you.
…
A I see what you mean. So you move the tyre along your arm, down the body, and you step out of it one leg at a time. Can you show me that again?
K Sure. Like this.
A Wow, that's difficult.
K The team has to work together to find a solution. It's also a race because there are two teams and they want to be the fastest.
A It's great. Er … let me make some notes.
K Would you like me to go through that again?
A Yes, please!

8.6
1 A I've started a blog, but I don't get any hits. Can you help me?
   B Sure. To get hits, you need to use tags.
   A Sorry, I don't follow you.
   B You can put special key words on your blog. This helps people find your blog. For example, if you write about art, use the art tag. Look, click here … and add the tag. Do you see how it works?
   A Yes, that's fine. Thanks.

2 A You need to arrange a Russian visa. This is the form you need to complete. Is everything clear?
   B Er, no. I have a problem. I might leave Russia and return to the country several times.
   A Do you know how many times you'll do that?
   B I'm not sure, two or three times.
   A In that case, get a business double entry visa. That gives you permission to leave and re-enter the country.
   B OK, that makes sense.

3 A When the wind is strong, pull this rope. That helps control the boat.
   B I don't understand how to use all these ropes.
   A Would you like me to go through the instructions again?
   B Yes, please. This is the first time I've been sailing in my life.
   A Don't worry, you'll soon understand it all.

9

9.1
O=Olivia Hammond, J=Jules Goldsmith

O … You've been involved in the Olympic organization for some time, so I'm sure you know a lot about how the Olympics makes money from sponsorship.

Can you tell us what was the original Olympic policy concerning sponsors?

J Sure. Well, up to 1972, the Olympics had very little connection with business. The International Olympic Committee, or IOC as it's known, wanted the Olympics to be amateur rather than professional. Avery Brundage, who was the President of the IOC from 1952 to 1972, actually refused to allow corporate sponsorship. After Brundage retired, things began to change and the committee started to accept some sponsorship: over the next eight years it made about $45 million from sponsors. Then in 1980, Juan Antonio Samaranch became IOC president. Samaranch was the person who introduced a policy called TOP, which stands for 'the Olympic Programme'. The Olympic Programme, which Samaranch designed to encourage sponsorship, had dramatic results. During the 1984 Summer Olympics, which were held in Los Angeles, the IOC received $225 million in sponsorship deals.

O Wow! That's a big difference. Could you explain how the Olympic Programme works? How do you become a sponsor?

J Well, within the Olympic Programme, there are different levels of sponsorship. The sponsors the IOC chooses are given different marketing rights. The main sponsors are called the Worldwide Olympic Partners. In the 2012 Olympics, there were 11 Worldwide Olympic Partners, such as Coca-Cola and Samsung. They each paid $100 million to become Partners. This gave them exclusive global marketing rights to the Games, so they could use the Olympic symbol, the five rings, in their publications and advertisements.

O I see. Did the Partners play any other role?

J Yes, they also supplied important services for the Games. For example, Acer, who was a Worldwide Olympic Partner in 2012, provided the computer network for the entire Olympic complex. Omega – you know the company that makes watches – was another Partner. They provided more than 400 tonnes of timing and scoring equipment.

O You mentioned that there are other levels of sponsorship? What are they?

J As well as Worldwide Partners, there are also domestic sponsors. These are chosen by the Olympic Committee of the nation that is hosting the games. In London there were seven of these companies, such as Adidas, and BMW, who each paid around £40 million. After that, there were two other levels of sponsorship in London: seven 'supporters' who paid £20 million, and finally 28 'suppliers' who paid around £10 million.

O And what happens to the money that the IOC gets from sponsors?

J Well, over 90% of the revenue which the games generate is given to organizations within the Olympic movement, such as the Olympic teams and athletes. The remaining 10% is used to cover the IOC's administrative costs.

O I see. You also mentioned broadcasting rights for television and other forms of media. This must also generate a lot of money.

J Yes, it does. Broadcasting revenue increased from about $1 million in 1960 to over $1.7 billion in 2008. Also, the amount of media coverage has grown enormously. The BBC, who the IOC awarded the TV rights for the London Games, broadcast around 5,800 hours of television. That was more than twice the number of hours which were broadcast in the Beijing Games. In the future, the amount of media coverage will only increase.

9.2

1 Salma is our team leader. I think she's great at motivating people. She's very good at seeing what people's strengths and weaknesses are and she gives people jobs that suit their abilities. She also offers help and support when it's needed. She's very good at explaining things so that they're easy to understand. I've seen her give presentations a number of times and was really impressed.

2 Javier works in our web design department. He's always full of ideas about how to make our website more attractive. His designs look so fresh and innovative. I'm very envious of people like Javier. They just seem to have this natural ability to come up with new and interesting ideas.

3 Olga works in the Finance Department. She's very reliable. She's got a lot of experience so you don't need to tell her what to do or give her many instructions. She's happy working on her own and she always seems to get the job done. I think she has a very positive attitude to work.

4 I've been working with Tomas for a couple of years now. We're in the same team at work. As a work colleague, he's great. He's really supportive of other members of the team and always offers his help and advice to the rest of the team. He's good at seeing what needs doing and will tell you if an idea is unrealistic. If you want sensible advice, he's the guy to go to.

5 I think Jae Min will go far in her career. She was recently promoted to a senior management position and she's only 28. I think she hopes to be a CEO one day and I bet she'll get there! She puts in very long hours. She's always the first in the office in the morning and the last to leave each night.

9.3

1 I think it was winning our first sales contract in Mexico. I worked really hard to persuade the client to sign, and a lot of business followed as a result.

2 I'm not a very organized person, but I've recently been working on this. I got a new smartphone a few months ago and it's changed my life. I can now keep track of my appointments more easily using the calendar on my phone. I also find that it helps me to use my time more productively, so when I'm waiting for a bus, or having a coffee, I can check my work emails or email clients. It all saves time.

3 I can speak Spanish and Portuguese, so I think that will be useful in communicating with your South American branches. I've also had a lot of experience of managing teams. I've been told that I'm a good communicator, and I like to think that I'm good at motivating the people I work with.

4 There were some big changes in the company I was working for, and I felt it was time for me to develop in a new direction. I also wanted to improve my IT skills and my current job has allowed me to do that.

5 The salary is very attractive. I've just bought a new house so I need to earn more than in my current job.

6 I was very impressed with your website. I like the modern feel to it, and from what I've seen, that seems to be true of the entire organization. I can see that you want to expand into South America, where I imagine your products and services will work well.

7 No, I don't have any questions thank you. You've told me everything I need to know.

8 I had a problem with a colleague I was working with. We just didn't seem to be getting on. It worried me a lot because everything I did seemed to annoy him. In the end, I took a very simple step: I asked him if he had any problems with the way we were working, and what we could do to improve the situation. He apologized immediately and said it wasn't me, but a personal issue he had. He was going through a divorce at the time. We actually became good friends.

9.4

O=Oliver, N=Nicole

O Nicole?
N Hello, Oliver. Thanks for calling.
O No problem.
N Right … Let's look at the transport situation for the annual meeting. There's no metro, so I was wondering whether you could send some information about the buses to everyone. Timetables, routes …
O Well, I'd like to, but the problem is that the buses may go on strike too.
N I see. Would you mind booking some coaches for our guests then?
O No, I'm happy to do that. Could you tell me how many people are coming?

N Certainly. Thirty-eight people are coming through Charles de Gaulle airport.
O Uh-huh.
N Another 25 people are coming via the airport at Orly. Do you think you could book one coach for both groups of people?
O No, I'm afraid we won't be able to do that because the airports are quite far apart.
N That's true.
O We'll need two separate coaches, but it'll be expensive.
N Don't worry, it's fine.
O OK. I'll book them.
N Thanks, Oliver. There's one more thing. The Managing Director, Ms Boule, is coming by train. She arrives at Gare du Nord.
O OK. I'm coming by train too with Barry, our new Sales Director. We're arriving at … let me see … Gare Saint-Lazare. I've already arranged a taxi.
N Do you mind booking a taxi for us as well?
O That's no problem. A taxi for one person at Gare du Nord and a taxi for two people at Gare Saint-Lazare.
N OK. Thanks for sorting this, Oliver. What would we do without you?

9.5
N=Nicole, R=Rick
N Unfortunately, the company has some budget problems so we need to save money. Would you mind flying to the meeting in Paris on a budget airline?
R No, I'm happy to do that.
N Before we discovered the budget problems, we had hoped to book you a hotel too, but that will be expensive. So do you think you could fly back the same day?
R Don't worry, it's fine. I think it's important to save money too.
N I was also wondering whether your team could travel on public transport instead of by taxis.
R Mm, I don't think that will be possible because there's a strike on the day of the annual meeting.
N That's right. I forgot. Could you send an email to everyone about that?
R Certainly. Leave it with me.

9.6
1 A We need someone to translate our website pages into Russian. Could you ask Ivan to do that, please?
  B I don't think that'll be possible. Ivan's on a six-month contract in Brussels at the moment.
  A OK, well … Can you arrange a translation agency to do it, please?
  B I'd like to, Ava, but the problem is that I don't know any translation agencies.
2 A I had hoped to run the training course for our new employees, but now I have to go to London on business. Would you mind running the course for me?
  B No, don't worry, that's fine.

3 A Unfortunately, the conference in Miami has been cancelled due to the hurricane. Do you think you could cancel our flights?
  B We won't be able to do that because we've already printed our boarding passes.
4 A Something's come up. We're going to do the product launch in Chennai, not in Delhi. Would you mind contacting the press to tell them? Here's the new address.
  B Certainly. Leave it with me.

10

10.1
A=Alexander, B=Bruno, C=Charlotte
A Welcome to today's programme where we are discussing famous partnerships. Bruno, who would you like to mention first?
B Well, I love their product and I respect their values, so I would like to talk about Ben Cohen and Jerry Greenfield.
A And we know them better as?
B Ben and Jerry, the world's best ice-cream makers.
A Could you tell us a little about their early days?
B Of course. They actually met in a gym class at the age of 12. They were friends at school, but then went on to different colleges. They met up again in the late 70s and decided to go into business together. At first they thought of the bagel business, but the equipment for making bagels is very expensive so instead they decided on ice cream.
A If they had started a bagel business, they mightn't have been so successful.
B Possibly, but we'll never know.
A What did they know about ice cream?
B Ben had worked as an ice-cream seller before going to college, but they both decided to they take a correspondence course in ice-cream making at Penn University. It cost $5 and was a great investment.
A And were they immediately successful?
B Pretty much. They chose a college town, which meant there were a lot of potential customers. There was no ice-cream shop, so there was no competition, and they made different ice creams every day depending on what was available.
A What was different about their ice cream?
B Because Ben had a rare condition which means he has very limited taste and smell, he put big chunks in the ice cream, of cookie and fruit, and so on. This made the taste unique.
A So it would have been a completely different story if he hadn't had this condition.
B Exactly.
A And are they still involved in the business?

B They sold it to Unilever in 2000, but 7.5% of profits goes to the Ben and Jerry Foundation which donates money to good causes.
A An interesting pair. What about you, Charlotte?
C How about Paul McCartney and John Lennon? Together they wrote more number one songs than any other songwriters. They were also part of the greatest pop group ever, the Beatles. They met in 1957. Paul heard John playing with his band the Quarrymen at a church festival in Liverpool. A friend called Ivan introduced Paul to John and John invited Paul to join the band.
A So if Paul hadn't gone to the event, he wouldn't have met John.
C That's right.
A Who was the next to join?
C George Harrison. Paul knew him and wanted him to join as lead guitarist, but John thought he was too young. Paul arranged for George to play guitar on a bus and John heard him and thought he was so good he invited him to join the group.
A So if George hadn't got that bus, John would never have heard him play. Amazing.
C I know. They then got a new manager, Brian Epstein, who tried to get them a recording contract. After an audition, Decca Records rejected the band with the comment: 'Guitar groups are on the way out, Mr Epstein.'
A Decca should have signed the Beatles when it had the chance.
C Absolutely. Instead, the Beatles signed to EMI and made their first record. Unfortunately, the producer, George Martin, was not happy with the drummer, Pete Best. So they had to find a new drummer, and that was Ringo Starr. If Pete Best had been a better drummer, he could have become a superstar. The rest is history.

10.2
1 If they had started a bagel business, they might not have been so successful.
2 So if Paul hadn't gone to the event, he wouldn't have met John.
3 So if George hadn't got that bus, John would never have heard him play.
4 Decca should have signed them when it had the chance.
5 If Pete Best had been a better drummer, he could have become a superstar.

10.3
1 You should've offered her a bigger share.
2 She shouldn't have accepted his offer.
3 They should've offered them a contract.
4 If they'd gone to different schools, they'd have started companies with other people.
5 If he hadn't demonstrated his computer, he wouldn't have met Steve.

10.4
Mariam
My first job after I left university was as an editor in publishing. It was interesting,

152 Scripts

but I was never keen on spending all day in an office. Also I never enjoyed working at a computer all day. Who does, right? Anyhow, I spoke to my friend about this and told her that I was thinking of taking some time out, and maybe going travelling. She suggested doing some charity work and put me in touch with an organization in Bolivia. So, I left my job and went to Bolivia. I worked on a project, teaching underprivileged children reading and writing skills. It really changed my life. While I was there, I had time to think about what I really wanted to do. I had always loved gardening – I enjoy being out in the open air. When I got back to the UK, I enrolled on a one-year landscape gardening course. It was great. I really felt that I'd found my 'thing' – you know, what you really want to do. After finishing the course, I managed to get some work experience with a landscape design company in Bristol. They offered me a job afterwards and I've ended up working there for three years now. I love my job. I work long hours in all weather conditions, but I can't think of anything else I'd rather be doing.

Liam
I used to be a marketing manager for a drinks company. Working in marketing is interesting but very busy. After we had our second child, my wife and I decided to make some changes to our lives. My wife works as a lawyer and she wanted to carry on working, but with two small children, it was difficult to manage our work and family commitments. She made more money than me so it didn't make sense for her to quit her job. Anyhow, I had an idea. I offered to stay at home and look after the kids. She was really surprised but, when we looked at the finances, we realized that it was possible. So I quit my job to take care of the kids. I loved being with the kids, but it was exhausting – way more tiring than my old job! While I was looking after the kids, I felt quite isolated. It's quite hard to meet people, especially when you're a man, and I really missed going in to the office and the social interaction that brings. Anyway, I decided to set up a club and website for 'stay at home dads'. It has proved to be very popular and we now have several clubs across the country – we're trying to set up a similar network in some other countries. We charge members to join and also receive some money from advertising and sponsorship. I don't earn as much from the website as I did in my old job, but it's easy to spend time with my family now. I had planned to go back to a marketing job after the kids went to school, but now I'm not sure. I like the independence and flexibility that my new job brings.

Beatrice
My first career was in events management. I used to organize large corporate events, like trade fairs, and product launches. At first, it was a lot of fun. I enjoy meeting people and I'm pretty good at organizing things, so it seemed like the perfect job for me. But there were some downsides. Managing events involves working long hours. You need to work evenings, and there are lots of weekends away. When I was young, this was fine, but after I got married, my husband and I found that we hardly ever saw each other, and when we did, I was always exhausted. I realized that I needed to make a few changes. I was 32 at the time and the thought of changing career was scary. Obviously, I was afraid of not having any money, but also other things. Changing career meant leaving a good job, learning new skills, making new friends… all that. But still, I needed to do it. So, I did! I've always been interested in cooking and food, but it was just a hobby. Working in events management, you often need to organize the food for events, so I had a good idea of how catering companies worked. So I decided to start my own catering company. We specialize in providing the food for events, such as weddings, corporate dinners, things like that. It's great because I work at home most of the time – so I can spend time with my partner – but I'm also involved in making an event special for my clients. It was a big change, but I'm so happy I did it.

10.5
Conference call 1
R=Renata, S=Sergio, M=Magda, H=Hanif
R   OK, everyone, this is Renata speaking. I think we're all here now. Can everyone hear OK? [Yes, yes.] Good. Well, I'm pleased you could all attend the meeting, even if it is remotely from your offices! As you know, my name's Renata Ribeiro. I'm the Head of IT for Brazil. I hope you all got the agenda I sent round by email. We're meeting today to discuss a possible new IT project between our companies. As you don't know each other, I'm going to ask you all to introduce yourselves. Also during the meeting, as we can't see each other, can you please say your name before you speak? It will help us all to communicate more easily. And also, if you want to speak to a particular person, please say their name first. So, first of all, I have Sergio Carvalho with me here in Brazil. Sergio, can you start us off?
S   Sure. Sergio here. Hello, everyone. Nice to talk to you all. I'm Sergio. I'm the Head of Finance in the Brazilian office.
R   Thanks, Sergio. Magda, would you like to say something next?
M   Yes, of course. Hi, my name's Magda Vega. I am the IT Manager in Argentina.
R   Thanks, Magda. This is Renata again. Last but not least, we have Hanif. Hanif, would you like to introduce yourself? … Hanif, are you there? … Hanif? … Sorry, Hanif. I think there's a problem with the line. Please go ahead.
H   Thanks, Renata. Hi, Magda, Sergio. My name's Hanif Kirani. I'm the Head of IT for IT Solutions in South Asia.
M   Magda, here. Good to talk to you, Hanif.
H   And you too, Magda … Sorry, this is Hanif. By the way, you all sound a little quiet. Could you turn up the volume a little?
S   Sergio, here. Is that better?
H   Thanks, Sergio. Yes, much better, thanks.
R   OK, Renata here again. Right, let's get started. Magda, would you like to say something about the IT operation in Argentina?
M   Magda again. Sure. Well, our IT network was set up about eight years ago for …

Conference call 2
J=Junko, B=Boris, G=George, T=Tom
J   OK, this is Junko. Let me just show you one of the ideas we had for a new company logo. I'll just hold it up for you.
B   Sorry, Junko, this is Boris. Can I just stop you there? The picture's breaking up. I'm not sure we can all see it. George, can you see it?
G   Yes, it's fine here. It looks good. I like the design you've used, and the colours.
B   Hold on, before you go on, we need to sort out the technical problem. Tom, did you want to come in on that? You're the technical man.
T   OK, let me have a look. Maybe if …
J   Hi, Could I just say something?
B   Yes, Junko. Go ahead.
J   Perhaps I should email it to you. It might be quicker.
B   That's a good idea. Tom, did you want to say something?
T   I was going to suggest exactly that …

10.6
V=Valerie, J=Jordi
V   Jordi! Jordi! Long time, no see!
J   Valerie! It's great to see you. You got here OK, then?
V   Yes. It was a long flight from the States but I'm here now. This conference is enormous, isn't it?
J   Yeah. It's a huge event. So, is everything OK in the Seattle office?
V   Fine, No problems. How's everything going here in Barcelona?
J   Very well. Business is good in Spain at the moment.
V   I'm not surprised. Our new apps are great. We're selling hundreds of downloads. These are good times for the app industry.
J   Well, let's hope our new smartphone game will be a success.
V   I hope so. It's important that we have a successful launch at the conference.
J   Absolutely. There are journalists from all over the world.
V   That's true. … So how are things at home? Are Maria and the kids OK?
J   I have some news actually. We're expecting baby number three!

V Congratulations! That's fantastic. I had no idea. I haven't seen you in ages.
J Thanks. We're really excited too.

10.7
V=Valerie, D=David, A=Anthony, G=Greg, J=Joanna, B=Belinda

1   V David Mills.
    D Valerie. Long time, no see.
    V How are you? Are you still working at Slipstream Apps?
    D Yes, I am. I got a promotion actually. I'm now a project leader.
    V Really? So your game apps were a big success?
    D Well, yes, but I can't tell you any more, Valerie. You're the competition!

2   A Valerie?
    V Anthony! I haven't seen you since we left university. How are you?
    A I'm very well, thanks.
    V What have you been doing since I last saw you?
    A I moved to California. I live in the San Diego area now.
    V You don't say.

3   V Hey, Greg.
    G Valerie. Good to see you.
    V We only speak by Skype these days.
    G True.
    V So what happened with our India project in the end?
    G It's on. In the end, the programmers in India accepted the deal. It's going to be a big success for our company.
    V Yeah, I think so too.
    G Sorry, I have to go now, but I'll see you at the office. OK?
    V OK!

4   J Valerie!
    V Joanna! I thought I'd see you here at the congress. How are things at Microsoft?
    J Actually, I changed jobs again last year. Now I'm at Apple.
    V Good for you. You know, if you want to change jobs again, you can always come back and work with us.
    J Ha ha! Thanks for the offer, but I'm very happy at Apple for the moment.
    V Oh, well.
    J Look, I have a presentation now, but I'll see you later. OK?
    V I'll be right here.

5   V Thanks for that radio interview you did for us, Belinda. Our website got lots of hits after that.
    B Really? It's good to know that people are listening to the show! Your new game sounded great. How did that project go?
    V We ended up creating eight different versions of the game. We had a special one for the US market, the Middle East, and others.
    B I'm pleased it was a success.
    V It really was.
    B Well, I have another interview to do now.

    V Oh, OK. It was lovely to meet you again.
    B You too. Let's speak soon.

10.8
E=Emilio, P=Pierre, M=Marina, R=Rose

E Hello, everyone. I think we're all here now. Hi, Pierre. Hello, Rose. Can you both see us OK?
P Hi, Emilio. We can hear you OK, but there's a problem with the picture. It keeps breaking up.
M Hi, Pierre. This is Marina. I'm just going to check that the camera is plugged in correctly. … How's that? Any better?
P Hi, Marina. Yes, much better, thanks. We can see you now. Ah, it looks like a beautiful day there!
M Yes, it is. It's 35 degrees outside! Hi, Rose. How are you?
R Hi, Marina. I'm well, thanks. Thanks for setting up this meeting, Emilio. We got the agenda that you emailed.
E Great. Well, in that case, let's get started. The first point on the agenda is the technology conference in Seattle next month. Marina, did you want to say something about this?
M Yes, thanks Emilio. Well, as you know …
R Sorry to interrupt, Marina. Could I just say something?
M Sure, please go ahead.
R I was talking to Pierre about the conference and I think I'm going to attend. It would be useful to see what our competitors are doing. It's still possible to register for it, isn't it?
M Great! Yes, you can still register online. It will be nice to see you again – in person, I mean!
R OK, great. Thanks. I'll register today. Anyway, sorry, please go on with what you were going to say.
M Well, as you know, we're planning to promote our new line of tablets at the conference, so I'd just like to take you through some of the events we've organized. First of all, we're going to …

154   Scripts

Answer key

1

Grammar pp.6–8

2 1 She uses Facebook.
2 He posts adverts on the site. The process is quicker than traditional ways, and it's free.
3 They plan to promote events and offers, etc. using Twitter and Facebook feeds, and a blog.

3 1 F: He's a social media manager.
2 T
3 F: He's very busy.
4 F: He's developing the mobile device side of their marketing.
5 T
6 F: It's going very well.
7 F: He works quite a lot of weekends too.
8 F: He generally enjoys his job.

4 1 you do
2 involves
3 areas
4 business
5 current project
6 are working
7 going
8 typical
9 enjoy

Focus

1 d 2 a 3 c 4 b
Present Simple a, d   Present Continuous b, c

5 1 stay
2 are staying
3 always goes
4 is going
5 is developing
6 develop
7 am trying
8 tries
9 sometimes wait
10 am waiting

6 1 do … think; 'm using
2 's; 's, prefer
3 Do … know; 'm checking
4 does … start; starts, 's starting
5 's; isn't, 's making
6 's … doing; 's having
7 do … have; have, have

8 1 F: People want time without technology.
2 T
3 F: A group of resorts in Antigua, Grenada, and St Lucia have banned mobile phones from their beaches.
4 T

Vocabulary pp.9–10

2 2 click
3 log in
4 chat
5 upload
6 link
7 download
8 post
9 access

3 1 i 2 c 3 e 4 a 5 f 6 g 7 d
8 b 9 h

5 She mentions 1, 2, and 4.

6 1 upload
2 online
3 identity theft
4 log in
5 access
6 posting

Work skills p.11

2 1 Adam
2 Silvia
3 Ken
4 Silvia
5 Ken
6 Adam

Functions pp.12–13

2 1 last ~~month~~ year
2 ~~sports~~ technology website
3 their blog ~~Twitter~~
4 her ~~friend~~ colleague

3

Pete Shen	Diane Smith
San Diego	LA
technology journalist	marketing manager
computer programmer	journalist

5 1 familiar
2 charge
3 deal
4 work
5 save
6 follow

Focus

Meeting	Talking about your work
I'm sorry, I don't remember your name.	I'm in charge of marketing a new laptop for our company. I'm based here in Santiago.
Introducing another person	
Would you like to meet my colleague, Diane Smith?	
Sharing contact details	
My email address is Pshen (all one word) at pshen dot com.	

6 1 c 2 a 3 d 4 f 5 b 6 e

Review

Grammar pp.14–15

1 1 are using
2 spend
3 is growing
4 send
5 check

2 1 'm posting
2 use
3 specializes
4 allows
5 claims
6 's growing
7 have
8 like
9 is expanding
10 'm looking
11 's travelling
12 wants
13 think

3 1 'm trying
2 'm having
3 'm looking
4 want
5 's only showing
6 'm just checking
7 takes

Vocabulary pp.15–16

2 1 F: Most people use a blogging site to host their blog.
2 T
3 F: You can upload photos.
4 F: Blogs are usually informal.
5 T
6 F: Post comments on other people's blogs.
7 F: Update your blog once a week.
8 T
9 T

3 1 log in
2 uploaded
3 access
4 click
5 downloaded
6 update
7 posted
8 link
9 chat

Work skills p.16

1 1 London
2 Uncrossed Wires
3 cross-cultural relations (between China and Europe)
4 consultancy services in Human Resources
5 travel and squash

Answer key 155

Functions p.17

1
1. with
2. Previously
3. currently
4. to meet
5. Give

2
1. hotel
2. advertising
3. IT / computers

3
1. to meet; Pleased to; in charge
2. isn't it; don't remember; meet … again; based in
3. familiar with; my card

2

Grammar pp.18–20

2
1. She designs buildings / She's an architect.
2. She was born in Baghdad.
3. She's lived in London since 1972.
4. She's had her own business since 1980.
5. She's won the Stirling Prize twice.
6. the Sumerian deserts
7. She's been working on projects in Korea, China, Italy, and France, and on the Central Bank of Iraq.

Focus
We use the **Past Simple** for finished actions and situations in the past.
We use the **Present Perfect Simple** or **Present Perfect Continuous** for actions and situations that began in the past and continue to the present.
We use the **Present Perfect Simple** for past actions with results in the present.
We usually use the **Present Perfect Simple** when we want to focus on the result or completion of the action.
We usually use the **Present Perfect Continuous** when we want to focus on the activity rather than the completed action.

4
1. have been doing
2. hasn't had
3. been writing
4. Have you been
5. has won
6. Have you ever climbed
7. have never gone
8. was launched
9. have been waiting
10. has designed

5
1. F: She was born in Lebanon.
2. T
3. F: She's been living in Beirut.
4. T
5. T
6. T
7. T

6
1. jobs have you had since you left college
2. was your first job
3. do you do
4. do you work for
5. have you been working there
6. have you been on business

8
1. What've you; I've been
2. What's she; She's done
3. Has she been; she hasn't, She's been
4. What's; It's been

Vocabulary pp.21–22

2
2. Ask for advice
3. Make a financial plan
4. Know your customer
5. Location, location, location

4
1. carry out
2. set up
3. put off
4. find out
5. point out
6. look after
7. sort out
8. look into
9. break down
10. put together

5
1. set it up
2. sort them out
3. look into
4. broken it down
5. look after
6. carried it out
7. found out
8. pointed it out
9. put it together
10. put me off

6 separable: break down, carry out, find out, point out, put together, put off, sort out
inseparable: look into

8
1. after
2. down
3. off
4. off
5. on
6. up
7. over
8. on

Work skills p.23

3
1. F
2. T (ahead of schedule)
3. T
4. T
5. F
6. F
7. T
8. F

4
1. make
2. item
3. help
4. move on
5. specific
6. fill us in
7. discuss
8. sum up

5 He follows tips 1, 2, 3, 4, 5, 7, 8.

Functions pp.24–25

1
1. to discuss the window displays for the autumn collection
2. fashion / retail
3. autumn
4. models wearing the clothes in a shop window

2 colours: red, orange, yellow (not black, white, blue)
mannequins: man, woman, child (not three men)
model: dog (not cat)

3
1. yet
2. I'd
3. with
4. I'd

4
1. our main clothing
2. June
3. lighting
4. designer
5. Colin

5
1. handle
2. able
3. covered
4. leave

Focus

Checking progress	Delegating
Have we ordered the bikes yet? Have we covered everything?	Britta, I'd like you to handle that. Can I leave this with you?
Agreeing to do something	Saying you can't do something
Leave it with me. Yes, I can handle that.	I'd rather not because I have a lot of work. I won't be able to do that because I'll be in New York.

6
1. How are we doing
2. Is anyone free
3. I won't be able to do that
4. Leave it with me
5. I'd like you to
6. I can do
7. Have we covered

7
1. I can handle that.
2. I'm not free, I'm afraid.
3. Who's responsible for recruitment?
4. Louise, can I leave this with you?
5. I'd rather not go to the meeting because I have too much work.

Review

Grammar p.27

1
1. grew up, haven't been
2. emigrated
3. has lived
4. opened
5. didn't employ
6. has opened
7. opened
8. has given
9. hasn't had, booked

2
2. When did your parents emigrate to Chicago?
3. How long has your brother lived in Chicago?
4. When did he open his first pizza shop?
5. How many staff did he employ in the early days?
6. How many pizza shops has he opened since the early days / then?
7. When did he open his most recent pizza shop?
8. How many people has he given work to over the years?
9. How often has he had a holiday

3 2 's happened
3 's left
4 did … happen
5 gave
6 's been
7 've known
8 did … find out
9 told
10 spoke
11 did … say
12 's found
13 had
14 've offered

Vocabulary pp.27–28

1 1 h 2 g 3 e 4 f 5 c 6 d 7 b
8 a

2 1 turned up
2 turn off
3 looking into
4 put me off
5 took over
6 turned it down
7 sort out
8 pointed out

3 1 her business plan
2 The concept isn't new.
3 yes
4 put together a marketing plan
5 He missed his last deadline.
6 Paulo; read the paper

4 1 carry out
2 looked into
3 pointed out
4 put you off
5 put together
6 break it down
7 sort out
8 turns up

Work skills p.28

1 1 f 2 e 3 a 4 c 5 g 6 b 7 h
8 d

2 1 Rita
2 adverts for the newspaper campaign, adverts for the radio
3 The target market listens to these stations the most.
4 He's contacted some writers, had a meeting with them, and discussed some ideas.
5 He worked with them on the last radio campaign.
6 the TV campaign

Functions p.29

1 1 Is anyone free to go
2 Yes, I can do that
3 How are we doing with
4 I won't be able to do that
5 Have we covered everything
6 Yes, I can handle that

2 1 ✓ 2 ✗ 3 ✗ 4 ✓

3 1 a yet   2 a look   3 a handle   4 a for
    b leave   b rather   b afraid   b Leave

3

Grammar pp.30–32

3 1 wireless telephone circuits, newspaper colour photographs, ready-cooked meals, fast traffic within the city, electric light and growth of vegetables
2 It's unlikely that all traffic will be below ground or above ground level.
3 There will probably be subway systems or overground monorails, and it's likely there'll be a car-free zone.
4 using natural light, without fresh water
5 It will grow very fast in the next hundred years.

Focus

c	b, h, k	e, f, i	a, g, l	d, j
0% impossible		possible		certain 100%

4 1 I am sure we will prevent malaria by 2050.
2 It is likely that people will grow taller in the future.
3 It is unlikely that the earth will cool down in the next 50 years.
4 I am sure there won't be a colony on Mars in my lifetime.
5 We might / may (be able to) fly from New York to Tokyo in less than two hours.
6 Oil reserves will probably / are likely to run out by 2050.
7 We probably won't find intelligent life on another planet.
8 It is possible that print newspapers will disappear.
9 There might / may be a direct train line between the UK and China by 2100.
10 Cars will definitely become hands-free.

6

	Yolanda	Dmitri	Haruka
1	probably won't	it's possible	might
2	probably won't	definitely won't (don't think I'll have a family)	definitely will
3	it's unlikely	probably will	it's unlikely

Vocabulary pp.33–34

2 1 He lost the game and the amount of rice he had to pay doubled on every square.
2 It says that the power of computer microchips doubles every 18 months.
3 a smartphone
4 Because computers are faster.
5 UK = 40%, Finland = 80%
6 Because there is greater competition between research departments for funding.

3 2 We closed down our factory in England. *As a consequence, we have managed to lower our production costs significantly*.
3 Belinda's quit her job *because she wants to start her own company*.
4 *Due to the rising price of copper, our manufacturing costs have increased*.
5 The new law has *led to a reduction in crime*.
6 The marketing campaign *resulted in a 15% increase in sales*.
7 The fall in share prices in 2008 *was the result of the banking crisis*.
8 The factory will *cause more pollution in the surrounding area*.
9 We've recently spent more money on advertising; *as a result, sales of our new smartphone have risen*.
10 The development of the business park *will create hundreds of jobs in the area*.

4 1 sport and 3-D television
2 people living alone
3 people retiring abroad
4 digital publishing

5 1 Because of / Due to
2 Due to / Because of
3 As a consequence / As a result
4 result in / lead to
5 the result of / because of / due to
6 lead to / result in
7 As a result / As a consequence
8 cause / result in / lead to

Work skills p.35

2 1 Singapore
2 late afternoon on Monday 1 October
3 Tom
4 a B   b A   c C

3 a 1, 5, 10   c 2, 7, 9
   b 4, 6, 11   d 3, 8, 12

Functions pp.36–37

2 1 merge
2 insurance
3 Dave's company: USA; Elke's company: Switzerland

3 1 three
2 managers
3 the mountains
4 August 30th

5 1 August 31st
2 August 30th
3 September 4th
4 September 3rd

6 1 1 Are you free
     2 all day
     3 rest of the team
   2 1 convenient for
     2 with my PA
     3 tomorrow
   3 1 on vacation
     2 in September
     3 the date
   4 1 about the meeting
     2 wedding
     3 me fine
     4 pencil

Focus

1   1 b   2 c   3 d   4 a
- a   That should be fine / I can make …
- b   I'm afraid that August is no good for me … / I can't make …
- c   Are you free on … / Is … good for you / Does that sound OK to you?
- d   I'll get back to you / I can't confirm the date now / Let's pencil in …

8   1 convenient for you   5 As soon as
     2 busy then   6 pencil in
     3 don't we meet on   7 sounds good to
     4 can't make

Review

Grammar p.39

1   1 will definitely   6 may / might
     2 may / might   7 will definitely
     3 think … will   8 probably won't
     4 definitely won't   9 definitely won't
     5 probably won't   10 will probably

2   1 There **will definitely be** more …
     2 … I'm not **sure**.
     3 It's **possible**, but …
     4 … in cities **will increase**.
     5 … cars **might increase**.
     6 **I'm sure** we will …

Vocabulary pp.39–40

1   1 Due to   5 As a consequence
     2 resulted   6 caused
     3 because   7 because
     4 led   8 the result

2   2 He's bought a new laptop because his old laptop is broken.
     3 As a result of a rise in orders, we need to take on more staff.
     4 Due to heavy snow last night, the road is closed today.
     5 An increased demand for natural gas has led to a rise in gas prices.
     6 She has to wear glasses because of her poor eyesight.
     7 The decision to close the factory resulted in many job losses.
     8 As a consequence of eating a lot of junk food, he has put on weight.

Work skills p.40

1   1 Can you just confirm   4 you want to add
     2 if that's OK with you   5 to seeing you
     3 I've attached   6 Best wishes

2   Example answer
Hi Nico
Thanks for your email.
I'd like to confirm that I can attend the meeting tomorrow in Paris. I'll be arriving at Charles de Gaulle at 10 a.m. My flight number is AF134. Can you just confirm that someone will meet me at the airport?
And can you let me know the meeting room and the time of the meeting?
I've attached a new agenda with some additional points.
I'm looking forward to seeing you tomorrow.
Best wishes

Functions p.41

1   1 should   5 in
     2 for   6 make
     3 as   7 me
     4 for

2   1 I can't confirm if 16th May is OK right now.
     2 I'm afraid that tomorrow afternoon is no good for me.
     3 I can make an 8 a.m. meeting on Wednesday.
     4 Why don't we meet on 18th May?
     5 She'll get back to you next week.
     6 Does 7 p.m. in the Jasmine Garden restaurant sound OK?
     7 I'm busy all day tomorrow.
     8 Are you free at lunchtime on 15th October?

3

Conversation	1	2	3	4	5	6
Agreeing	✓					✓
Saying not convenient				✓	✓	
Waiting on a decision		✓	✓			

4

Grammar pp.42–44

2   1 1753   5 €11
     2 5.2 million   6 1,700
     3 60,000 m^2 7 Alexander McQueen
     4 *Mona Lisa*

3   1 oldest   5 better
     2 a little older   6 as many as
     3 less expensive   7 more popular
     4 most famous   8 least popular

Focus
One-syllable adjectives
We add **-er** to the end of the adjective to make the comparative.
We add **-est** to the end of the adjective to make the superlative.
Two-syllable and three-syllable adjectives
We put **more / less** before the adjective to make the comparative.
We put **most / least** before the adjective to make the superlative.

4   1 the most   6 older
     2 bigger   7 most beautiful
     3 smaller   8 as good
     4 as old   9 more interesting
     5 as many   10 less expensive

6

1st syllable stress	2nd syllable stress	3rd syllable stress
interesting	relaxing	educational
dirty	exciting	independent
dangerous	expensive	international
beautiful	enjoyable	
	professional	

Vocabulary pp.45–46

1   Geography: in western part of Japan's main island Honshu; surrounded by three mountains; Kamogawa river passes through the centre of the city
Climate: sub-tropical, with mild winters and hot and humid summers
Business / Industry: important centre for information technology and education
Places to visit: temples (Kinkaku-ji), castles (Nijo), geisha district (Gion), bamboo forests (Arashiyama)
Places to stay: hotels (including capsule hotel); ryokan
Food: kaiseki ryori, shojin ryori

2   2 fascinating   8 amazing
     3 surprising   9 disappointed
     4 annoyed   10 interesting
     5 stunning   11 pleased
     6 boring   12 surprised
     7 tired

3   1 a   interested, annoyed, tired, disappointed, pleased, surprised
        b   fascinating, surprising, stunning, boring, amazing, interesting
     2 Adjectives describing how we feel end -ed; adjectives describing something that causes the feelings end -ing.

4   1 ed   2 ing   3 ing   4 ed   5 ing   6 ed
     7 ing   8 ed

6   1 traditional   5 humid
     2 cosmopolitan / famous /   6 lively
        lively / modern / popular /   7 delicious
        traditional   8 modern
     3 ancient / famous   9 popular
     4 famous

Work skills p.47

1 1 pie chart 3 slide with prompt words
2 line graph 4 table

2 a 3 b 2 c 4 d 1

3 1 line graph 2 pie chart 3 table

4 1 shows 4 represent
2 indicates 5 look at
3 see 6 describes

5 1 follows: b, d, e, f, g, h, i; doesn't follow: a, c, e (extract 2)

Functions pp.48–49

1 1 two weeks
2 January, February, October, November
3 $4,500

2 1 a seven-day tour 3 no one signed up for it
2 rains a lot

4 Lamu, Mount Kenya, Lake Nakuru National Park

5 Route = Nairobi → Mount Kenya → Lake Nakuru National Park → the Great Rift Valley → Masai Mara Game Reserve → Nairobi

6 1 island 4 zebras
2 diving 5 balloon
3 fly

Focus
Asking for opinions
What are your views?
Giving opinions
In my view, the balloon ride should be an extra thing.
Agreeing
Definitely.
Disagreeing
I'm not sure about that.
Recognizing someone's point of view
I can see where you're coming from, Sumiko.

7 1 What do you think about 4 I completely
2 From a marketing 5 I think we should
3 I see where Bradley is 6 that's a good

Review

Grammar pp.50–51

1 1 The Eiffel Tower is taller than Big Ben. Big Ben isn't as tall as the Eiffel Tower.
2 The Taj Mahal is older than the Sydney Opera House. The Sydney Opera House isn't as old as the Taj Mahal.
3 The Colosseum is older than the Taj Mahal. The Taj Mahal isn't as old as the Colosseum.
4 The Eiffel Tower has more visitors than the Sydney Opera House. The Sydney Opera House doesn't have as many visitors as the Eiffel Tower.
5 The Burj Khalifa is taller than the Eiffel Tower. The Eiffel Tower isn't as tall as the Burj Khalifa.
6 The Taj Mahal has fewer visitors than the Colosseum. The Colosseum has more visitors than the Taj Mahal.
7 The Burj Khalifa is more modern than the Sydney Opera House. The Sydney Opera House isn't as modern as the Burj Khalifa.
8 The Colosseum is shorter than Big Ben. Big Ben isn't as short as the Colosseum.

2 Example answers
1 The Eiffel Tower is a lot taller than Big Ben.
2 The Taj Mahal is much older than the Sydney Opera House.
3 The Colosseum is far older than the Taj Mahal.
4 The Eiffel Tower has slightly more visitors than the Sydney Opera House.
5 The Burj Khalifa is much taller than the Eiffel Tower.
6 The Taj Mahal has slightly fewer visitors than the Colosseum.
7 The Burj Khalifa is a bit more modern than the Sydney Opera House.
8 The Colosseum is much shorter than Big Ben.

3 1 the finest 4 the greatest
2 the largest 5 the most visited
3 the tallest 6 the most famous

Vocabulary pp.51–52

1 a 4 b 5 c 6 d 1 e 3 f 2

2 1 ed 2 ing 3 ing 4 ed 5 ed 6 ing
7 ed 8 ing

3 1 lively 5 delicious
2 famous 6 cosmopolitan
3 humid 7 ancient
4 traditional 8 popular

Work skills p.52

1 1 a 2 d 3 c 4 b

2 1 shows 5 look
2 see 6 shows
3 see 7 look
4 look 8 indicate

Functions p.53

1 1 should; definitely 4 think; view
2 view; sure 5 opinion; point
3 Personally

2 1 ✗ 2 ✓ 3 ✗ 4 ✗ 5 ✓ 6 ✓

3 1 I don't 4 In
2 mean 5 that's
3 completely 6 from

5

Grammar pp.54–56

2 1 a trawler man f (racing car) pit crew
b astronaut g American football player
c cabin attendant h businessman
d rugby player i arctic researcher
e doctor

3 1 a 2 g 3 f 4 d 5 i 6 c

4 1 to protect their hands from ropes and sharp objects
2 Jorge
3 a lot of the rules and clothes are different: not allowed to wear a helmet, but allowed to wear padding; not allowed to wear gloves
4 Keira
5 cabin attendant

5 1 don't have to 5 can't
2 have to 6 mustn't
3 must 7 needs to
4 allowed to 8 Can

Focus

It's necessary	have to, must, need to
It's not permitted	mustn't, not be allowed to, can't
It's not necessary	don't have to, don't need to
It's permitted	can, be allowed to

7 Example answers
2 airport: Hand luggage mustn't be larger than … / Liquids have to be placed in a 20cm x 20cm plastic bag.
3 shop: You have to / must pay by credit card only.
4 building site: You must / need to wear a hi-visibility vest.
5 office building: You have to / must wear your identity card at all times.

6 church: You can't wear bright colours / shorts or mini-skirts / shawls or wraps. You must / have to wear appropriate colours. You must cover your shoulders. Ladies must cover their knees.
7 website: You don't have to / need to pay for delivery.
8 shop/bank: You can't / aren't allowed to wear hoodies.
9 (dinner) party: You have to dress smart casual.
10 airport: You have to / must place your coats and jackets in the tray.

10 1 We speak languages and we wear clothes.
2 Rules are things you have to do and you mustn't do. Conventions are things you don't have to do, but are advisable and expected.
3 wear a suit or a dress to a cabinet meeting; wear white kit at Wimbledon; wear a tie in some restaurants; don't wear the same colour dress as the bride at weddings; wear shirts in bars in the USA

Vocabulary pp.57–58

2 1 red 6 blue
2 white 7 Black
3 blue 8 black
4 green 9 grey
5 red

4 yellow 4 red 1 black 5 green 2 blue 3

5/6

un-	in-	im-
unusual	invisible	impossible
unhappy	inefficient	immoral
unlucky	incapable	imperfect
unknown		
untidy		

il-	ir-	dis-
illegal	irresponsible	dissatisfied
illegible	irregular	disorganized
illogical	irrelevant	dissimilar
		dishonest

7 1 p, m, l, and r
2 Examples: unbelievable, unavoidable; indecisive, indifferent
3 Example: disrespect, dislike; discontinue, disobey

8 1 illegal 4 immoral
2 dishonest 5 untidy
3 irrelevant 6 inefficient

9 1 b 2 a 3 d 4 c 5 e 6 f

10 1 eco-friendly 4 co-produce
2 cybercrime 5 ex-president
3 anti-smoking 6 E-commerce

Work skills p.59

2 1 h 2 f 3 c 4 b 5 e 6 g 7 d 8 a

3 1 4 b 5 2 f
2 6 g 6 8 a
3 7 d 7 3 c
4 1 h 8 5 e

4 1 a to reschedule his meeting with Simone Parker
   b 076013962
2 a to return Paolo's call
   b a train

5 1 h, 2, 6, 4 2 3, 8, 7, e

Functions pp.60–61

1 1 b 2 a 3 c 4 e 5 d

2 1 public transport 4 basic phrases
2 Taxis 5 amazing shops
3 helicopter 6 Park

4 a 2 b 5 c 4 d 6 e 1 f 3

Focus

Asking for advice and suggestions	Giving advice and suggestions
Do you have any advice?	You should definitely …
What do you think I should do?	One thing you should be careful about is …
Do you have any suggestions?	How about …?
	Why don't you …?
	Have you considered …?

Accepting ideas: a, c, d
Rejecting ideas: b, e, f

5 1 What books or magazines from your country do you recommend?
2 Do you think we should wear gloves and a scarf tomorrow?
3 Where do you think I should go for a coffee after class?
4 Do you have any advice for learning English vocabulary?
5 Do you have any suggestions for a typical gift from your country?

6 1 be; for 4 definitely; a
2 going; sounds 5 getting a coach; I'd
3 on; not 6 I'd; of

Review

Grammar pp.62–63

1 1 have to 6 need to
2 don't need to 7 can
3 must 8 don't have to
4 allowed to 9 are not allowed to
5 don't need to 10 must

3 2 Do you have to wear a suit?
3 Do you have to be on time?
4 Do you have to call your manager if you are going to be late?
5 Can you / Are you allowed to use your computer for personal emails?
6 Can you / Are you allowed to make personal phone calls in work time?
7 Are you allowed to bring your children to work?
8 Do you need to wear a uniform?
9 Do you have to bring in your own lunch?
10 Do you need to bring your own coffee?

4 Example answers
1 You mustn't smoke.
2 You can't use your mobile phone.
3 You must remove your laptop from your hand luggage.
4 You don't have to say what goods you have brought into the country.
5 You must wait here for a taxi.
6 You have to pay here.
7 You need to pay extra for service.

Vocabulary pp.63–64

1 1 tidy, known, lucky 4 visible, efficient, capable
2 perfect, moral, possible 5 legal, logical, legible
3 regular, responsible, relevant 6 honest, organized, similar

2 1 illegible 3 impossible 5 unlucky
2 invisible 4 disorganized 6 irresponsible

3 1 eco- 2 co- 3 anti- 4 ex- 5 cyber 6 e-

4 1 red 3 white 5 blue
2 Black 4 red 6 green

Work skills p.64

1 1 hold 5 catch
2 getting 6 like
3 take 7 give
4 cutting 8 put

2
1. Sales
2. Manuel's colleague
3. out of the office
4. 6.30
5. about the sales trip next week
6. 0731 8972

Functions p.65

1
1. advice
2. suggestions
3. careful
4. How
5. avoid
6. should
7. considered
8. better
9. why

2
1. I like the sound of that
2. I'm not keen on travelling
3. Thanks for the tip
4. I'd rather not pack
5. is a good idea but

3 1 A 2 R 3 A 4 R 5 R

6

Grammar pp.66–68

4
1. Two South African engineers: Pettie Petzer and Johan Jonker.
2. They wanted to help people in Africa who had to carry water in buckets.
3. The water goes in the wheel rather than in a container on top.
4. He heard about it when he was watching the news on TV.
5. It took a long time for people to have access to safe / clean drinking water.
6. The holes in the filter were small enough to remove all bacteria and viruses.

Focus
1   1 saw   2 were working   3 had struck
a 2   b 3   c 1
a was watching
b had seen, had tried
c invented, faced, decided, wanted, started, realized, was, had, saw, had to, took, designed

6
1. F: She got up at 3 a.m.
2. T
3. F: She fell over.
4. T
5. F: She had already missed several classes the week before.
6. F: After she had found out about the organization, she talked to her mother.
7. T

7 Example answers
2. Who had done the same thing when Lila was younger?
3. What happened while Lila was walking home?
4. What did Lila tell her teacher?
5. How often had Lila been late for lessons?
6. What did she do after she had found out about an organization that could help?
7. What was there in Lila's village by the end of the following year?

9
1. was watching
2. had lost
3. had
4. had carried
5. installed
6. had worked
7. were walking
8. had found

10
1. He had the idea while he was discussing optical lenses with a colleague.
2. They could be adjusted by the wearer to correct their own vision.
3. 40,000 glasses have been made so far.
4. Silver met Henry while he was working on an early project in Ghana.
5. He had been forced to retire because he could no longer see to thread the needle of his sewing machine.
6. After Henry had adjusted the glasses, he was able to thread a needle and go back to work.

11 Student A: 1 merry-go-round   2 storage tank   3 pipe   4 water underground   5 tap
Student B: 1 sun's energy   2 fresh water   3 fresh produce

Vocabulary pp.69–70

2
1. 140 litres: It takes 140 litres to grow, produce, package, and ship the beans you use to make an espresso.
2. It's the 'hidden' water used in the production of food and goods.
3. 150 litres a day
4. Because a huge amount of water is used in beef production.
5. Because of the growth of cities and rising populations.
6. improve agricultural performance, e.g. through better use of fertilizers and pesticides; improve management of water supply, e.g. more waste-water recycling, better methods of desalination so we can use sea water in agriculture
7. take a shower instead of a bath, fix leaky taps, eat hamburgers less often

3/4/5

-ment	-tion	-ance	-al
improvement	production	performance	removal
development	solution	appearance	appraisal
management	reduction	assistance	refusal
agreement	definition	disappearance	denial
encouragement	exploration	guidance	survival
payment	explanation	resistance	
investment	satisfaction		

6
1. satisfaction
2. payment
3. guidance
4. performance
5. solution
6. improvement
7. denial
8. survival

Work skills p.71

3
1. developing new technologies for use in water purification
2. the problem of water purification; the research carried out to find a solution; what is needed to put the solution into practice

4 tips 1, 2, 3, 4, 8, 9

5

beginning	middle	end
Today, I'm going to talk to you about … Good morning everyone and thank you for coming. Let's begin with … My name is …	Now let's move on to the second section … My next point deals with …	That brings me to the end of my talk. Does anyone have any questions? Thank you for listening. So to sum up … I'd like to leave you with one last point to think about …

Functions pp.72–73

2
1. internet, mouse, speakers, antivirus

3 1 c   2 d   3 a   4 b

4
a could, might, may
b must
c can't

5
1. working
2. like
3. fault
4. before
5. caused
6. try
7. wrong
8. need
9. solution

Focus

Describing problems	Asking about problems	Discussing solutions
The internet isn't working. There's a problem with … Something's wrong with …	How long has it been like that? Have you noticed it before? What do you think caused it?	Why don't we try …? What we need to do is … One solution is to …

6 a 2   b 1   c 4   d 3

7 1 It keeps making; Have you noticed; What you need
   2 Something's wrong; How long has it been; Why don't we put
   3 a problem with; tried using; isn't working
   4 happened; do you think; looks like

Review

Grammar p.75

1 1 e   2 c   3 b   4 a   5 d

2 1 were studying, decided, had both failed, were feeling
   2 were watching, had never seen, found, decided
   3 left, flew
   4 had been, travelled
   5 started, were carrying, met, wanted, bought
   6 got, decided, had sold, bought, floated
   7 were floating, saw, came, didn't attack
   8 reached, had had
   9 had experienced, had never been done
   10 didn't go

3 1 were studying
   2 established
   3 invented
   4 came up with
   5 led
   6 had
   7 was ploughing
   8 imagined
   9 had already invented
   10 became
   11 had been
   12 ran
   13 (had) started
   14 were thinking of
   15 retired
   16 had run

Vocabulary p.76

1 1 improvement
   2 denial
   3 assistance
   4 removal
   5 performance
   6 production
   7 explanation
   8 development
   9 definition
   10 appearance
   11 satisfaction
   12 reduction

2 1 definition
   2 removal
   3 explanation
   4 reduction
   5 production
   6 appearance
   7 assistance
   8 satisfaction
   9 improvement
   10 performance
   11 development
   12 denial

Work skills p.76

1 1 f   2 g   3 d   4 a   5 b   6 e   7 h   8 c

Functions p.77

1 1 What do you think caused it?
   2 Have you tried asking Michelle?
   3 Have you noticed it before?
   4 Why don't you try offering two meals for the price of one?
   5 How long has it been like that?

2 1 d   2 c   3 a   4 b

7

Grammar pp.78–80

1
	Matt	Grace
1	✓	
2		✓
3	✓	
4	✓	✓
5	✓	✓
6	✓	✓

4 1 yes
   2 yes
   3 very likely
   4 yes
   5 something completely different
   6 yes

5 1 I'll work really hard
   2 I'd say 'Yes'
   3 I'll probably do some training
   4 I'll really need to save some money first
   5 I'd probably do the same sort of job somewhere else
   6 it would have to be good

Focus
We form the Zero Conditional with *if* + **Present Simple**, Present Simple.
We form the 1st Conditional with *if* + Present Simple, **will** + **infinitive**.
We form the 2nd Conditional with *if* + **Past Simple**, *would* + infinitive.
We use the Zero Conditional to talk about things that are generally **true**.
We use the 1st Conditional to talk about future outcomes based on **likely** or possible conditions.
We use the 2nd Conditional to talk about future outcomes based on **unlikely** or imaginary conditions.

7 1 offers
   2 would it be
   3 gives
   4 would you do
   5 moved
   6 will you be
   7 could
   8 will you do

Vocabulary pp.81–82

2 1 £800
   2 the first day of each month
   3 He thought he had more than £2,407 in his account.
   4 £80
   5 his credit card bill
   6 £500

3 1 standing order
   2 account number
   3 transfer
   4 balance
   5 withdraw
   6 direct debit
   7 debits
   8 deposited

4 1 lend = give money to someone, to pay back later; borrow = receive money from someone, to pay back later
   2 deposit = put in; withdraw = take out
   3 standing order = an instruction to your bank to pay somebody a fixed amount of money from your account on the same day each week / month; direct debit = an instruction to your bank to allow somebody else to take an amount of money from your account on a particular date
   4 debit = take money from; credit = put money in
   5 open = start; close = end
   6 in credit = have money in your account; overdrawn = more money has been taken out of the account than you have put in

5 1 e   2 a   3 f   4 b   5 d   6 c

7 1 c   2 b   3 a   4 d   5 e

8 1 F   2 T   3 T   4 T   5 T   6 T

Work skills p.83

1 IT Consultant; the ability to design, test, install and monitor new systems; knowledge of Mandarin; experience in a similar role

2 a 3, 4   b 1   c 6   d 2   e 5

3 It is more formal, e.g. no contractions, length of sentences, the salutation and ending used.

4 1 b   2 e   3 f   4 g   5 c   6 d   7 a

Functions pp.84–85

2 1 They are health and safety consultants and they offer first aid courses.
   2 Students' own answers
   3 Students' own answers

3 1 What we can offer you
   2 We can (also) offer you a discount
   3 We cannot offer this discount unless

4 1 **Some** of Martina's colleagues …
   2 … people return **every year** …
   3 … **two** accidents
   4 **Martina** will organize …

    5 … in **three months**
    6 a discount of **15%**

5 1 important   5 sorry
    2 propose   6 return
    3 fine   7 deal
    4 main

Focus
Asking about requirements
What's the most important thing for you?
What are your main concerns?
Putting forward a proposal
What I propose is a package of beginner course plus refresher courses.
Negotiating
In return, would you consider a further discount?
Agreeing to a proposal / request
That would be fine for us.
It's a deal!
Rejecting a proposal / request
I'm sorry, but that's not possible.

7 1 A   2 A   3 R   4 A   5 A   6 R

8 1 In return   4 would be
    2 a deal   5 unless we
    3 afraid that   6 not possible

Review

Grammar p.87

1 1 c   2 e   3 a   4 d   5 b

2 1 didn't exist   5 went
    2 put   6 don't read
    3 could   7 give up
    4 will check, won't relax

3 1 would probably find   6 offered
    2 knew   7 don't take
    3 work   8 moved
    4 will probably   9 will become
    5 would make   10 stop

Vocabulary pp.87–88

1 1 pay   4 enter
    2 deposited   5 withdrew
    3 set up   6 transfer

2 1 25-04-43; 9723678   5 her salary
    2 £500   6 £150
    3 Her account is overdrawn.   7 her rent
    4 −£105.65

3 1 check   6 shares
    2 transfer   7 savings
    3 set up   8 PIN
    4 outgoings   9 open
    5 withdraw   10 interest

Work skills p.88

    1 in response   5 attached to
    2 a Front Desk Manager   6 qualification
    3 Post Ref   7 experience
    4 you will see   8 available for

Functions p.89

1 1 We cannot give you a discount on golf equipment unless you are a member of the sports club.
    2 We can offer you a special price of $20 per ticket.
    3 Can you help with my presentation? In return, I'll help you with your website.
    4 What is your priority here?
    5 I'm afraid a 15% discount wouldn't be possible.

    6 What we propose is a price of $20 …
    7 What are your main concerns?

2 1 R   2 A   3 A   4 A   5 R

3 1 I'm sorry, but that's not possible
    2 Yes, that would be fine for me
    3 Are you happy with that?
    4 We can agree to that.
    5 I'm afraid that wouldn't be possible

8

Grammar pp.90–92

1 1 the Mayans
    2 more than 2,000 years ago
    3 cacao
    4 Côte d'Ivoire, Ghana
    5 flour

2 1 Central America and Mexico
    2 It was introduced by the Spanish general, Hernán Cortés.
    3 It was drunk.
    4 Europe
    5 Chocolate is not as popular in Asia.
    6 It is likely that more chocolate will be consumed as Asian economies grow.
    7 Thousands of children in West Africa are being forced to harvest and pack cacao beans.

Focus
… products **will be consumed**. = will *future*
Less than 1% of the trillion dollars **has been used** … = Present Perfect
Thousands of children **are being forced** … = Present Continuous
Chocolate **was** first **produced** … = Past Simple
… they **are paid** very little. = Present Simple
1 *be* + past participle.
2 the object
3 the agent

4 1 was set up   9 have been described
    2 produce   10 are launching / have launched
    3 are sourced   11 will offer / are going to offer
    4 is made   12 will be taken
    5 have expanded   13 will love
    6 opened   14 will find
    7 sells   15 is currently being updated
    8 appeared

5 Example answers
    2 How do you produce chocolate?
    3 Where are your beans sourced from?
    4 How is the chocolate made?
    5 Where have you expanded since 2006?
    6 When did you open your first chocolate café?
    7 What does the café sell?
    8 Where did the café appear last year? / Has the café ever appeared on network TV?
    9 What have you / has the company been described as?
  10 What have you launched this week?
  11 What will you / are you going to offer next year?
  12 What will visitors be taken on?
  13 What will people love?
  14 What will people find on the website?
  15 What is currently being done to the website?

6 1 Chocolate was brought to Europe … by the Spanish.
    2 Sugar was added to the chocolate by the Europeans as …
    3 The first chocolate bars in Britain were made by J.S. Fry.
    4 Up to the 19th century, chocolate was drunk by rich people rather than …
    5 Chocolate-making businesses were started by the Swiss, Italians, and British …
    6 Family names were often used for the brand by company founders, for example Hershey, Cadbury, and Lindt.

7 Around 70% of the world's cocoa is produced by African countries.
8 Only 3% of the total amount of chocolate consumed is eaten by African consumers.

8 1 Student A: 1 d 3 f 5 e 8 c 9 a 11 b
Student B: 2 e 4 d 6 a 7 b 10 f 12 c

Vocabulary pp.93–94

2 1 Design 5 Packaging
2 Materials 6 Distribution
3 Production 7 Retail
4 Testing

3 1 shape, size, materials
2 40% plastic, 40% metal, 20% glass and other materials
3 various suppliers
4 the clarity
5 It's designed to reduce the amount of waste produced and to protect the contents during transportation.
6 air, sea, road (plane, ship, lorry)
7 product demonstrations, advice before and after purchase, customer service (repair, refunds, and replacements)

4 1 develop 7 production
2 distribution 8 pack
3 process 9 transportation
4 extract 10 advertise
5 assemble 11 demonstration
6 test 12 replacement

7

	recyclable	reusable
+	saves raw materials	saves raw materials
	saves money	reduction in the amount of rubbish produced
–	expensive process	not all products are as reusable as glass
	some materials can only be recycled a limited number of times	older products are less efficient than more recent models

Work skills p.95

3 1 d 2 f 3 g

Functions pp.96–97

2 1 Happy sundaes 3 Get in gear
2 The Picasso picture show

3 Example answers
1 is making all the decisions
2 he arrived late
3 is talking too fast

4 1 a mean 2 a follow 3 a through
b works b explain b makes
c show c with c clear

Focus

Checking someone understands you	Saying you understand
Do you see how it works? Would you like me to go through that again? Is everything clear?	I see what you mean. Yes, I'm with you. OK, that makes sense.
Saying you don't understand	Asking for clarification
Sorry, I don't follow you.	Can you show me that again? Can you explain what you mean by …

6 1 people 5 legs
2 bicycle 6 leg
3 hands 7 solution
4 position 8 race

7 Can you explain what you mean by …
Do you follow me?
Yes, I'm with you.
Do you see how it works?
I see what you mean.
Can you show me that again?
Would you like me to go through that again?

Review

Grammar pp.98–99

1 1 was opened 6 was launched
2 have been served 7 are being / will be invited
3 was employed 8 is being / will be held
4 are used 9 will be given
5 are cooked 10 has been invited

2 2 pizzas have been served since then
3 was Lucy employed previously
4 are used in her pizzas
5 are pizzas cooked
6 was launched
7 are customers being invited / will customers be invited to the restaurant tonight
8 is being / will be held next week
9 will the cooking demonstration be given by
10 who has been invited as well

3 3 One of the big pizzas companies previously employed Lucy.
8 Lucy Franks herself will give it.

4 2 come 8 named
3 has become 9 was served
4 will be eaten 10 have been established
5 will eat 11 is coloured
6 are eaten 12 have tried
7 was invented 13 is being eaten

Vocabulary pp.99–100

1 a distributed e production
b design f packed
c retail g materials
d tested

2 a 6 b 1 c 7 d 4 e 3 f 5 g 2

3 1 development 7 test
2 process 8 packaging
3 distribution 9 advertise
4 produce 10 demonstration
5 extraction 11 replacement
6 assemble 12 transport

4 1 produce(s) 4 replacement
2 extraction 5 transportation
3 demonstration 6 assembly

Work skills p.100

1 1 e 2 a 3 b 4 c 5 d

2 1 emails, texts, accounts
2 meetings, trade fairs, conferences
3 colleagues, customers, clients, friends
4 colleagues, customers, clients, friends
5 paperwork, exercise, research, accounts
6 coffee, photocopies
7 emails, texts, documents

Functions p.101

1 1 Can you explain what you mean by
2 Can you just clarify what
3 Would you like me to go through that again
4 Do you follow me
5 I don't understand how to

6 Can you show me that again

2 a 3 b 1 c 2

3 1 don't follow
2 it works
3 Is everything
4 that makes
5 how to
6 go through

9

Grammar pp.102–104

3 1 F: It changed in 1972.
2 T
3 F: Acer provided the computer services.
4 T
5 F: 90% of the money goes to the athletes and the Games.
6 T

Focus
1 c, d, e, f, g
2 a, b
1 who, which
2 defining
3 non-defining
4 g; object

4 1 which ND
2 who / that D
3 who ND
4 which / that D
5 which / that D
6 who ND
7 which ND
8 which / that D

5 1 Avery Brundage, who was an Olympic athlete, was the fifth president of the IOC.
2 Women's boxing, which featured 36 competitors, was included in the Olympics for the first time in 2012.
3 The Orbit, which was designed by Anish Kapoor and the engineer Cecil Balmond, is a 115-metre-high tower in the middle of the Olympic Park.
4 The Olympic tennis matches, which were very popular, were held at Wimbledon.
5 Mo Farah, who was born in Somalia, is the Olympic 10,000 metres and 5,000 metres champion.

6 1 d 2 e 3 g 4 h 5 b 6 f 7 c
8 a

Vocabulary pp.105–106

1 1 e 2 b 3 a 4 c 5 d

3 1 IT
2 retail
3 sales and marketing

4 2 team players
3 good communication skills
4 talented
5 hard-working
6 self-motivated
7 ambitious
8 creative
9 good leadership skills
10 practical

5 1 good leadership skills, good communication skills
2 creative, talented
3 independent, self-motivated
4 team player, practical
5 ambitious, hard-working

6 reliable – unreliable
sensible – reckless
hard-working – lazy
enthusiastic – unenthusiastic
experienced – inexperienced
laid-back – uptight

7 1 laid-back
2 lazy
3 reliable
4 reckless
5 experienced
6 enthusiastic

Work skills p.107

3 a 3 b 2 c 4 d 5 e 8 f 1 g 6
h 7

4 Yes: 1, 2, 3, 4, 6, 8   No: 5, 7

Functions pp.108–109

1 1 It's the (company's) annual meeting.
2 the management teams and important fundraisers
3 Most guests would get to the venue by metro.
4 There'll be a strike on the day of the meeting, so travel by metro won't be possible.

2 Charles de Gaulle airport: 38, coach
Orly airport: 25, coach
Gare du Nord: 1, taxi
Gare Saint-Lazare: 2, taxi

3 1 whether; I'd
2 booking; to
3 Could; Certainly
4 could; do
5 Do; no

Focus
1 Something's come up.
2 Unfortunately, …
3 We had hoped that …, but …

Making requests	Agreeing
I was wondering whether you could …	I'm happy to do that.
Would you mind booking …?	Certainly.
Could you tell me …?	That's no problem.
Do you think you could book …?	**Declining**
Do you mind booking …?	Well, I'd like to, but …
	No, we won't be able to do that because …

4 1 Unfortunately
2 Would you mind
3 I'm happy
4 we had hoped
5 do you think
6 I was also wondering
7 that will be possible
8 Could you send

Review

Grammar pp.110–111

1 1 ND: The 2012 World cup, which was held in South Africa, was …
2 D
3 ND: The IT conference, which will take place in Berlin, starts …
4 ND: Usain Bolt, who broke the 100 metres world record at the Beijing Olympics, also …
5 D
6 D

2 The relative pronoun can be left out in sentences 2, 5, and 6.

3 1 who fixed my shower
2 that I bought in the sales
3 I sent you
4 that set up our IT system
5 I'm presenting the paper to
6 Angela is talking to

4 1 The Titanic, which was built in Belfast, sank in 1912. / The Titanic, which sank in 1912, was built in Belfast.
2 Marius, who works for NASA, is an electrical engineer. / Marius, who is an electrical engineer, works for NASA.
3 Our company, which was founded in 1982, now has factories all across the world. / Our company, which now has factories all across the world, was founded in 1982.
4 Cairo, which has a population of about 9 million people, is one of the largest cities in the world. / Cairo, which is one of the largest cities in the world, has a population of about 9 million people.
5 My manager, who speaks four languages fluently, is Russian. / My manager, who is Russian, speaks four languages fluently.
6 Thomas Edison, who invented the light bulb and the phonograph, held 1,093 US patents in his name. / Thomas Edison, who held 1,093 US patents in his name, invented the light bulb and the phonograph.

5 1 which / that / Ø
2 which / that / Ø
3 who
4 who
5 who / that
6 who
7 which / that
8 which
9 which / that
10 which
11 who
12 which / that / Ø

Vocabulary pp.111–112

1
1. experienced
2. enthusiastic
3. independent
4. talented
5. unreliable
6. practical
7. uptight
8. hard-working

2
1. creative
2. experienced
3. self-motivated
4. team player
5. good leadership skills
6. ambitious
7. hard-working
8. good communication skills
9. independent
10. laid-back

Work skills p.112

1
2. an achievement
3. questions
4. our organization
5. this job
6. your last job
7. weaknesses
8. situation

2 a 1 b 7 c 6 d 8 e 2 f 5 g 4 h 3

Functions p.113

1
1. I was wondering if / whether you want to have a meeting tomorrow.
2. Would / Do you mind working at the weekend?
3. Could you give me your ID number?
4. I'd like to do some research, but I don't have enough time!
5. Something's come up.
6. I'm happy to chair the meeting.

2 1 R 2 A 3 R 4 A

3
1. ask
2. will
3. I'd
4. hoped
5. running
6. fine
7. Unfortunately
8. think
9. able
10. come
11. mind
12. Certainly

10

Grammar pp.114–116

1
William Harley – Arthur Davidson
Coco Chanel – Pierre Wertheimer
Charles Rolls – Henry Royce
Ben Cohen – Jerry Greenfield
Steve Jobs – Steve Wozniak
Bill Hewlett – David Packard
Wilbur Wright – Orville Wright
Neil Armstrong – Buzz Aldrin
John Lennon – Paul McCartney

2
1. the Homebrew Computer Club
2. a microcomputer
3. The Byte Shop
4. Longchamp Racecourse near Paris
5. perfume (Chanel No. 5)
6. her shareholding in Les Parfums Chanel

3
1. a bagel business
2. They chose a college town, which meant there were a lot of potential customers; there was no ice-cream shop, so there was no competition, and they made different ice creams every day.
3. Some of the profits go to the Ben and Jerry Foundation, which donates money to good causes.
4. at a Church festival in Liverpool
5. on a bus
6. It rejected the band because it thought guitar groups were on the way out.
7. Because the producer George Martin wasn't happy with him.

4
1. had started
2. wouldn't have met
3. hadn't got
4. should have
5. could have become

Focus
We use the 3rd Conditional to talk about the **imaginary** past.
We use the **Past Perfect** in the *if* clause.
We use **would** + **have** in the main clause.

We use *should have* to talk about the **best** thing to do.
We use *shouldn't have* to talk about the **wrong** thing to do.

5 1 e 2 h 3 f 4 a 5 g 6 b 7 d 8 c

6
1. should've
2. shouldn't have
3. should've
4. they'd gone, they'd have
5. hadn't, wouldn't have

7
1. should have practised
2. shouldn't have offered
3. should have realized
4. shouldn't have sold
5. shouldn't have sold
6. shouldn't have criticized

8 Example answers
1. had 29 years' flying experience, he might not have been able to land the plane safely
2. co-pilot training, he couldn't have taken the controls
3. into the aircraft, the engines wouldn't have stopped
4. they wouldn't have had to do an emergency landing
5. they could have reached an airfield
6. all 155 passengers might not have escaped

Vocabulary pp.117–118

2

	1st career	2nd career
1 Mariam	editor	landscape gardener
2 Liam	marketing manager	clubs and website for 'stay at home' dads
3 Beatrice	events management	catering company

3
1. a doing b being c to get
2. a to meet b to spend
3. a organizing b not having c to start

4/5

-ing	Examples	
after prepositions	good at organizing afraid of not having keen on spending thinking of taking interested in cooking specialize in providing involved in making	
after some verbs	enjoy being suggested doing going travelling	loved gardening ended up working meant leaving
infinitive	Examples	
after adjectives	hard to meet easy to spend	wanted to do difficult to manage
after some verbs	managed to get decided to start proved to be trying to set up	planned to go back used to organize need to work

6
1. playing
2. to apply
3. making
4. to break into
5. to cut
6. to use
7. managing
8. giving
9. to learn
10. going

8
1. to change
2. to have
3. identifying
4. to do
5. to meet
6. asking
7. earning
8. to work
9. to work
10. managing
11. to make
12. having
13. appearing
14. doing

Work skills p.119

3
1. conference call 1 = teleconference; conference call 2 = videoconference
2. teleconference = a possible new IT project; videoconference = a new company logo

4 1 teleconference: all except the fourth guideline
videoconference: second, fifth, eighth, ninth guidelines
2 teleconference: a problem with the line – Hanif introduces himself again; everyone sounds quiet – turn up volume
videoconference: picture breaks up – Junko emails the logo

5 1 there
2 volume
3 ahead
4 to say
5 This
6 here
7 breaking
8 sort out
9 come in
10 something
11 This
12 say

Functions pp.120–121

2 company, family, the economy

3 1 Seattle
2 Barcelona
3 creates apps and games
4 to launch a new smartphone game

4 a 4 b 1 c 5 d 2 e 3

5 1 got a promotion
2 moved to
3 In the end
4 changed jobs
5 ended up

Focus
1 Meeting someone again
2 Asking for news
3 Giving news about yourself
4 Saying goodbye

6 1 I haven't seen you in ages.
2 How's everything going?
3 I got a promotion.
4 What happened with
5 In the end
6 Are you still working at
7 changed jobs
8 I have to go now
9 I'll see you later
10 was lovely to meet you again

7 1 How's everything going?
2 Are you still doing that English course?
3 What have you been doing since I last saw you?
4 How are things at work?
5 What happened with your last project in the end?

Review

Grammar pp.122–123

1 1 If I hadn't bought an expensive car, I would have been able to afford a holiday.
2 If they had realized red and yellow were bad luck colours, they wouldn't have bought red and yellow flowers.
3 If I hadn't left my mobile at home, I would have called you.
4 He wouldn't have got a bonus if he hadn't worked very hard last year.
5 If we had listened to the instructions, we wouldn't have gone to the wrong room.
6 I would have given the waiter a tip if I had known service wasn't included.
7 If I hadn't lost my temper with my boss, I wouldn't have lost my job.
8 If we had made a better offer, we would have won the contract.
9 If my flight hadn't been delayed, I wouldn't have stayed at the airport hotel.
10 If he had gone on the course he would have know how to use the new software.

2 2 We should have checked the weather.
3 We shouldn't have taken too many clothes.
4 We shouldn't have booked tickets to the wrong airport.
5 We should have told our hosts when we were arriving.
6 We shouldn't have forgotten to take a phone or laptop.
7 We should have packed some suncream.
8 We should have taken some presents for our hosts.

3 Example answers
2 If we had checked the weather, we would have known about the hurricane.
3 If we hadn't taken too many clothes, our suitcases wouldn't have been so heavy.
4 If we hadn't booked tickets to the wrong airport, we would have arrived on time.
5 If we had told our hosts when we were arriving, someone would have met us.
6 If we hadn't forgotten to take a phone or laptop, we would have contacted our families.
7 If we had packed some suncream, we wouldn't have got sunburnt.
8 If we had taken some presents for our hosts, we wouldn't have felt embarrassed.

4 Example answers
2 If I hadn't overslept, I wouldn't have missed the bus.
3 If I hadn't missed the bus, I wouldn't have been late for work.
4 If I hadn't been late for work, my boss wouldn't have fired me.
5 If my boss hadn't fired me, I wouldn't have gone to a café to think things over.
6 If I hadn't gone to a café, I wouldn't have bought a paper.
7 If I hadn't bought a paper, I wouldn't have seen the advert for a diving instructor.
8 If I hadn't seen the advert, I wouldn't have called the company.
9 If I hadn't called the company, I wouldn't have got an interview.

Vocabulary pp.123–124

1 1 flying
2 learning
3 managing
4 to get
5 to carry
6 to buy
7 to have
8 designing
9 to help
10 seeing

2 1 experimenting
2 to start
3 mixing
4 to start
5 to get
6 creating
7 selling
8 to do
9 to get
10 to borrow

3 1 They made their jams for their friends.
2 The started selling their jams at the Borough Market in London.
3 They were good at creating unusual flavours.
4 A supermarket chain was interested in selling their jams.
5 It was hard to supply the supermarket's order because they were still making the jams in their apartment, and it was also difficult to get enough money to pay for the ingredients and jars.
6 Friends and family lent them money.

Work skills p.124

1 a 1, 7, 8   b 2, 4, 9   c 3, 5, 6

2 1 videoconference
2 The picture keeps breaking up.
3 four
4 the technology conference in Seattle next month
5 She wants to find out if it's still possible to register for the conference.
6 the events at the conference to promote their new line of tablets

Functions p.125

1 1 c 2 e 3 a 4 f 5 d 6 b

2 1 Long; going; promotion
2 things; changed; moved
3 happened; ended; later

Alastair Lane

INTERNATIONAL EXPRESS
INTERMEDIATE
Pocket Book

OXFORD
UNIVERSITY PRESS

Contents

Pocket Book Guide	3
Grammar	4
Vocabulary	11
Work skills	22
Functions	28
Classroom language	37
Grammar terms	38
Irregular verbs	40

Pocket Book Guide

Here is some information about the Pocket Book.

1 There are short examples of conversations for each section of the Student's Book. You can listen to these conversations using the audio files. The audio is on the DVD-ROM in your Student's Book Pack. Here are some suggestions.

  1 You can practise your listening. Just play the audio and listen. Listen a little bit every day to improve your listening skills.

  2 You can practise your speaking. You can take the **B** part and answer **A** in each conversation.

  3 You can practise your pronunciation. Listen carefully to how the people speak. Copy their pronunciation.

  4 You can improve your memory. Cover the **B** line. Then read the **A** line. Repeat until you can remember the **B** line.

2 You can check the notes in the Student's Book for each language point. The reference page is at the end of each section.

3 You can use the *Classroom language* section in class. Keep your Pocket Book on your desk and check the right phrase to use to ask questions, check meaning, and so on.

4 The *Grammar terms* section gives you some more study words about grammar.

5 The *Irregular verbs* section gives you a reference for common irregular verbs in the Present Perfect, Past Perfect, the Passive and Past Simple.

6 Take the Pocket Book with you to work. Keep it on your desk. Practise when you have spare time. Use it when you make a phone call or before you meet someone.

7 Take the Pocket Book on business trips or on holiday.

Grammar

UNIT 1 Present Simple and Present Continuous

1. **A** How *do* you *get* to work?
   B I *usually drive*.
2. **A** What products *does* your company *make*?
   B We *manufacture* pipes and tubes.
3. **A** What *is* Sara *working* on at the moment?
   B She's *organizing* the sales conference in Dubai.
4. **A** Lots of young people *are leaving* the country to look for work.
   B I *understand* why they are doing that. There aren't any jobs here.
5. **A** *Do* you *know* if there is chilli in the soup?
   B I'm not sure but it *smells* very spicy.
6. **A** *Do* you *have* a nice hotel room?
   B Yes, we do. We*'re having* a great time.
7. **A** *Do* you *remember* the name of our sales rep in Dublin? Is it Dana?
   B No, I *don't think* it's Dana. Maybe it's Diana.
8. **A** Are Stefanie and Trevor in the office today?
   B No, they *aren't* in today. They*'re doing* a training course.

Reference: Student's Book **p.14**

UNIT 2 Past Simple; Present Perfect Simple and Present Perfect Continuous

1. **A** When *did* you *start* working for Credit Suisse?
   B I *started* working here in 2009.
2. **A** *Did* you *speak* to Francis yesterday?
   B No, I *didn't*. I *didn't see* him in the office.
3. **A** How long *have* you *lived* in Denmark?
   B I*'ve lived* here for seven months.

4 A How long *have* we *had* a sales office in Japan?
B We*'ve had* an office in Tokyo *for years*. It's *been* there *since 1988*.

5 A James looks really tired today.
B Yes. He*'s been working* all night.

6 A *Have* you *been travelling* a lot?
B No, I *haven't been travelling recently* because we*'ve just had* a baby.

7 A *Has* the company website *been getting* a lot of hits?
B Yes, it *has*. Lots of people *have been visiting* the news page.

Reference: Student's Book **p.26**

UNIT 3 *will, may, might, be likely / possible*

1 A *Will* people *stop* using digital cameras in the future?
B No, they *won't*. Most people *will probably use* their phones to take pictures, but for professional pictures, you *will need* a proper digital camera.

2 A It's *possible* that my company *will go* out of business next year.
B *Will* you *look* for a new job?
A Yes, I *will*.

3 A *Will* the new database be ready for April?
B Probably not. The developers say it *might be* May.

4 A How many journalists *will be* at our product launch?
B There *will probably* be about twenty people.
C Carole White of Business News *will definitely attend* the launch. She told me last week.
A Great. What about the TV companies?
B *It's unlikely that* the TV companies *will be* at the launch. However, some radio journalists *might come* and they*'ll probably ask* us for an interview.
A Good. I*'m sure that* Martina *will give* them an interview. She likes talking to the press.

5 A We've asked four people if they want to retire early from the company. What do you think *they'll do*?
  B Well, Georgina Scott *definitely won't retire*. She wants to stay. And *I don't think* Oswald Buhler *will retire* – he loves his job.
  A I see. *I think* Rosa and Torsten *will leave* the company. They only have six more months before the end of their contracts.

Reference: Student's Book **p.38**

UNIT 4 Making comparisons

1 A Is Stonehenge *older than* the Egyptian Pyramids?
  B Yes, it is. Stonehenge is *a lot older* than the Pyramids. It's about 2,000 years older.
  A So is Stonehenge *the oldest* monument on Earth?
  B No, it isn't. There are other ones. For example, the Gobekli temple in Turkey is *much older than* Stonehenge. It may be 6,500 years older.
  A That's incredible.

2 A What's *the cheapest day* to fly to Paris?
  B Tuesday *is cheaper* than other days of the week. Avoid Saturday. That's *the most expensive day*.
  A Right. What's *the best* time to fly?
  B The morning. Normally, early morning flights are *less expensive* than afternoon or evening flights.
  A So the afternoons are *busier* than the mornings?
  B That's right, especially between 2 p.m. and 9 p.m. In fact, Friday afternoon is *the worst time* to fly. It's *the busiest time* of the week.

3 A What's the *best* way to travel from Paris to Marseilles?
  B The plane is *faster* than the train, but I prefer to go by rail.
  A Why?
  B The plane is *slightly more expensive* than the train, but the train is *far more comfortable*.

A What about a coach?
   B The coach is the *cheapest* option, but it isn't *as good as* the train for working.

4 A Let's look at our sales figures.
   B Right. Sales this month are *slightly higher* than last month.
   A Good. What about our sales teams?
   B The London team was the *most successful*. Their sales rose by 15%.
   A How about Madrid?
   B Their results were *worse* than expected, I'm afraid.

5 A How is the Italian market doing?
   B It's doing OK, but it's not growing *as fast as* the German market.
   A How about the UK?
   B It was our *biggest* market last year, but the situation is *more difficult* this year because of the euro.

Reference: Student's Book **p.50**

UNIT 5 Modal and related verbs: *have to, must, need to, be allowed to, can*

1 A *Can* you *use* Facebook or Twitter at work?
   B No, we *aren't allowed to use* any social networking sites.

2 A When *do* we *have to pay* our electricity bill?
   B We *have to* pay before 1st January.

3 A *Can* we *use* the tennis courts at the hotel?
   B Yes, you *can*, but you *must wear* the correct shoes.

4 A *Does* Roger *have to go* to the meeting tomorrow?
   B Yes, he *does*. He *has to go* because our clients want to meet him.
   A How about Erica? *Does* she *need to go*, too?
   B No, she *doesn't have to go* if she doesn't want to.

5 A *Do* we *need to bring* any food to the party?
   B No, you *don't need to* bring anything. There will be lots of food there.

6 A *Are* we *allowed to take* photos during the factory tour?
   B Yes, that's OK. You *don't need to ask* for permission in the factory. However, you *mustn't take* any photos in the research centre. That's top secret!

7 A *Can* anyone *access* your website?
   B No, you *can't access* it without a password. You *must register* first.

Reference: Student's Book **p.62**

UNIT 6 Past Simple, Past Continuous, Past Perfect

1 A What *did* you *do while* you *were waiting* for your flight?
   B I *bought* a present for my daughter while I *was looking* round the shops.

2 A John is going to leave the company!
   B Yes, I know. He *told* me while we *were having* lunch.

3 A Was your flight on time?
   B No, it was late because the previous flight *had been delayed*.

4 A Anita looked very happy this morning.
   B Yes, she *was* happy because she *had just signed* a new contract.

Reference: Student's Book **p.74**

UNIT 7 Zero, 1st, and 2nd Conditional

1 A Is the hotel swimming pool open every day?
   B Yes, but it's outdoors. So *if it rains*, we *close* the pool.

2 A *If you see* Svetlana this afternoon, *will you ask* her to call me?
   B Yes, *I'll ask* her *if* I *see* her.

3 A *If* I *were* you, *I'd look* for a new job.
   B I don't really want to. If I got another job, I *wouldn't get* as much money.

Reference: Student's Book **p.86**

8 Grammar

UNIT 8 Passives: Present Simple, Present Continuous, Present Perfect Simple, Past Simple, *will*

1. **A** Where *are* pistachio nuts *produced*?
   B They*'re grown* in Iran, Turkey, and the USA.
2. **A** Who *was* the website *designed by*?
   B It *was designed by* a guy in Korea.
3. **A** Why did you get the train to work today?
   B My car*'s being repaired* so I can't drive at the moment.
4. **A** Has the new photocopier *arrived* yet?
   B Yes, it*'s* just *been delivered*.
5. **A** Where *will* next year's conference *be held*?
   B It*'ll be held* in Seoul.
6. **A** Why *has* the meeting *been cancelled*?
   B Because lots of people *have been delayed* by the weather.

Reference: Student's Book **p.98**

UNIT 9 Relative clauses

1. **A** The woman *who was working* part-time suddenly quit.
   B Is she the one *who had* a problem with her visa?
   A I think so.
2. **A** Is this the door *which we need to repair*?
   B No, it's the other door *that doesn't open*. The one on the left.
3. **A** Rafael Nadal, *who won the 2013 French Tennis Open*, comes from Mallorca.
   B Really? I didn't know that.
   A Yes, he comes from Manacor, *which is a town on the east of the island*.

4 A Our holiday was great but it was often over 35 degrees, *which was too hot.*
B Really? We went to Berlin, *which was beautiful.* Most days, it was about 25 degrees, *which was just right.*

Reference: Student's Book **p. 110**

UNIT 10 3rd Conditional; *should / shouldn't have*

1 A Bill Hewlett and Dave Packard chose their company name by tossing a coin. *If* Packard *had won,* they *would have called* their company Packard-Hewlett.
B Really? I never knew that. So that's why it's called HP today.

2 A Nicola left the company because she wanted to be a sales manager.
B I know. If *we'd promoted* her, she *would have stayed* with us.

3 A We were lucky that the weather was nice yesterday.
B Yes, if *it hadn't been* sunny, we *wouldn't have had* a barbeque.

4 A The negotiation failed because our competitor offered £30,000 more than us.
B We *should have offered* the company more money.

5 A Camilla is furious because you complained about her on Facebook.
B I know. I *shouldn't have written* that message. I didn't know she looked at my Facebook page.

Reference: Student's Book **p.122**

Vocabulary

UNIT 1 Social networks and the internet

1 A I've forgotten my password so I can't *access* the company website.
B It's OK. I can *log in* with my password, and we can look at it together.

2 A What happens if I follow this *link*?
B It goes to a website where you can *chat* about travel and things like that.

3 A I've *uploaded* some photos onto our shared folder at work.
B Great! I'll *download* them onto my laptop later.

4 A Did you read my latest *blog* post?
B Yes, I did. I loved it. I really liked the *link* to the website about China.

5 A The computer is showing a message. It says it needs to *update* your antivirus software.
B It's OK. Just *click* on 'accept'. It happens all the time.

UNIT 2 Starting a new business; phrasal verbs

1 A I'm trying to *set up* my own company, but it's really difficult. There's so much paperwork.
B Don't let the paperwork *put* you *off*. I can help you with that.

2 A I'm *putting together* a financial plan for my new company. Do you have any advice?
B Yes, *find out* how much you have to pay in company tax. That can be very expensive.

3 A What research *did* you *carry out* before you chose the location for the new factory?
B We got a team of consultants *to look into* the various options.

4 A I don't think people will understand our presentation. We need to *break* the information *down* so it's easier to follow.
  B I see what you mean. OK. Don't worry. I'll *sort* it *out*. I'll rewrite it tomorrow.

5 A I'm *looking after* the visitors to the resort this afternoon.
  B Oh good. Don't forget to *point out* our new squash court. I want them to see that.

6 A I'm really scared of flying, especially the moment when the plane *takes off*.
  B You *take after* your father. He was the same. He was terrified of flying.

7 A We interviewed one person today and he *turned up* twenty minutes late.
  B Did you *take* him *on*?
  A Yes, we did actually. His CV was perfect so we didn't worry about the time.

8 A Can you *turn* the TV *on*, please?
  B Sure. Why?
  A I want to watch the sports news. I heard that my football team wanted to sign a new manager, but he *turned* them *down*.

9 A A big multinational has *taken over* my company and now everything has changed.
  B Really? How?
  A Well, for example, they're really serious about saving money. We have all these new rules, so when you leave work, you have to *turn off* your computer, and *turn off* all the lights and things like that.

UNIT 3 The speed of change; describing cause and effect

1. **A** *Because of* the strong wind and rain, all flights into and out of the country have been cancelled.
   B Really. What *caused* all this bad weather?
   A It's *due to* a tropical storm passing through.

2. **A** Our sales results are very poor this year and *as a consequence*, we'll have to close two of our factories.
   B Oh, no. What happened?
   A Sales are down *because* of the recent economic problems. We also lost a really important customer this year. *As a result*, our sales fell 65%.
   B Closing the factories will *lead to* lots of job losses.
   A I know. It could *result in* 600 people losing their jobs.

UNIT 4 City descriptions; -ing vs -ed adjectives

1. **A** I'm really *annoyed* that the air conditioning isn't working.
   B I know. And it's so *humid* today too.

2. **A** Did you stay in a *traditional* hotel in China?
   B No, they were all fully booked. We were so *disappointed*.

3. **A** What did you think of the *modern* buildings in Tokyo?
   B They were *stunning*! It was like being in a sci-fi movie.

4. **A** Istanbul is great, isn't it? It's such a *cosmopolitan* city.
   B Yeah, Istanbul was *amazing*. We had such a great trip.

5. **A** In Albi, in France, you can visit a museum dedicated to the artist Toulouse-Lautrec.
   B Is it any good?
   A Yes, it's very *interesting*. We saw lots of his *famous* paintings.

6 A They say the clubs in the old town are *the liveliest*.
   B Really? I think the clubs there are *boring*. I prefer the clubs in the port.

7 A The food in that restaurant was *delicious*, wasn't it?
   B Yes, and I was *pleased* to see lots of traditional dishes on the menu. I love trying food like that.

8 A Have you visited the *ancient temple* yet?
   B Yes, and we had a guided tour. It was *fascinating*. The guide told us all about the history of the building.

9 A I'm *surprised* that there are lots of other tourists here.
   B Me too. I didn't know it was such a *popular resort*.

UNIT 5 Colours and colour idioms; prefixes

1 A The company *is in the red*.
   B Really? By how much?
   A We owe the bank $20,000.

2 A How are the company finances?
   B Very good, actually. We've been *in the black* all year.

3 A In the UK, *white* goods means things like fridges and washing machines.
   B Really? In the United States, it might mean things like sheets and pillows.

4 A You tell me that you often feel angry and frustrated at work?
   B That's right, doctor. Sometimes, I just *see red* and I get furious. I don't know why.

5 A My boss came into work and asked me to move to Hong Kong. I couldn't believe it!
   B So she just asked you *out of the blue*?
   A That's right. I didn't expect it at all!

6 A What sort of things are available on the *black market*?
 B Things like cigarettes from other countries.

7 A Do you think internet companies should share people's personal information?
 B I'm not sure. It's a *grey area*, isn't it.

8 A Do you remember *Black Monday*?
 B Yes, I do. I was working for an investment firm at the time.

9 A Have we got the *green light* for our project yet?
 B No, we're still waiting to hear from the committee.

10 A We're really stuck on this project.
 B I agree. What we really need is some *blue sky thinking*.

1 A How is your relationship with your *ex-husband*?
 B Actually, we now have a very good relationship! I was very *unhappy* when we were married. He was always working and we argued a lot. But now we're friends again.

2 A My dream is to become a pilot, but I think it's *impossible*.
 B My cousin is a pilot for BA. If she can do it, I'm sure you can.

3 A There's a man who does the same job as me and he gets paid more money. Isn't that *illegal*? It's discrimination against women.
 B Yes, it is. That doesn't happen at my company.

4 A Why was he *disqualified* from the competition?
 B I don't know. I think he was very *unlucky*.

5 A The *ecotourism* business is very successful in Scotland.
 B Yes, the travel companies *cooperate* really well with the local communities.

6 A Luke is really *disorganized*, isn't he?
 B I know. He never replies to *emails*. It's very *irresponsible*.

7 A The government are very *anti-smoking*, aren't they?
 B So am I! I hate the smell of cigarettes. It's so *unpleasant*.

8 A Is *cybercrime* a big problem?
B Yes, internet security companies are *incapable* of stopping all the hackers, viruses, and other problems.

9 A Look at this menu. It's *illegible*.
B I know. How are we going to order any food?

10 A I knew a guy who ran an *e-commerce* company, and he actually stole €100 from lots of different people. They ordered things from the site, but he never delivered them.
B That's just *immoral*. It's only a small amount but it's still stealing.

UNIT 6 Water footprint; noun formation

1 A I hear that there is some *resistance* to longer working hours.
B That's right. The *refusal* to work more hours is threatening the *survival* of the company.
A And our bonuses.

2 A I tried to talk about *job satisfaction* in my *appraisal*, but no-one was listening.
B I know. *Management* don't seem to care, do they.

3 A Our client needs some *assistance* with their *investments* in Asia. Any suggestions?
B Vanessa Chan can give you some *guidance*. She's an expert on the Asian markets.
A That's great.

4 A *Consumption* of our cherry soda is really down this year.
B What's the best *solution*?
A Maybe we should just stop *production*.

5 A What happened in the fraud case?
B The company CEO issued a *denial* of the charges against him.

6 A Our sales team's *performance* has been poor this year.
B I agree. We need to see a big *improvement* in the next quarter.
A It's a tough market. The sales team need some *encouragement*. Maybe we should them offer a bigger bonus.

7 **A** There's been a big *reduction* in the number of wild bees.
   B I know. Their *disappearance* is a big mystery.

8 **A** This textbook is very useful. It's got *definitions* of all the key words.
   B Yes, and the explanations are really clear.

UNIT 7 Money and finance

1 **A** I suggest that you *deposit* some money every month into *a savings account*.
   B How much *interest* does it pay?
   A About 5% per year. You can pay by *standing order* too, so it's easy to deposit the same amount every month.
   B OK. In that case, I'd like to *open a savings account*, please.

2 **A** I'm *overdrawn* again. Every month, I owe the bank about €300.
   B It's the same for me. My account is never *in credit* at the start of the month. I just have so many *outgoings*.
   A I think everyone is in the same situation. My bank *balance* is always in the red.

3 **A** I have a lot of *savings* at the moment.
   B Then you should invest them. Buy *shares*. If you don't invest, the value of your savings will fall because of *inflation*.
   A I don't want to buy shares. I think I'll put the money in a *pension scheme*.

4 **A** Do you use *online banking*?
   B Yes, of course. It's so easy to *transfer money*. You just need the account number.
   A I don't know. I use *telephone banking*. I think it's safer.
   B That's so old-fashioned. Online banking is better. You immediately know if someone debits or credits your account.

5 A I'd like to apply for a *mortgage*.
   B Certainly. How much do you need to *borrow*?
   A About €100,000.
   B Do you have an *account* with us?
   A No.
   B Well, if you open an *account* with us, we can offer you a low-*interest* mortgage and very reasonable home *insurance*.
   A Great.

UNIT 8 Product journey

1 A How many people are involved in the *assembly* of your bicycles?
   B About forty people. We *assemble* the bikes here in the UK, although we *produce* the parts in China.
   A So the first part of the *production* is in China?
   B That's right. We then *transport* the parts here by sea. The *transportation* costs are relatively low.

2 A I love the *packaging* on your new line of crisps.
   B Thank you. The *package design* is by a company in Korea.

3 A How long does *distribution* to the retail outlets take?
   B It takes about three days to distribute items to our European customers and about a week to Asia.

4 A We need a new *advertisement* for our men's shampoo line.
   B Why do you want to *replace* the old campaign?
   A We've *advertised* the shampoo in the same way for ten years.

5 A How do you *extract* copper from the old computers?
   B The *extraction* is all automatic. Special recycling machines process everything. I can *demonstrate* how they work if you like.
   A Yes, please, a *demonstration* would be great.

UNIT 9 Describing personal qualities at work

1 A Rita is very *ambitious*. She wants to be the CEO one day.
  B Yes, she has *great leadership skills* and she's *very hard-working*. I think she can do it.

2 A So we have Tom and Sara as candidates to run the children's summer camp. I thought Sara was *enthusiastic*. She really wanted the job.
  B Yes, I thought she was a good candidate too. Tom was too *laid-back*. He might be a bit *unreliable*.

3 A I think Sandor is so *talented* as a designer.
  B Oh, yeah. He is incredibly *creative*. His ideas for our new necklaces were amazing.
  A Everyone is *enthusiastic* about the designs. I think they're going to be a real success.

4 A I was thinking of asking Frida to be the new head of Quality Control. She's completely *reliable*.
  B That's true, but she's a little bit *inexperienced*. She's only worked for us for eighteen months.
  A That's not a problem. She's very *self-motivated* so she'll quickly learn the job.

5 A The staff have been complaining about Duncan. They say he's really *lazy*. He doesn't do any work and spends two hours at lunch.
  B I know, and you can't criticize him because he gets really *uptight*.
  A We should ask him to leave the company but he's so *experienced*.

6 A We cannot work with this advertising company. They're completely *reckless*. They make shocking adverts just to win industry awards.
  B I agree. How about the Harris and Paul Agency. They're very *sensible* and they don't take risks.
  A I'm not sure about that. I worked with Charles Harris a few years ago and he was really *unenthusiastic*.

7 **A** Let's ask Josef and Clara to give the presentation together. They both have *great communication skills*.
   B Yes, but Josef is very *independent*. He doesn't like working with other people.
   A He can be a *good team player* too, though.

UNIT 10 Changing careers; -ing vs infinitive

1 **A** I'm *thinking of going* freelance but I'm *afraid of losing* my monthly salary.
   B If you're *interested in doing* that, talk to my sister. She's a freelancer and she can give you some advice.

2 **A** Last year, I *decided to do* the Inca Trek in Peru. I *enjoyed doing* it, but it was tough.
   B Really? It must be *hard to walk* and carry your bags.
   A Actually, the porters carried our bags.
   B But I guess it *wasn't easy to put up* the tents.
   A Actually, they did that too.

3 **A** We're *planning to have* an office party this summer. Either in July or August.
   B I *suggest holding* it in July because lots of people are on holiday in August.
   A OK. Will you organize it? You're *good at arranging* social events and things like that.

4 **A** I *missed going* to the Milan Fashion Show this year.
   B I know. Poor you. I *managed to speak* to Alessandro Spinelli and he *offered to produce* some new designs for us.
   A That's great.

5 **A** We *hope to finish* the first stage of the project by next month but we're a bit short of people.
   B Right. Well, I *don't mind helping out*.
6 **A** We *aim to expand* our sales in Slovakia next year.
   B That's a good idea. We *need to increase* business across Eastern Europe.
7 **A** We're *planning to arrive* at your office at about 3 p.m.
   B Excellent. We're *looking forward* to meeting you.
8 **A** The number of visitors to the ski resort is *likely to rise* over the next few years.
   B That's good news. People really *enjoy coming* here. It's a perfect family resort.
9 **A** I *expect to visit* our new suppliers in Bangladesh soon.
   B Really? *I'd like to go* with you. Is that possible?
10 **A** Fernanda has *decided to recruit* some new sales representatives.
   B I know. I *want to talk* to her about it.
11 **A** My brother and I are *planning to cycle* across South America.
   B Really. I can't *imagine doing* anything like that.

Work skills

UNIT 2 Team meetings

1. **A** Shall we start the meeting? Oh, is Jackie here?
   B No, she can't make the meeting today.

2. **A** The first item on the agenda is the new company logo. Michael?
   B Right, I wanted to talk about the suggestions from the public for the new logo.

3. **A** OK, that's everything on the logo. Let's move onto the next point. We don't have enough people for the product launch next week.
   B Would you like me to help? I'm free on Thursday and Friday.

4. **A** We've had some complaints about late deliveries to customers.
   B Really? Could you be more specific, Carmen? How late were they?

5. **A** The next item on the agenda is the new staff language courses. Lola, would you like to fill us in on what's happening with that?
   B Certainly. We're arranging courses for thirty people in Russian and basic Chinese.

6. **A** Does anyone have anything they would like to add regarding the language courses?
   B No, I don't think so.
   C No, I'm OK.
   A OK, that's the end of the meeting. To sum up, we will see designs for the new logo next week. Carmen will look into the problem with the late deliveries and report back to us. And the new language courses are all under control. Great work, everybody.

UNIT 4 Presentations 1: using visual aids

1 A Let's look at this graph. The horizontal axis shows the last eighteen months. The vertical axis shows the rise in sales.

2 A This pie chart represents the main markets for the olive oil sector. If you look at the purple segment, you will see that 60% of our sales are in the Middle East.

3 A This table shows the number of students at the university's Department of Engineering. Each cell here represents the number of students on each course.

4 A Let's look at this graph. As you can see from the way that the line falls, we are not doing well at the moment. This arrow shows the moment when we lost our main customer in South Africa. That was the beginning of the problem.

5 A This slide shows the cost of our products. The red numbers indicate the change in prices from last year.

UNIT 5 Telephoning

1 A Could I speak to Herta Sorensen, please?
  B Yes, certainly. Hold the line, please … I'm sorry, her line's busy at the moment. Would you like to leave a message?
  A Yes, please. Could you tell her Andrew Parker called? It's about our meeting next week. I'd like to reschedule it.
  B OK, I'll pass on your message, Mr Parker. Does Herta have your number?
  A Yes, she does.

2 A Hello. Could you put me through to Alicia, please?
  B I'm afraid she's on another line. Could you hold on a moment?
  A Actually, I'm in a bit of a hurry.
  B OK. Can I take a message?
  A No, it's OK. I'll call back later.

3 A Hi. Shelly? It's Gianni here.
  B Gianni, hi! Thanks for getting back to me! How are you?
  A I'm fine, thanks. I'm calling because … and …
  B Sorry, Gianni, you're breaking up. Can you repeat that?
  A Sorry, yes, I'm calling about … and … so …
  B Sorry, I didn't catch that.
  A I … and …
  B Gianni? Hello? Your phone's cutting out. I'm on a train. Can I call you back later today?
  A Yes, fine. I'll be here in my office all day.

4 A Hello, Chieko?
  B Oh, Olga. Thanks for getting back to me. Did you find out the information that I needed?
  A Not yet, but I'll have all the figures for you by two o'clock. Can I give you a call later today?
  B Actually, it's nine p.m. here in Japan, so tomorrow would be better for me.
  A OK. I'll send you an email this afternoon, and then I'll call you tomorrow. OK?
  B Great.

UNIT 6 Presentations 2: structuring a talk

1 A Good afternoon, everyone, and thank you for coming. My name is Kevin Lai. Today, I'm going to talk to you about business opportunities in Indonesia.

2 A I've divided my talk into three sections. First, we'll look at the economic situation in Indonesia. Secondly, I'll talk about the country's manufacturing industry. Finally, I'll talk about the legal situation. Let's begin with a quick overview of the Indonesian economy.

3 A Does anyone have any questions? No? OK. Now let's move onto the second section of my talk: manufacturing in Indonesia.

4 A My next point deals with the law regarding foreign employees in the country.

5 A I'd like to leave you with one last point to think about. The government is very keen to encourage foreign companies to come and work in the country.

6 A So to sum up, Indonesia is one of the fastest growing economies in the world at the moment. This is the perfect time to set up your business in Jakarta or anywhere else in the country. Thank you for listening.

UNIT 9 Job interviews

1 A What do you think your key skills are?
B I'm very experienced in project management.

2 A What do you think your main weaknesses are?
B I'm sometimes quite impatient, but now that I have more experience, it's not such a problem.

3 A Why did you leave your last job?
B I left to do a two-year Masters in Business Management.

4 A Why do you want this job?
B I love running training courses and I could do a lot of staff training in this role.

5 A Can you tell us about a difficult situation you've had at work and how you dealt with it?
B Yes. Last year, we had an impossible deadline for a project. I knew that we could not do quality work in the time available, but the client insisted. In the end, we had a big meeting and I explained our position. The client agreed and we changed the dates.

6 A Can you tell us of an achievement of which you are proud?
 B In my last company, I arranged our sponsorship of a local girls' football team. We got a lot of good publicity for the company and we really improved our relationship with the local community.

7 A What do you know about our organization?
 B Well, I've read your website and a number of news stories, so I'm familiar with your big deal with Nissan.

8 A Do you have any questions for us?
 B Yes, could you tell me something about a typical day at work?

UNIT 10 Teleconferencing and videoconferencing

1 A Hi, Matthias? I think we're all here now. Hi, Amelie and Joseph. Can everyone hear OK?
 B Hi, Yvonne. I can hear you fine.

2 A Before we start, can you please say your name before you speak? It will help us all to communicate more easily. Also, if you want to speak to a particular person, please say their name first. So, first of all, I have Harry with me here in Dallas. Harry, can you start us off?
 B Sure. Er … Well, it's Harry here.

3 A Sorry, Matthias? Before we continue, we need to sort out this technical problem.
 B Oh? What's wrong? Everything looks fine my end.
 A We can hear you, but there's a problem with the picture. It keeps breaking up, so we can't see your slides.
 B Oh, sorry. Wait a minute … I'm just going to check that the camera is plugged in correctly. How's that?
 A Oh yes, that's much better.

4 A Joseph, would you like to say something about the situation in Spain?
 B Yes. Er, well this is Joseph speaking. Here in Spain, things are looking good.

5 A Could I just say something here?
  B Sure, Amelie, go ahead.

6 A Matthias, did you want to say something?
  B Yes, I was going to suggest that we arrange a face-to-face meeting for next month.

7 A Yvonne? … Yvonne? Are you there?
  B Yes, I am.
  A You sound a little quiet. Could you turn up the volume a little?

8 A So, I think we should move our head office from Lyon to Paris.
  B Amelie, do you want to come in on that? You know Paris very well.

Functions

UNIT 1 Networking

1 A It's Harriet Richards, isn't it?
   B Yes, that's right. I'm sorry, I don't remember your name.
   A It's Fabian Adamski. We met at the Paris Air Show last year.
   B I remember now. How are you, Fabian?

2 A Katrina, I'd like you to meet my colleague Alan Short.
   B Pleased to meet you, Katrina. I'm in charge of marketing in your country.
   A Really? Well, I'm pleased to meet you too. Here's my card.
   B Thank you. Here's mine.

3 A Where do you work, Fabian?
   B I'm based in Warsaw. Currently, I'm recruiting a new sales team for Poland.
   C Really? I remember you worked in Vilnius before.
   B That's right. I worked for Air Lithuania.

4 A Are you familiar with SAP?
   B Yes, I am. But I'd like to know more about it.
   A OK. Would you like to meet the Head of IT?
   B Yes, please. That would be great.

5 A Could you give me your email and I'll save it on my phone?
   B OK, it's ianjackson (all one word) at amc dot com.

Reference: Student's Book **p.17**

UNIT 2 Checking progress; delegating tasks

1 A How are we doing with the preparations for the New Year sales?
   B Everything's fine, but we still need to order the signs for the shop windows for all 62 branches.
   A Who's going to look after that?
   B I'll do it. Leave it with me.

2 A Have we got the contracts for the summer temporary staff yet?
  B No, not yet.
  A We need them soon. Can you deal with that, Rui?
  C Yes, I can do that.

3 A OK, that's nearly the end of the meeting. Have we covered everything?
  B No, we need someone to show some visitors around on Friday. Is anyone free to do that? Margaret?
  C I won't be able to do that because I have another meeting.
  B Victor?
  D Friday afternoon? Sorry, I'm not free then.
  B Nick?
  E I have visitors coming on Friday and I have to go to the airport. I think my assistant is free. I'll ask him.
  B Really? Can I leave this with you?
  E Yes, leave it with me.

4 A Alberto, we need translations of our website into six different languages. I'd like you to handle that.
  B OK, no problem.

Reference: Student's Book **p.29**

UNIT 3 Making arrangements

1 A We need a meeting to arrange next year's budget. Is Thursday 20th June convenient for you?
  B I'm afraid the 20th is no good for me.
  A Are you free on the 21st?
  B That should be fine. Let me check with my PA. I'll get back to you this afternoon.

2 A Why don't we meet on Wednesday at 11 a.m.?
  B Yes, I can make Wednesday at 11. Uma should be at the meeting too, so we need to check the time with her.
  A OK. I'll pencil in 11 on Wednesday for now. Will you speak to Uma?
  B Yes, I'll ask her. As soon as I know, I'll let you know.

3 A We need to have a meeting to choose a new company to clean the offices. Is next Monday good for you?
  B Sorry, I'm busy then.
  A How about Thursday?
  B Yes, that should be fine.

4 A Have we got a date for a meeting with the Managing Director yet?
  B I'm sorry, no. She knows about the meeting but I can't confirm the date or time right now.

Reference: Student's Book **p.41**

UNIT 4 Giving opinions

1 A What do you think about manufacturing our products in India?
  B From a financial point of view, it's an excellent idea.

2 A Jeffrey wants to change the company name. What's your opinion on that?
  B I completely agree. Our name is really old-fashioned.

3 A I don't think we should expand into the Chinese market.
  B I'm afraid I disagree. I think there are huge opportunities there.

4 A Personally, I think the Quality Control team is doing an excellent job.
  B I'm sorry, but I don't agree. Our customers returned 100 cables last quarter because they didn't work properly.

5 A I think we should appoint two new managers. We have too much work at the moment for just three people.

B I take your point but I think the situation will be different next year. We could have too many managers then.

6 A We need to hire a new person to handle negotiations with the government. We're not winning any big contracts.
  B I see what you mean. Who is the best candidate, do you think?
  A In my opinion, it's Moira Stevens.

7 A We shouldn't only recruit experienced staff.
  B That's a good point. Many of our best employees came here direct from university.
  A On the other hand, it is expensive to train people who don't have experience.
  B I see what you mean, but young people have lots of energy and new ideas.

Reference: Student's Book **p.53**

UNIT 5 Giving advice and suggestions

1 A I want to try a traditional Thai dish. What do you recommend?
  B How about trying the fried rice? I particularly like the fried rice with crab.
  A I'm not keen on seafood, actually.
  B Ah, OK. Why don't you try the rice with chicken?
  A Good idea. I like the sound of that.

2 A I have a free afternoon in Budapest. What do you think I should do?
  B You should definitely go for a walk on Margaret Island. It's a lovely island in the river between Buda and Pest.
  A That sounds like a good idea.

3 A I'm visiting London next month. Do you have any advice?
  B Have you considered getting an Oyster card? You can use it to pay for all public transport in the city.
  A Oh, great! Thanks for the tip.

4 A We're going on holiday to Italy but we want to do something different. Do you have any suggestions?
  B Yes. Have you considered agriturismo? It's where you stay on local farms with families. It's more fun than a hotel.
  A That's an interesting idea.

5 A Is there a lot of crime in the city centre?
  B Yes, there is. One thing you should be careful of is pickpockets on buses. I'd leave your camera here.
  A I'd rather not, actually. I'd like to take some pictures while I'm here.
  B OK, but you'd better leave your passport in the hotel. If someone stole that, you'd be in big trouble.
  A Right. Do you think we should take a little cash with us?
  B Yes, that's good idea. but leave your credit cards.
  A OK. Thanks for the advice.

Reference: Student's Book **p.65**

UNIT 6 Describing problems and finding solutions

1 A The microwave's not working properly.
  B What's wrong?
  A It keeps making a strange noise and the food isn't cooking. Look, it's cold.
  B Have you noticed it before?
  A Yes, it was making a strange noise yesterday too.
  B What we need to do is buy a new one.

2 A Hello. How can I help you?
  B I just bought a train ticket online, but I can't print the final ticket. There's something wrong with the website.
  A Have you tried opening the files in another web browser, like Internet Explorer or Google Chrome?
  B Let me try that … Ah. OK. That works. What do you think caused it?
  A Sometimes the program doesn't work with some browsers. It's a very common problem.

3 A The internet's down at the moment.
 B Really? How long has it been like that? It works on my computer.
 A About five minutes. I was watching a video online and it suddenly stopped.
 B Why don't you try restarting your computer?
 A OK, let's see if that works.

4 A The car's broken down.
 B What happened?
 A It just didn't start this morning.
 B It looks like a problem with the engine. We need to call the garage. Leave it with me. I'll do it now.

Reference: Student's Book **p.77**

UNIT 7 Discussing and reaching agreement

1 A What's the most important thing for you?
 B We need a hotel that can provide quality accommodation for 100 VIP guests.

2 A What's your priority here?
 B We need a shipping company that can deliver these products to market before February 28th. That is our number one priority.

3 A What are your main concerns?
 B We're concerned about the exchange rate. The contract is in dollars, but we are paid in euros. This could make a big difference over a five-year contract.

4 A What I propose is a price of €1,200 for all the catering at the wedding.
 B That would be fine for us.

5 A The original price for security at your company was $3,000 a month. You're an important customer so we can offer you a discount of 7.5% for next year if you can agree to a three-year contract.
 B We can agree to that.
 A Great! It's a deal!

6 A Thank you for offering to reduce the cost of your broadband service. We've had some better offers, however. In principle, would you consider a further discount?
  B I'm afraid that wouldn't be possible. But we can offer you faster broadband for the same price.

7 A Would you agree to a pay rise if I moved to Boston?
  B I'm sorry, but that's not possible. However, we can offer you relocation expenses of $2,000 to help you move home from Philadelphia.

Reference: Student's Book **p.89**

UNIT 8 Checking understanding and clarifying

1 A I don't know how to add a video to my presentation.
  B It's very easy. You click here and here, and then add the video like this. OK? Would you like me to go through that again?
  A Yes, please, can you show me that again?
  B Yes. It's like this. Do you see how it works?
  A OK. I see what you mean.

2 A So that's how you post a blog on the company website. Do you follow me?
  B Yes, I follow you.

3 A If you follow these instructions, you can make a company conference call. Are you with me?
  B Yes, I'm with you. It's all clear.

4 A This is how we plan to do viral marketing.
  B Can you explain what you mean by 'viral marketing'?
  A Of course. Viral marketing is advertising by getting the public to talk about your product, especially online.

5 A I'm writing some bills for customers for the first time. Can you just clarify what I need to do?
B Right. Every bill needs a reference number. This number needs to be unique so we can track payments.
A OK, that makes sense. How do I get the reference numbers?
B You get them from this program. Like this. OK? Is everything clear?
A Sorry, I don't follow you. Where did you get the user ID?
B That's your number. It's on your company swipe card.
A I see. Thanks!

Reference: Student's Book **p.101**

UNIT 9 Changing plans

1 A Eduardo, something's come up. I can't give the presentation tomorrow. Do you think you could do that for me?
B Yes, no problem. I'm happy to do that.

2 A I was wondering whether you could do the interviews on Friday?
B Sorry, I won't be able to do that because I'm visiting our call centre.

3 A Sam can't show the visitors from Munich round the university tomorrow. Do you think you could manage it for her?
B I'd like to, but I'm not free tomorrow. I have an all-day meeting.

4 A We had hoped to fly to Glasgow, but there's a strike that day. Do you mind getting the train? It's a five-hour journey.
B Don't worry, it's fine. I can work on the train.

5 A Could you book the conference centre for our product launch?
B I don't think we have enough money in the budget for that.

6 A The meeting's starting in five minutes and the drinks machine's broken. Do you think you could get some coffees from Starbucks for me?
B Certainly. I'll go now.

Reference: Student's Book **p.113**

UNIT 10 Catching up

1 **A** Hi, Kazuko! I haven't see you in ages.
   B Ben. Long time, no see. How are things at Moulinex?
   A Actually, I changed jobs last June. I'm at Fagor now.

2 **A** So, Daniela, are you still working at Thompson Construction?
   B Yes, I am, but I changed jobs last year. I'm a production planner now.

3 **A** How are things at PepCo?
   B Great. I got a promotion last year. I'm now working at the Head Office.

4 **A** So, Brendan, how's everything going?
   B Great, thanks. And you?
   A Everything's fine with me. What have you been doing since I last saw you?
   B I've been developing a new product for our markets in North Africa. It's very exciting.

5 **A** What happened with our project to build schools in Africa?
   B In the end, it was a big success. We ended up building over twenty schools.

6 **A** Sorry, I have to go now.
   B OK. I'll see you later. It was lovely to meet you again.
   A You too. Let's talk again soon.

Reference: Student's Book **p.125**

Classroom language

Here are some phrases to use in the classroom.

Phrase	Translation
Could you say that again, please?	
How do you spell 'internet'?	
What does 'reception' mean?	
How do you say 'autobus' in English?	
What's the past participle of 'forget'?	
Sorry, I don't understand.	
What should I do?	
I don't know the answer to number 3.	
I'm not sure, but I think the answer is 'False'.	
I've finished.	
Who is my partner?	
Sorry I'm late.	
I need to leave early.	
Do you understand the instructions?	
Are you ready?	
Let's start.	
Is it my turn?	
I think you're right.	
I don't agree because …	
Are you sure?	
Maybe the answer is …	
What do you think?	

Grammar terms

Here are some grammar terms to help you with your studying.

Word	Definition
adjective	a word that describes a person or thing **Example** This drink is *hot*.
adverb	a word that tells you how, when or where something happens **Example** Please speak *slowly*.
article	*a* or *an* are indefinite articles, and *the* is the definite article **Example** There is *a* computer on *the* table.
auxiliary verb	a verb that is used with a main verb to make questions, negatives, etc. They also combine with *–ing* and past participles to make continuous and *perfect* forms. **Example** I *don't* know Henry. We*'re* working in room 911. *Have* you ever been to Sweden?
comparative	a form of adjective that compares two things **Example** The Bristol Hotel is *cheaper* than the Ritz.
conditional	a sentence that we make with *if*. It describes the possible effect or result of an action. **Example** *If* it rains, I'll take a taxi.
gerund	a noun that we make with the *–ing* form of the verb. **Example** *Walking* is great exercise.
infinitive	the basic form of a verb. The bare infinitive is the verb: *work*. Infinitives are also *to* + verb: *to work*. **Example** I'll *work* from home tomorrow. I want *to work* with you.
modal verb	an auxiliary verb that we use with a bare infinitive to show possibility, certainty, permission, etc. **Example** You *can't* take photos in the art gallery. It *might* rain tomorrow.
noun	a word that you use for a person, place, thing or idea **Example** My *company* has an *office* in *Munich*.

past participle	a form of the verb that you use with the passive and the present perfect **Example** The meeting is *cancelled* because Tony has *missed* his flight.
plural	more than one person or thing **Example** He has got *two jobs*.
possessive adjective	the form of a word that shows that something belongs to someone **Example** It's *your* notebook.
preposition	a word that tells you where, when, how, etc. **Example** He is travelling *from* London *to* Paris *on* 5th March.
pronoun	a word that you use in place of a noun **Example** *She* gave *it* to *you*.
singular	the form of the verb that shows there is only one person or thing **Example** There's one *man* in the meeting room.
superlative	a form of adjective that shows the highest degree of something **Example** Exxon Mobil is the *largest* company in the world.
tense	a form of a verb that shows time, for example, the Past Simple. **Example** The Past Simple of *do* is *did*.
verb	a word that tells you what somebody does or what happens **Example** She *lives* in Windsor and *works* in London.

Irregular verbs

Verb	Past Simple	Past Participle
be	was / were	been
beat	beat	beaten
become	became	become
begin	began	begun
break	broke	broken
bring	brought	brought
build	built	built
buy	bought	bought
catch	caught	caught
choose	chose	chosen
come	came	come
cost	cost	cost
cut	cut	cut
deal	dealt	dealt
do	did	done
draw	drew	drawn
drink	drank	drunk
drive	drove	driven
eat	ate	eaten
fall	fell	fallen
feed	fed	fed
feel	felt	felt
fight	fought	fought
find	found	found
fly	flew	flown

forget	forgot	forgotten
forgive	forgave	forgiven
freeze	froze	frozen
get	got	got
give	gave	given
go	went	gone
grow	grew	grown
have	had	had
hear	heard	heard
hide	hid	hidden
hit	hit	hit
hold	held	held
hurt	hurt	hurt
keep	kept	kept
know	knew	known
lead	led	led
learn	learnt	learnt
leave	left	left
lend	lent	lent
let	let	let
lie	lay	lain
light	lit	lit
lose	lost	lost
make	made	made
mean	meant	meant
meet	met	met
pay	paid	paid
put	put	put
read	read	read

Irregular verbs

ride	rode	ridden
ring	rang	rung
rise	rose	risen
run	ran	run
say	said	said
see	saw	seen
sell	sold	sold
send	sent	sent
set	set	set
shine	shone	shone
shoot	shot	shot
show	showed	shown
shrink	shrank	shrunk
shut	shut	shut
sing	sang	sung
sink	sank	sunk
sit	sat	sat
sleep	slept	slept
slide	slid	slid
speak	spoke	spoken
spend	spent	spent
split	split	split
spread	spread	spread
stand	stood	stood
steal	stole	stolen
stick	stuck	stuck
swim	swam	swum
take	took	taken
teach	taught	taught

tear	tore	torn
tell	told	told
think	thought	thought
throw	threw	thrown
understand	understood	understood
wake	woke	woken
wear	wore	worn
win	won	won
write	wrote	written

OXFORD
UNIVERSITY PRESS

Great Clarendon Street, Oxford, OX2 6DP, United Kingdom

Oxford University Press is a department of the University of Oxford.
It furthers the University's objective of excellence in research, scholarship,
and education by publishing worldwide. Oxford is a registered trade
mark of Oxford University Press in the UK and in certain other countries

© Oxford University Press 2014

The moral rights of the author have been asserted

First published in 2014
2018 2017
10 9 8 7 6 5 4

No unauthorized photocopying

All rights reserved. No part of this publication may be reproduced, stored
in a retrieval system, or transmitted, in any form or by any means, without
the prior permission in writing of Oxford University Press, or as expressly
permitted by law, by licence or under terms agreed with the appropriate
reprographics rights organization. Enquiries concerning reproduction outside
the scope of the above should be sent to the ELT Rights Department, Oxford
University Press, at the address above

You must not circulate this work in any other form and you must impose
this same condition on any acquirer

Links to third party websites are provided by Oxford in good faith and for
information only. Oxford disclaims any responsibility for the materials
contained in any third party website referenced in this work

ISBN: 978 0 19 459790 6

Printed in China

This book is printed on paper from certified and well-managed sources